SCOTLAND'S
ABBEYS AND CATHEDRALS

Also by Hubert Fenwick

ARCHITECT ROYAL
THE AULD ALLIANCE
SCOTLAND'S HISTORIC BUILDINGS
THE CHATEAUX OF FRANCE
SCOTLAND'S CASTLES

SCOTLAND'S
Abbeys and Cathedrals

HUBERT FENWICK

Photographs by the author

ROBERT HALE LIMITED
LONDON

First published in Great Britain 1978

ISBN 0 7091 6374 6

Robert Hale Limited
Clerkenwell House
Clerkenwell Green
London EC1R OHT

Photoset, printed and bound
in Great Britain by
REDWOOD BURN LIMITED
Trowbridge & Esher

CONTENTS

ILLUSTRATIONS

ACKNOWLEDGEMENTS

Plans and sections have been taken from *The Ecclesiastical Architecture of Scotland* by MacGibbon and Ross; and by courtesy of Mr Ronald Miller, who also read the proofs, a selection of prints have been reproduced from R. W. Billings, who visited Scotland in the first half of the nineteenth century and recorded the state of Scottish buildings of note before many of them disappeared or were altered beyond recognition. The prints chosen show, amongst other things, Glasgow Cathedral with a western tower, since demolished, and St. Magnus's Kirkwall before the present incorrectly designed steeple was added. Mr Alexander Heward, of Messrs Miller & Black, the Glasgow architects responsible for the most recent restoration, kindly supplied the photograph of work in progress to repair the vaulting. Other photographs are the author's.

GLOSSARY

AISLE: Division of church from nave, choir or transepts; often chapel containing family tombs.
AMBULATORY: Walk-way behind altar.
APSE: Rounded or polygonal end of choir or chancel of church.
ARCADE: Line of arches, sometimes blank (blind).
ASHLAR: Dressed stone
ATRIUM: Court, or large porch in front of church.
AUMBRY: Wall cupboard. Often used to house sacred vessels.

BALDACCHINO: Canopy of woven material over altar.
BARREL-VAULT: Semicircular roof of stone or timber.
BOSS: Ornamental cover at intersection of vault ribs.

CALEFACTORY: Monks warming-room.
CAMPANILE: Detached bell tower.
CHANCEL: Altar space.
CHAPTER HOUSE: Business room in monastery.
CHEVET: Chancel or ambulatory with radiating chapels.
CHOIR: Space between chancel and nave where monks sang the offices.
CIBORIUM: Domed canopy over altar supported on columns.
CLERESTORY: Upper window space of nave.
CLOISTER: Square enclosure with covered walk in monastery.
CORBEL: Projection in stone or timber to support walls or beams.
CROSSING: Space at centre of east–west axis of church often with tower above.
CROW-STEPS: Stepped gable ends.
CRUCIFORM: Plan in form of cross.

CUSP: Small projection dividing the underside of window arches into leaves (foils).

DECORATED: English Gothic architecture of the first half of the fourteenth century.

DOG-TOOTH: Ornamental star shapes in deep relief, usually around doorway.

DORSAL: Back of altar.

DORTER: Monks' dormitory.

EARLY ENGLISH: Gothic style in Britain of thirteenth century.

FESSE-CHEQUEY: Horizontal band across armorial shield with querboard pattern of alternate squares.

FILLET: Narrow band running down shaft or along moulding.

FLAMBOYANT: Late-Gothic architecture with 'flame' motive.

FLÈCHE: Slender spire, usually of timber at centre of roof.

FLYING BUTTRESS: Arch transmitting weight from wall to free-standing buttress.

FRATER: Monks' dining-hall.

GALILEE: Chapel or raised tribune at entrance to church, often with singing gallery.

GROINED VAULT: Gothic vault without ribs.

HAFFIT: Wood or stone end supports, i.e. pew end.

LANCET: Narrow window with pointed arch typical of early Gothic period.

LIERNE VAULT: Ancillary between main ribs, not springing from walls or central pillar.

LUCARNE: Roof window, usually of stone.

NARTHEX: (*See* ATRIUM).

NAVE: Part of church west of crossing, reserved for lay brothers in abbey.

OGEE: Ogival shape in which convex and concave curves combine.
ORIEL: Projecting window.

PARLOUR: Room in monastery where conversation was allowed.
PEND: Arched entrance.
PERPENDICULAR: English Gothic style in late-Gothic period.
PISCINA: Wall basin with drain, usually near altar.
PRESBYTERY: End of church reserved for clergy.
PULPITUM: Stone screen between lay and clerical parts of church.
PYX: Ornamental vessel to contain the Reserved Sacrament in aumbry or hanging from dome of ciborium.

REFECTORY: Dining-hall.
REREDORTER: Latrines.
REREDOS: Screen behind altar.
RIB: Part of framework supporting vaulted roof.
ROMANESQUE: Buildings derived from Roman and characterized by use of rounded arches.
ROOD: Screen, sometimes with loft above for choir, at west end of chancel.

SACRAMENT HOUSE: Late-Gothic aumbry, or wall 'tabernacle' to contain Reserved Sacrament.

SADDLEBACK ROOF: gable-ended roof.
SALTIRE: Diagonal cross.
SEDILIA: Seats for priests or monks on south side of altar.
SQUINT: Hole allowing view of altar from outside.
SLYPE: Covered passage.

TRANSEPT: Projecting bay of church on either side of crossing.
TREFOIL: Three-leafed, hence quatrefoil (four), cinquefoil (five) etc.
TRIBUNE: (*See* Galilee.)
TRIFORIUM: Arcaded passage between clerestory and nave arches.
TYMPANUM: Space between door lintel and arch.

VAULT: Arched roof.
VESICA: Oval or fish-shaped opening, pointed head and foot.
VOUSSOIR: Wedge-shaped arch stone.

WATERLEAF: Simple leaf motive used on capitals to columns in Early English architecture.
WATERTABLE: Projection in wall to throw off water.

INTRODUCTION

UNLIKE ENGLAND, where scores of cathedrals and quite a few abbatial buildings survive and are, taken together, the country's principal architectural heritage, in Scotland only two cathedrals out of ten existing before the Reformation, no abbeys and only one priory survive in anything like their original form. Indeed St Mungo's in Glasgow is the sole medieval cathedral remaining unrestored on the Scottish mainland, St Magnus, at Kirkwall, in Orkney, being the other survivor, a Viking foundation unique in Britain. The priory at South Queensferry, really a friary, belonged to the Carmelite order, and its church, protected by the local laird, whose ancestors founded it, is still in use, though not by friars. Of romantic ruins we have enough, some of them, such as Dryburgh and Melrose, are renowned throughout the world, having been imbued with literary and other associations by Sir Walter Scott, who lies buried near Earl Haig of Bemersyde at Dryburgh. Yet despite the depredations of time and a particularly contentious religious history, Scotland retains in varying degrees of wholeness a quite remarkable residue of medieval ecclesiastical architecture which deserves to be better known. Not all the damage, incidentally, can be laid at the door of the Reformers, or even their latter-day interpreters, the Covenanters, for the Border abbeys suffered much from English philistinism and local ignorance. Nietzsche's strictures about peasant fear and hatred of beauty certainly apply to some folk north of the Border, though in defence of Luther, whom he specially attacked, one must admit he and his followers did not destroy church buildings *per se*, and they at least kept the music, otherwise we should never have had Bach.

The very uniqueness of what remains in Scotland gives it a special place, a uniqueness of architecture linked to a very unique history, as witness the survival in Galloway of part of the stone church erected by Scotland's first bishop, St Ninian, in the early fifth century, before the Roman legions had left Scotland's shores.

Ninian, who was a friend and disciple of St Martin of Tours and was consecrated bishop in Imperial Rome, was buried in his tiny cathedral church, his 'Candida Casa', or 'White House', another church, the medieval cathedral-priory at Whithorn, being erected above. The saint's tomb then became one of the chief pilgrimage centres in North Britain. St Ninian's mission to the Picts and Britons preceded that of St Columba to Iona by more than a hundred years, and that of St Augustine to Kent by two hundred. His disciples were scattered when the Romans departed, though not wiped out, and amongst them was Kentigern, or Mungo, the 'loved one' as he was called, whose church stood on the present site of Glasgow Cathedral.

As for Iona and the Irish mission to the Picts in the sixth century, the significance of that is directly related to the collapse of Roman power and the ability of the Celtic monks not only to keep the flame of faith alive during the Dark Ages but to carry the torch to regions that would otherwise have passed into pagan control. One thinks first of St Aidan's mission to Northumbria, and then of the cells set up on the continent of Europe, in the Vosges Mountains and the Jura, and beyond, at the famous monastery of St Gall; and of the mission of St Columban, who died at Bobbio, near Piacenza in the Appenines. His library is now in the Vatican. The Celts were more given to learning than to keeping strict rules; they were not the precursors of medieval monasticism and their bishops were pastoral and not diocesan. All this, of course, is part of world history and not peculiar to Scotland or Ireland, but unfortunately while their work can be traced in several fine structures in France, Switzerland and Italy, practically the only authentic remnant of the monastery of St Columba at Iona is part of the cashel, or mound-like boundary wall. The monastery was sacked several times by the Danes, its wooden buildings totally destroyed, and the later structures belong to a thirteenth-century Benedictine foundation on a new site. Probably the oldest stone monument still standing at Iona is St Martin's Cross, which is Celtic in form and design and dates from the tenth century.

With the sacking of Iona by the Danes the Celtic monks went with their books and relics to the mainland, finding a resting-place at Dunkeld, in Perthshire, in the midst of Pictland. There a cathedral was subsequently erected which was the metropolitan church of the land until the tenth century. Central Scotland was evangelized by St Adamnan, a follower and the biographer of St Columba, who founded a church near Blair Atholl, one which is still in use, though the actual building is not more than five or six hundred years old. St Adamnan's kirk, standing in a field about a quarter of a mile from the main road north to Inverness is virtually unknown and does not figure in the guide-books, though it is built on a seventh-century site and has a continuous history since before the Reformation. Architecturally speaking, however, we must go elsewhere for substantial evidences of Early Christian building in Scotland. Dunkeld Cathedral is of much later vintage, but at Brechin, in eastern Pictland, we find what is probably our best-preserved and most interesting stone building of the pre-Norman era. Brechin Cathedral has been twice rebuilt, the first time in the most banal manner imaginable, but its battlemented tower is medieval, as is its west doorway, while more in the present context is the 'Pictish' round tower on its south side, Pictish in respect of its probable commissioning by a Pictish King, but Irish in its general form. Opinions differ as to the precise date of the latter, most making it tenth century, though Dr James Richardson, first Inspector of Ancient Monuments in Scotland, has ventured to suggest earlier beginnings. In the eighth century King Nechtan desired to romanize his church in usage and in architecture, and wrote to the abbot of St Peter's, Monkwearmouth, seeking help and advice, promising that if architects were sent he would build a stone church in the 'Roman' fashion and dedicate it to the 'Prince of Apostles'. Dr Richardson identifies two of the figures carved beside the tiny entrance to the round tower as the Saints Peter and Paul, which may mean that Nechtan's 'Roman' church was here. A similar association applies to the now ruined priory at Restennet, to the south of Brechin, the lower part of whose square tower is Saxon in detail. Restennet was afterwards revived by Augustinian canons and dedicated to St Peter. It is probable, therefore, that Northumbrian masons were engaged on more than one ecclesiastical foundation in the neighbourhood; they undoubtedly were in the twelfth century, when St Rule's or Regulus's Tower, part of the earliest cathedral-priory at St Andrews, was built in imitation of English models.

It is to Northern England too, and particularly Durham, that we must look for precedents in the design of the abbey at Dunfermline, founded by Margaret, Queen and Saint, and rebuilt by her son, David I, and the cathedral of Kirkwall, which is the finest example of Norman architecture in Scotland surviving, though of Viking foundation. Rognvald, Jarl (Earl) of Orkney, began Kirkwall Cathedral in honour of his murdered uncle, St Magnus; it stands apart from its contemporaries, being built to the designs of a Norwegian mason and to the command of a Norwegian ruler, and remained in the diocese of Trondheim until 1472. From Dunfermline the story is continuous throughout the twelfth and most of the thirteenth century, when we arrive in the era of Edward I and the Wars of Independence, when abbey and cathedral-burning was more in vogue than building, and the close links forged between English and Scots since the time of Queen Margaret were rudely broken. The feudal system was implanted in Scotland by Margaret's sons and heirs, and included the setting up of dioceses and parishes, with abbeys and priories to supplement the work of kirks and cathedrals. Dunblane Cathedral, which Ruskin so admired and which has been restored and partly rebuilt within living memory, was begun by David I, known as 'that sair sanct for the croun' on account of his numerous religious foundations that included the abbeys of Cambuskenneth, near Stirling, Dundrennan, in Galloway, Holyrood, forerunner of the existing palace, and the celebrated Border houses of Jedburgh, Kelso and Melrose.

Medieval monasticism sprang from St Benedict's Rule, reformed or unreformed, Dunfermline being orthodox while Kelso and Tironensian, Melrose Cistercian and Jedburgh, Cambuskenneth and Holyrood Augustinian, the latter being colonized with Austin canons from St Andrews, where the cathedral also held priory status. Throughout the twelfth and thirteenth centuries the number of religious houses grew, with William the Lion founding the great abbey at Arbroath and dedicating it to the newly martyred St Thomas à Becket, Inchcolm, the so-called Iona of the east, refounded by Alexander I on a Celtic site, and Pluscarden Priory, in Moray, resettled by Benedictines since the last war and in course of restoration. Nor were kings alone in pious works of this kind: the High Stewards, ancestors of the royal house of Scotland, founded Paisley Abbey for monks from Cluny, who were also settled at Crossraguel, in Ayrshire, by the Earl of Carrick, an ancestor of Robert Bruce. Hugh de Morville founded both Dryburgh and Kilwinning Abbeys in the mid-twelfth century, while Walter, Earl of Monteith, founded the romantically and securely sited priory of Inchmahome, made famous in later years by the sojourn there of the infant Mary, Queen of Scots. Curiously enough, of the former priory at Scone, from which St Andrews was colonized, nothing survives except the 'Stone of Destiny' at Westminster. Even that may not be genuine but merely a piece of local building stone palmed off onto Edward I by the canons in place of the talisman which had come originally from Ireland, and possibly from the Near East, as the Gaels migrated westwards and north in pre-historical times.

The last cathedral to be built as such before the Reformation was Fortrose, on the Black Isle, in the fifteenth century, and the last abbey was the New Abbey, also known as 'Dulci Corde', or Sweetheart, in Galloway, which dates from the fourteenth century and was the creation of the Lady Dervorguilla, last in the native Picto-Scottish line of royalty. She founded it in memory of her husband, John de Baliol, himself founder of Balliol College, Oxford. The abbey church stands almost to eaves' height and is surrounded by an enormous granite-boulder boundary wall. It was here that the last abbot, the legendary Gilbert Broun, functioned and remained *in situ* well into the reign of James VI and I, protected by the local laird who was of the old faith. Cathedrals and abbey kirks alike proved too large for Protestant worship, the conventual buildings often surviving as private houses, and either the choir or the nave, whichever was the smaller, being adapted to new usages. The rest became a quarry for the local people and much of the towns of Arbroath and St Andrews, for instance, were built of stone from their respective abbeys and priories. The architecture of these despoiled buildings, as can be seen by what remains, was indistinguishable in the main from English and French examples, but no Scottish cathedral matched the larger English ones in length. St Andrews nearly compared with Norwich, and Glasgow with Bristol, while Elgin, the most beautiful of all Scottish cathedral kirks, was no bigger than Ripon. What these churches lacked in dimensions, however, they undoubtedly made up for in historical interest and refined detail.

There were nine Scottish dioceses in medieval times, plus two under the respective jurisdictions of Trondheim and York; but at the height of the episcopal ascendancy of the seventeenth century this had become fourteen, with two archbishops and a contemporary Royal Caroline See of Edenburgen carved out of St Andrews. The older sees were represented by cathedrals in Glasgow, Dunkeld, Dunblane, St Andrews, Aberdeen, Brechin, Dornoch, the cathedral of Caithness, Fortrose, for Ross, and Elgin, for Moray. Whithorn was eventually detached from York and served as the seat of the Bishop of Galloway, and St Magnus, Kirkwall, became independent of Trondheim when the Norwegian dioceses of Argyll and the Isles were separated, with Lismore representing Argyll and a rebuilt Iona the Isles. Edinburgh was created in 1633, with the High Kirk of St Giles becoming a cathedral until the setting up of the Presbyterian system in 1690. The disestablished Episcopal church now has seven bishops with cathedrals in Aberdeen, Dundee, Edinburgh, Glasgow, Inverness, Oban and Perth, with the tiny Cathedral of the Isles, Britain's smallest, on the Isle of Cumbrae. None of these are of any antiquity, though St Mary's in Edinburgh is usually considered the masterpiece of Sir George Gilbert Scott. It is certainly the largest church in Scotland containing a bishop's chair, and the minuscule Cathedral of the Isles is undoubtedly amongst William Butterfield's happiest and most ingenious designs. Both architects did other buildings in Scotland, but none quite up to the standard of the two mentioned above, while Sir Ninian Comper re-edified the interior of St Andrew's Cathedral in Aberdeen to mark the 150th anniversary of the consecration in 1784 of the first American bishop in Aberdeen, by three Jacobite bishops of the Scottish Episcopal Church.

Of the pre-Reformation cathedrals in Scotland, Glasgow and Kirkwall alone survive in anything approaching their original state, and Glasgow lost its two western towers in the nineteenth century. Dunblane has been restored, as has Brechin. Dornoch and Iona have been more or less rebuilt, while the parish kirk on Lismore boasts few remnants of its more ancient use. Elgin and St Andrews are toothy ruins, the latter more than the former, as are all our abbeys except Pluscarden, which is in course of restoration, and Paisley, which was partly rebuilt by Sir Robert Lorimer after an earlier restoration. Apart from these some attractive conventual buildings have survived, especially where they have been turned into private residences. The commendator's, or secular abbot's houses at Melrose and Arbroath are still roofed, and at Pittenweem the fourteenth-century gatehouse remains, together with the former Prior's lodging, which is actually the oldest inhabited parsonage in Scotland. More interesting still, and almost complete in its half-mile circuit, are the priory walls at St Andrews, with three ports, or gates, and thirteen towers, surely a unique survival in Britain. Then there are a number of bishop's palaces and castles to be seen, one at Dornoch being an hotel, another, on Lord Southesk's estate at Kinnaird, recently restored as a private house. It dates in part from the fourteenth century and was the *palatium nostrum* of the Bishops of Brechin. The archiepiscopal castle at St Andrews, in which Cardinal Beaton was murdered with John Knox amongst the interested spectators, is badly crumbled, but part of the archbishop's country seat at Monimail still stands, as does Provan Hall, erstwhile retreat of the clergy of Glasgow Cathedral, now in the hands of the National Trust for Scotland. Thus, while Scotland's ecclesiastical heritage is much depleted, what there is deserves our attention, and is of such a standard that it almost, but not quite, wipes out the memory of the damage inflicted on it. One cannot excuse this damage, it was practically all wilful, yet Melrose, whether seen in the moonlight or not, can be very moving, and the vision of roofless Elgin, set on its broad green beside the Lossie, can compare with anything in England or on the Continent.

ONE

Pre-Norman Foundations

THERE CAN be little doubt that the first authenticated stone cathedral, abbey or priory built in Scotland dates in its origins from the fifth century and was erected in Galloway by stone masons from Tours at the behest of St Ninian, the first Scottish bishop. Ninian is reputed to have visited Rome and there been consecrated by the Pope in 394 before returning home via the valley of the Loire, where he met and came under the influence of St Martin, hence, presumably, the dedication of his cathedral to that Gallic holy man. Ninian's church, which predates the departure of the Roman legions by some years, was called 'Candida Casa', or White House, probably after its masonry, which was composed of split stones set in clay, but also possibly on account of the white plaster with which the walls were daubed, some of which has survived to this day. It was the practice so to cover churches in early times, right up to the end of the pre-Norman era, the whiteness being symbolic of Christian purity and rebirth, and not particularly for beauty's sake. It is curious, however, how far we have gone in the other direction, scraping walls, woodwork and everything else scrapable, making our churches naked and cold where once they were bright and warm; I speak figuratively, since in the Middle Ages they must have been bitterly cold in winter. Having little if any light, the plastering of the interiors and their painting with the Bible stories in fresco served twin purposes: the enlivening of the atmosphere and the spreading of the Gospel to a largely illiterate population. The television of the Dark Ages one might say; and there was certainly no 'dim religious light'.

The walls of St Ninian's 'Candida Casa' actually still stand to the height of a few feet near the east end of the ruins of a latter day priory-cathedral, erected in the twelfth century by Fergus, Lord of Galloway, and covering the saint's tomb, a normal practice. This later building served as the cathedral of the revived diocese of

'Candida Casa' which was attached to the archdiocese of York almost until the Reformation. It was further enlarged and partly rebuilt in the thirteenth century, when Canons Regular, or Austin Canons, came from Prémontré, in France, to serve as clergy, making the church both bishop's seat and priory at the same time. A canon, of course, is a clergyman attached to a church who, while not necessarily resident, does have fixed duties, and the Austin or Augustinian Canons Regular were so named because they followed a monastic rule. In the rebuilding portions of the previous church were re-used, including a handsome Romanesque doorway which was reset and today marks the old entry into the nave from the west, while the more ancient foundations became submerged, thus preserving some remarkable treasures. In recent years a number of exceedingly significant and important discoveries have been made by the Ministry of Works, now the Department of the Environment, engaged in strengthening the lower walls of the ruined medieval cathedral-kirk. These show definite proof of the survival of St Ninian's 'Candida Casa', and resulted in the unearthing of fifth-century bones, together with later relics contained in three bishop's tombs, with vestments, rings, crooks and chalices. These have been removed elsewhere, as have other treasures found throughout the country, raising the question of whether this sort of discovery should not be treated differently.

The archaeologists and keepers of museums say that valuable 'finds' can be better examined and protected in Edinburgh or some other big city than on or near the sites on which they are found, but one is always in two minds about the subject, and especially when it comes to the digging up of graves; and how long should we leave the dead in peace before letting the diggers loose to rummage about at will? There is also the problem of relating 'finds', even non-tomb 'finds' to the place of discovery and their original use. The case of the St Ninian's Isle treasure found in Shetland raised this matter most forcibly. Here a great deal of silverware was found within a tiny ruined church, itself enclosed within an earth boundary wall, the whole dating from the eighth century. The Shetlanders pleaded eloquently, and with much support from well-wishers on the Scottish mainland, for their treasure either to be left where it was unearthed or placed in a special museum in Lerwick, but to no avail. It all went to Edinburgh, but with the proviso, squeezed out of the authorities, that it should be on view in Shetland periodically.

The distance from St Ninian's Isle in the far North to his 'Candida Casa' in the extreme South-west must be almost as far as between any two points in Scotland, and demonstrates how widespread was the influence of the first Scottish bishop, both during the last days of Imperial Roman rule and afterwards. It is known, for instance, that he founded churches near Stirling, in the Carse of Gowrie, and in Angus, while at Culross, in Fife, his disciple Serf brought up the future St Kentigern, whom he nicknamed 'Mungo', or loved one. Mungo subsequently evangelized the Strathclyde district, founding what became the diocese of Glasgow and the first church on the site of Glasgow Cathedral. This perhaps explains the close links between the dioceses of Glasgow and Galloway, which united represent the oldest Scottish episcopal see. It would, of course, be idle to pretend that either St Mungo's little church of heather and log or St Ninian's white stone cathedral were not ravaged by the Danes, the former utterly destroyed, the latter ruined; or that their missions continued uninterrupted into the Dark Ages. On the other hand, so far as 'Candida Casa' is concerned, there has been a church built of masonry on the same Gallovidian site, and there still is one, since the days of the Caesars, a record which surely cannot be matched anywhere else in the United Kingdom, and in very few places abroad. It became so holy a venue in the Middle Ages that kings and queens, including the ineffectual Edward II of England on his way to defeat by Bruce, made solemn pilgrimages to it, almost to the eve of the Reformation. Indeed its very holiness was one reason for its utter sacking by the Reformers, who specially disliked such places as idolatrous and wicked, so that in similar vein they made their way across the sea to wreck Iona.

Today the village of Whithorn, whose parish kirk stands not far from the remains of 'Candida Casa' and its despoiled successor, is not particularly inspiring and has nothing to suggest a shrine, or a Scottish Walsingham. However, the entrance to the priory ruins is through a pend, or arch, of an attractively whitened building, with the remnants of Gothic masonry protruding and the properly tinctured arms of the King of Scots and a late fifteenth-century bishop of Galloway decorating it. In the vicinity, by the sea, is St Ninian's Cave, and at Isle of Whithorn there is a small chapel formerly thought to have been on the site of the original 'White

House' but itself of a later vintage. Further to the west, at Kirkmadrine, two fifth-century crosses marked with the signs of two contemporary bishops served, until taken indoors at the behest of the Ministry of Works, as gateposts to the local church; and it was on this south-western shore, not far from Whithorn, that the famous illuminated Lindisfarne Gospels were recovered from the waves after having fallen from a boat taking fleeing Northumbrian monks to Ireland via 'Candida Casa'.

The existing Cathedral of St Mungo in Glasgow dates from the twelfth century, the first stone church on the site being dedicated in 1136, in the presence of David I, on the six hundredth anniversary of the original foundation. This new building was shortly afterwards destroyed by fire and another begun in 1197, under Bishop Jocelin, but even that was replaced a century later by a grander edifice, today represented by the choir and crypt. These were the work of Bishop Bondington and are amongst the finest examples of early pointed architecture in Britain, north or south. We shall return to St Mungo's, to its later nave and tower, in the appropriate chapter; sufficient to say here that the crypt, a masterpiece of Gothic vaulting and delicate detail, contains the shrine of St Mungo, or Kentigern, the central space with its four arched supports probably marking the original site of his burial, and possibly, therefore, of his rude log church roofed with heather. It is placed immediately below where the high altar once was in the same way as St Ninian's tomb in the erstwhile cathedral-priory at Whithorn.

In the fifteenth century Bishop Blacader became first Archbishop of Glasgow, a title only introduced in 1472, when the bishopric of St Andrews was raised to archiepiscopal status, partly in order to dispose of claims of primacy over the whole of Scotland by successive Archbishops of York. Glasgow followed in 1492, with St Andrews being 'Primate of all Scotland' and Glasgow 'Primate of Scotland', in imitation of Canterbury and York respectively. In practice the two were often joined, that is to say the Archbishop of Glasgow, was also Archbishop of St Andrews, a notable case being Gavin Dunbar, who was Primate and Lord Chancellor in the reign of James V. Robert Blacader, the new archbishop, was responsible for the aisle presently named after him, which is on a sort of mezzanine level, between the lower and upper churches, and was intended to be the crypt of an englarged south transept, the rest of which was never built. It is a splendid specimen of late Gothic, and again remarkable for the excellence of its workmanship. It is chiefly mentioned here because of an assumed connection with the story of St Mungo and the founding of the first church. As one enters the aisle one may notice overhead the carving between two spandrels, or ribs, in the vaulting, showing a man wrapped in a white robe, lying on a two-wheeled cart, with an inscription on either side, the topmost of which reads THIS-IS-YE-ISL-OF-CAR, while the bottom bears the single word FERGUS. Most sources associate this with the legend of Mungo and the hermit Fergus whom the saint found dying on the Campsie fells, to the north of Glasgow, and placed on a cart to which two wild bulls were yoked. The animals were left to go where they wished until they stopped, and there Fergus was buried and Mungo built his church. With this story in mind it is interesting to read the late Dr James Richardson's alternative explanation of the carving and its symbolism. In his view Fergus was the name of the carver, in which case a translation of the inscription might be 'This is the aisle of Carver Fergus', and the car, or cart, with the man or *vir*, on it, a play on the word carver. One has a feeling this may be as far-fetched as the traditional legend, yet both have a place in the saga of the founding and building of the finest and only surviving medieval cathedral on the Scottish mainland.

Like St Ninian's mission, that of St Kentigern was scattered by the Vikings and other pagan enemies, though the naming of the chapels and wells after Mungo rivals that of Ninian and covers a great deal of south and central Scotland. One thinks, for instance, of St Mungo's Well at Gleneagles, in Perthshire, itself meaning the glen of the church in Gaelic, and of the remains of a small church dedicated to Mungo at the eastern entrance to Culross, where he was educated. There was not complete darkness during the so-called Dark Ages, and it was not long before the flame of faith, taken to Ireland by Patrick, the son of a minor Roman official, returned to Scotland in the mission of St Columba to Iona. The sixth-century mission of an Ulsterman with royal blood in his veins was eventually to link up with the seventh-century one of St Augustine to Kent, the two meeting and merging in Northumberland. It is perhaps this aspect of Iona's role that gives it precedence over Whithorn as a religious site and place of pilgrimage in the modern world, though architecturally speaking there is not much at Iona, or indeed anywhere else in Britain, to compare in evoca-

St Martin's Cross, Iona

Iona Cathedral: the choir before restoration (from a drawing by R. W. Billings)

tive authenticity with the remnants of St Ninian's original fifth-century cathedral; and even Dr Samuel Johnson's emotional association of Iona with the Fields of Marathon does nothing to eradicate the facts of 'Candida Casa', its foundation and continuing existence to the present day.

One of the more permanent features of Celtic missionary settlements are the boundary, or cashel walls that surrounded them and helped to protect the wooden huts, one per monk, and the church, and a portion of such a wall has survived at Iona. Of a later era, but still pre-Norman, are a number of crosses, including St John's, which is damaged and had to be re-cast, and the celebrated St Martin's, which remains *in situ* and dates from the tenth century. It is Irish in ethos and design, as is the stump of what was once an Irish round tower. There are three of these known in Scotland, two still standing, one at Abernethy, a former Pictish stronghold, and another, more complete and interesting in details, beside the cathedral at Brechin in Angus. Before going on to describe this, however, and with it the Irish and Roman link-up in the centuries between St Columba's death and the arrival on the scene of Queen Margaret and the Anglo-Normans, we might as well stay a little longer at Iona, its associations, if not wholly so, being generally thought of as predominantly Celtic. The cashel wall is Columban, even if the round tower dates from three centuries after, while there is a plethora of crosses and gravestones, the ages of which range from late Romanesque times till the present day. They are in a special graveyard dividing the existing restored cathedral and the ruins of a Benedictine nunnery founded in the thirteenth century by the Lord of the Isles. Ever since early times it had been thought efficacious for the repose of the soul to be buried at Iona, and besides chiefs and their families, kings and saints as well as lesser mortals all lie in this sacred soil. The atmosphere of the island, peaceful because it lies sheltered from Atlantic winds, is calm and green, with white sands and outcrops of pink granite, the stone from which the nunnery and abbey were built. It is this atmosphere that contributes to Iona's attractions, to its mystical air, to legends that may be strong yet even here are probably no stranger than fact.

To the west of the restored church a rock called Tor Abb is thought to mark the possible site of St Columba's cell, while slightly to the south is St Oran's Chapel and burial ground. The

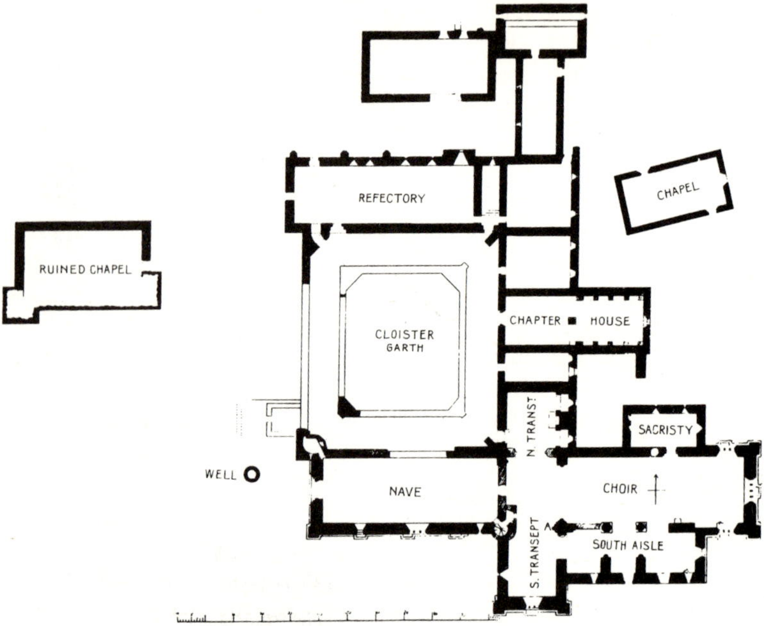

Iona Cathedral: plan

chapel consists of a plain stone shed with a typical Norman doorway, not unlike that re-set into the west end of the medieval cathedral-priory at Whithorn, only bolder in its chevron and 'dog-tooth' patterns and possessed of two recessed arches in place of four. It is said to have been built by Queen Margaret towards the end of the eleventh century, but probably dates from the later refounding of the monastery by the Benedictines in the thirteenth century. St Oran's Chapel has recently been restored and re-roofed and a 'dig' undertaken in the vicinity, when part of an ancient shrine was discovered together with a cross-slab bearing a Runic, or Norse inscription. That the Relig Oran site, as it is called, should, with the rest of Iona, have always shed its own particular aura is borne out by the determined attacks made upon it by the Reformers, who, though they destroyed both relics and objects of beauty utterly failed to eliminate the spirituality of the place. They reduced the Benedictine nunnery and newly finished Cathedral of the Isles to ruins, these ruins having remained exposed to the elements almost ever since, but less a prey to local acquisitiveness and vandalism than in many other parts of Scotland. Thus they have decayed gracefully, becoming more and more respected for their age and past history as time went on.

It was only natural that Samuel Johnson and James Boswell should have visited Iona on their tour, and that the perceptive doctor should have noticed that the ruined cathedral belonged to more than one period, indeed, the choir and tower were founded before the nave, the completed cruciform dating from the sixteenth century. Long before then, however, King Charles I had given what was a fairly considerable sum for its day, £400, towards the repair of the buildings. Unfortunately, none of the royal gift was spent as intended, and Iona abbey and cathedral remained roofless but picturesque until the end of the nineteeth century, when the eighth Duke of Argyll made the site over to the Church of Scotland, on condition the restored church should be available to other denominations. This part of the bargain has not been very obviously adhered to, perhaps because the other denominations have not been sufficiently demanding, and two of them have built their own chapels and hospices on the island for their own use. As a matter of fact the original idea, sponsored by the Duchess of Argyll and prompted from behind by the great Chinnery Haldane, Bishop of Argyll and the Isles, 'a second Saint Columba', was to return the buildings to the episcopal diocese, but the Duke got cold feet at the end of the day and compromised.

The former cathedral and abbey have been in the process of restoration and rebuilding for the past fifty years, the conventual quarters being taken in gradually by Lord MacLeod's Iona Community. Architecturally a number of unique features have survived, notably the internal flying buttresses on the south side of the choir, which were necessitated by the inexpert placing of late-Gothic clerestory windows immediately above the piers and not over the lower arches, as was usual. This fault undoubtedly adds to the picturesqueness of the interior and was one of the more romantic aspects of the old ruins. The piers themselves are round, suggestive of much earlier work, but reversals of style were fairly common in the fifteenth and sixteenth centuries in Scotland, when a return to roundnesses and simply constructed vaults followed the ending of the close cultural links with England that had pertained earlier. Scottish masons then found themselves left to their own devices, almost for the first time since the days of Queen Margaret. Some were able to cope, others were not, hence the dearth of good Gothic vaulting, the predominance of barrel instead of ribbed vaults, and the harking back to old-fashioned detail. This is especially noticeable at Iona, where the church contains much amusing carving, some of it displaying a quaint homeliness rarely found in religious buildings of so late a date, indeed it suggests Celtic origins. Most of it is debased Romanesque, but showing what may be termed latent Hiberno-Lombardic influences. The plan of the church, as indicated, is cruciform, with a central spireless tower, and that curious south aisle, complete with primitive lean-to roof. The external *tout ensemble*, however, though plain, fits in well with its island environment. It looked even better on that splendid occasion in 1963, when a number of priests of the Church of Ireland re-enacted St Columba's landing of 563 by crossing from Ulster in a replica of his coracle. On Iona they were received by the primus and bishops of the Scottish Episcopal Church and took part in a joint service in the ancient abbey and Cathedral of the Isles, with pilgrims from England and elsewhere led by the Archbishop of Canterbury.

In the ninth century the Celtic monks finally fled from Iona and at the invitation of Kenneth MacAlpine, first King of the Scots, settled at Dunkeld, bringing with them those relics which had escaped the grasp of the Vikings. At that time Dunkeld had already been evangelized and had its own monastery and early cathedral. Hard facts are difficult to come by and there exists more than one legend concerning its founding, by St Columba himself according to tradition. This is not impossible as he seems to have been all over the place, indeed, in so many and in such rapid succession that some historians have doubted his singularity and put him down as a composite person, a father-figure of the Scots as they progressed eastwards, ousting the native Picts as they went. In any event, from the ninth century Dunkeld became the headquarters of the old Celtic church and the Scoto-Pictish capital. The bishop was not diocesan, but pastoral, being kept in his place by the abbot and brought out when required for specific spiritual duties. The Celtic church was not very orderly, and at Dunkeld was particularly so, its abbots and monks marrying, becoming rather like their ultimate successors in the Roman obedience in the sixteenth century, when abbots *in commendam*, or commendators, drew the revenues of the abbeys without having any responsibility or place in strictly spiritual affairs. One of the early abbots of Dunkeld married the daughter of Malcolm II, their son actually inheriting the crown. Others belonged to notable local families, thus holding the land in their power; and this they continued to do right up to the Reformation and beyond. Bishop Robert de Cardeney, for example, whose recessed altar tomb survives in the south aisle of the ruined nave of the medieval cathedral, had for descendant a laird who assisted in the destruction of the building in 1571 and himself is thought to have removed the roof timbers for his own use. The appointment system, therefore, as it existed in pre-Norman Scotland, cannot have been wholly unlike that of the day when it was common for royal bastards to be made abbots and priors, even boy-bishops. These people fleeced the parish churches of their rightful dues and left the people destitute of regular and properly conducted services, the money going to the enrichment of their titular cathedrals and monasteries, and via them into the coffers of the most powerful and successful families, royal and otherwise.

The later Celtic church is often referred to as Culdee, the word coming from the Gaelic *Celi dé*, which means companions of God; and a quantity of misleading mythology attaches to it, especially that which seeks to prove the existence of some sort of church in Scotland outwith the authority of Rome and separate from the rest of Catholic Christendom. From this premise apologists go on to make out that the present Presbyterian kirk is descended from the Culdee church, in much the same way as some members of the Protestant Church of Ireland like to think they evolve from an establishment predating the advent of the Roman obedience in their country. So it goes round and round, becoming by degrees unalienable fact in the minds of those who wish it to be. The only thing one can say in mild support of such stalwarts is that during the Dark Ages, the period immediately following the fall of Rome, the power of the Roman church was weak and at times unenforceable, during which time the flame of faith was kept alive in remote areas by the Celtic church, a branch of the Church Universal nonetheless, and that that church sent missionaries to Italy, reaching the 'Eternal City' itself. The remoter Celts got progressively out of touch, however, with the rest of Christendom, and in the end became so wayward and degenerate that their virtual demise or at least thorough reformation was a foregone conclusion. The fact that they kept Easter at a different date, and cut their hair differently were only minor divergencies, lax attitudes towards spiritual authority and odd social habits clearly doomed them once order had been restored in Rome and the Goths and Vandals thrown back. Their original missionary organization had been sensible and effective and only broke down because it failed to accommodate itself to the needs of a fully evangelized community. In other words the very success of their early mission was its undoing, when they failed to adapt themselves to a situation of their own creating.

A description of the Culdees as they lived and worked at Dunkeld is given by Alexander Mill, or Miln, a prominent ancestor of the Mylne family of master masons, seven generations of whom served six successive kings of Scots, building amongst other things Parliament House for Charles I and Holyroodhouse for James IV and Charles II. Alexander Miln was a canon of Dunkeld under the episcopate of Bishop Brown towards the end of the fifteenth century and besides writing a history of the building of the cathedral was master of works there, as well as for the first stone bridge over the River Tay. He subsequently became abbot of the Augustinian abbey of Cambuskenneth, near Stirling, and in the reign of James V first President of the Court of Session, or Scottish Law Court. This institution was officially established in 1532, though there already existed the framework of law and James V merely regularized it by making the judges professional. At the same time he cunningly obtained the financial support of the Pope by appointing a majority of clerics as Senators of Justice, thus acquiring funds from which to pay the clergy, but which he diverted instead to his own use. Scots Law as then formalized was, and still is, based on Justinian's Pandects, on principle not precedent, and is, therefore, like Continental, or Roman Law, not English Common Law. Its present headquarters are in that same Parliament House John Mylne, Master Mason to Charles I, built in 1633, which has at its southern extremity a large stained-glass window depicting a mitred and croziered Lord Chancellor, Gavin Dunbar, Archbishop of Glasgow, laying a hand of blessing upon the Papal Bull held by a kneeling Alexander Miln, first President, in the presence of James V and his assembled court.

The cathedral, dedicated to St Columba, at Dunkeld, wherein Alexander Miln had his stall, was begun in the twelfth century on or near the site of the former Culdee settlement and under the aegis of Alexander I of Scots. The first bishop was also Abbot of Scone, itself once Celtic and the place where Scottish kings were crowned. The diocese was enormous, including Argyll and the Isles within its boundaries to the west, and Inchcolm, in Fife, to the east. Inchcolm is the Colm's Isle of Shakespeare's *Macbeth* and like Dunkeld is one of the sites where St Columba is said to have preached and founded a mission. It is certainly very ancient and possesses at one corner of the later monastery what purports to be an authentic Celtic monk's cell. This is entirely built of stone in the manner of a beehive dovecot, with overlapping stones for a roof, but rectangular and not round on plan. Others may say it is a dead house, or mortuary chapel. Be that as it may, Inchcolm, known to this day as 'The Iona of the East', was within the Columban diocese of Dunkeld until the thirteenth century, when Bishop John asked the Pope for a division of his jurisdiction and the diocese of Argyll was created, with the small cathedral on the island of Lismore serving as episcopal seat.

Dunkeld Cathedral as we see it today is not as old as might be supposed, the choir dates mostly from the fourteenth century, the nave wholly from that era and the chapter house and tower from

Dunkeld Cathedral and palace in the seventeenth century (from Slezer's Theatrum Scotiae*)*

the fifteenth; and although like Iona the walls are supported in places by robust round columns that suggest Norman work the oldest portion standing, an arcade in the thrice-rebuilt choir, was built by Bishop Richard in the thirteenth century. The rest of the choir was the creation of Bishop Sinclair, whose tomb survives, a hundred years later. The nave followed, with its 'antique' columns and quaint half-moon triforium arches suggestive of earlier styles. The splendid and complete tower was the last to be built, its lower, vaulted floor still showing traces of two paintings, on the north and west walls respectively, one depicting the *Judgement of Solomon*, the other the *Woman taken in Adultery*, both being thought suitable subjects for the Consistory Court which sat there. These pictures are almost unique in Scotland and it is curious how the reformers, who came to Dunkeld with full authority from the kirk in Edinburgh to destroy everything of even a slightly idolatrous nature, and to leave only the doors and windows undamaged, failed to deface these, unless, of course, the pictures had already received the coat of plaster which in recent years has been removed to reveal them.

The cathedral has no transepts, but a choir as long as the nave, and side aisles in the latter, where the only vaults were in the north aisle, the south being ceiled in timber. As we have seen, vaulting was not a Scottish forte, though paradoxically Scotland had more stone than timber, unlike England, where timber roofs are part of the glory of her medieval churches. The Scots would have preferred to build like the French, always in stone, had they not lacked the experience to construct large Gothic vaults which did not push the walls out or crush the foundations. Part of the trouble was the use of stone slab roofs which were themselves excessively heavy and weighed down vaults and walls below. Then there were the complications inherent in the construction of groined and ribbed vaulting, which many Scots masons clearly avoided for fear of making mistakes. Because of this timber was used more often to ceil larger roofs, stone vaulting being reserved for aisles and some transepts, or when used in naves and choirs made simply barrel shaped. Of the important Scottish cathedrals only Glasgow and Kirkwall were stone-vaulted, and in the case of the former, which had a nave vault, that collapsed and had to be replaced in timber, while at Kirkwall the miscalculations of earlier days has resulted in an overhaul of the roofing system becoming necessary, and the

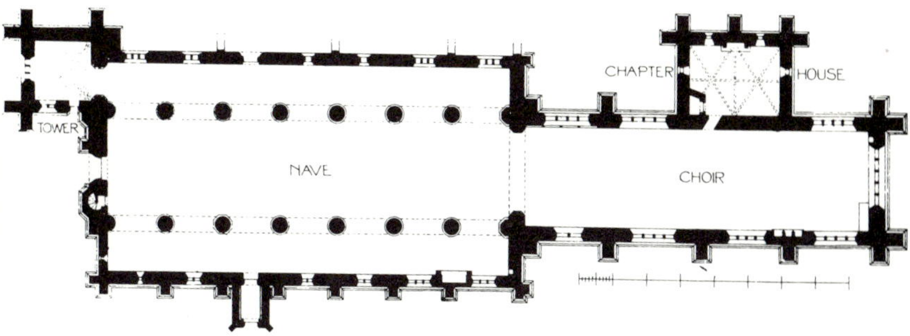

Dunkeld Cathedral from the south; plan of the cathedral

substitution of steel and concrete ties and beams to prevent disaster. Of the abbeys Holyrood and Melrose alone were completely vaulted in stone, though St Giles's High Kirk, in Edinburgh, nowadays granted honorary cathedral status, shows a variety of vaults, being the odd man out in every respect.

When the late-Gothic tower was added on the north side of the west front at Dunkeld the result was dreadful to behold, with a porch and door centred on the new total width, a large west window, now utterly devoid of tracery, centred on the original, and a top gable re-centred on the new door below. This architectural mutilation must be compared with that perpetrated by zealous lairds and their henchmen in the mid-sixteenth century, who, far exceeding their instructions, completely wrecked the building, going off with anything of value, including doors and pews and other objects they had been told to leave, and stripping the roof, as already mentioned. Thus in the seventeenth century, under a reformed episcopate, the first rebuilding of the choir was undertaken. This in turn came to grief during the Civil Wars, when the Covenanters attacked the kirk and nearby Dunkeld House, and defaced the figure of Alexander Stewart, fourth son of Robert II, the so-called 'Wolf of Badenoch'. His tomb behind the former high altar had somehow escaped earlier despoilers, possibly because it was not that of a bishop or other religious personage but a brigand like the despoilers. Then again, after a second rebuilding in the reign of Charles II, both house and choir fell victim to a further attack, when the choir was used as a strong point by government troops under Lt Col. Cleland in conflict with the supporters of James VII and II. The latter had won the Battle of Killiecrankie but lost their general, Viscount Claverhouse, better known as 'Bonnie Dundee', who was killed at the head of his cavalry. Colonel Cleland also lost his life and died of wounds in the choir of the cathedral, his men still fighting on, until, setting fire to the houses in the town by throwing burning woodwork down upon them, they finally drove the Highlanders out. There is another version of what happened which may perhaps be worth recalling since it shows the difference between the Highland and Lowland character, between Celt and Saxon if you like, for the former were said not to lock their doors, but left the keys unturned in their holes, so that the latter had only to lock them in before setting light to the houses and so disposing of them.

For the third time the choir at Dunkeld was rebuilt in 1691, and since then several times repaired, the adjoining chapter house becoming a mausoleum for the family of the Dukes of Atholl, and the much-altered remainder serving as the local parish kirk. The nave is ruined but picturesque in its grassy setting beside the Tay, half-enclosed by fine trees, the result of being in the erstwhile grounds of a large private mansion. Thus the cathedral is not surrounded and encroached upon by innumerable gravestones and pedestals as so many ancient Scottish churches are, and most memorials that do exist are either in the roofed choir or the roofless nave. Of these one might mention that to Colonel Cleland, and another to Bishop Sinclair, who built much of the choir and whose tomb is defaced rather more than that of the recumbent 'Wolf of Badenoch'. Pedants have suggested that since the armour in which Robert II's unruly son's effigy is encased is of a slightly later date than 1394, when the 'Wolf' died, the figure cannot be him; but this surely means that the tomb was not completed until some time after. It is certainly one of the best examples of its kind in Scotland and virtually unique in its present state, for apart from that of Princess Margaret, daughter of Robert III, in the former collegiate kirk at Lincluden, in Galloway, there are no recognizable royal tombs left in Scotland. There are two ancient carved stones in the choir, one depicting amongst other scenes Daniel in the lion's den; the other is a cross-slab of pink stone which must have been brought to Dunkeld from somewhere else, possibly Scone, or even by the Celtic monks as they fled from the west.

In the nave, near the westernmost arch dividing it from the south aisle, is the tomb of Count Roehenstart. This is not mentioned in the official guide-book, nor is the gentleman often mentioned in histories of the Royal Stuarts, though he was said to be the grandson of Prince Charles Edward, and, therefore, last in the male line of that ill-starred family. The inscription on the tomb states that it is 'sacred to the memory of General Charles Edward Stuart, Count Roehenstart, who died at Dunkeld on the 28th October 1854 aged 73 years'. There are a number of ambiguities and inaccuracies here not only as to the man's identity but in the details described. He was not a general so far as is known, nor did he die at Dunkeld, but at Stirling, as the result of an accident to the stagecoach in which he was travelling. His age is also suspect, as, of course, is his identity, about which we have very little to go on. He was not the son of Charlotte, Bonnie Prince Charlie's daughter, known in history as the Duchess of Albany, though he may have been the grandson of Clementina Walkinshaw, the Prince's mistress; but by whom? Count Roehenstart himself never stressed his claims, unlike others in the same field, notably the two Sobieski Stuart brothers, who were actually the sons of a British naval officer named Allan. They claimed to be the grandsons of Louise de Stolberg, the barren spouse of Prince Charles Edward, and played their parts up to the hilt. Indeed, it is chiefly to them that we owe many of our clan tartans, as accepted and regularized in the nineteenth century and illustrated by them in the *Costume of the Clans*, which appeared in 1845 for the centenary of the Jacobite rebellion. As for 'General' Charles Edward Stuart, Count Roehenstart, it is perhaps fitting, if he was in fact the last scion of his royal clan, that he should have been laid to rest in the nave of the old cathedral at Dunkeld, once the metropolitan see of Scotland and an early capital.

Dunkeld lies at the very point where Highland and Lowland traditions and interests meet, which made it not too safe either as a capital or a cathedral town, and by the twelfth century it had lost its pre-eminence on both scores, the capital having become wherever king and court happened to be, at Scone, Stirling or Edinburgh, the metropolitan see moving with St Columba's relics to St Andrews, which brings us to the spread of the Andrean cult and its eventual supplanting of the Columban. The story is intriguing and characterized by conflicting versions, the least credible asserting that St Regulus, or Rule, brought a relic of the apostle direct to Scotland from Patras, in the fourth century, being miraculously driven ashore on the coast of Fife near where the town of St Andrews now is. Bearing this in mind it is curious how it took until the fourteenth century for the symbolic saltire cross on which St Andrew is usually shown as martyred to be officially adopted, at a period when the Scottish church was beginning to demonstrate its independence of York, proceeding to create two archbishoprics, one of Glasgow and the other of St Andrews, the overall primacy going to the latter. We also have the legend of the Battle of Athelstaneford, *c.* ninth century, on the eve of which the Scottish king is said to have beheld a vision of the blue in the sky parted by a white St Andrew's cross, which he took to be a portent of victory. In practice he was roundly defeated not at Athelstaneford, in East Lothian, but many miles away on the shores of the Solway Firth.

The Andrean cult had almost certainly arrived in Scotland by the ninth century and probably came via St Augustine, whose favourite saint Andrew was; the first church founded in Kent by Augustine, at Rochester, was dedicated to St Andrew, and all the way up to Hexham, in Northumberland, is a trail of such dedications, coupled with a number honouring St Peter. It was at Hexham that St Cuthbert, the shepherd boy from Melrose, succeeded his mentor and former abbot of Melrose, Eata, as bishop, and via Hexham that monks from Yorkshire percolated into the borderland and further north throughout the early medieval period. Hexham Cathedral itself was sacked by the Danes and supplanted by York, only to be revived as an Augustinian priory, dedicated to St Andrew, in 1113. Seven years later Alexander I of Scots, himself still claiming Northumbria as part of his domains, invited the Augustinians to Scone; and in 1144 the Abbot of Scone, formerly Canon of Nostell in Yorkshire, founded the cathedral-priory of St Andrews.

At Bywell, on the Tyne between Corbridge and Newcastle, stand two ancient churches, one dedicated to Andrew, the other to Peter, and it is interesting to note how even in Scotland, before St Andrew became the country's patron, St Peter almost rivalled his elder brother in popularity. This, of course, reflected the influence of York, which was afterwards resented and finally rejected by the Scottish church. It is illuminating to recall, however, that the first stone church built in Scotland 'in the Roman manner', after St Ninian's tiny 'Candida Casa', honours St Peter. It dates from the eighth century, when Nechtan, King of the Picts, is said by the Venerable Bede to have written to Ceolfrid, Abbot of Monkwearmouth and Jarrow, seeking clarification on various points on which the Celtic church differed from that of Rome on doctrine and usage, and asking for masons and architects to come and build a stone church 'amongst his people in the manner of the Romans', promising to dedicate it to the 'Prince of the Apostles'. The Northumbrian abbot obliged by sending St Boniface himself, and we are told this important emissary stayed for some time in what was to become in the twelfth century the Augustinian priory of St Peter at Restennet.

The masons and architects would seem also to have arrived in

Restennet Priory. The broach spire is later work

due course, as witness the lower portion of the existing tower of ruined Restennet Priory, which has close affinities with northern English work, including a doorway with a semi-circular arch supported by large voussoirs, or prominent stones at the base of the arch, which might have derived either from St Peter's, Monkwearmouth, which is likely, or from some other Northumbrian church, Corbridge, for example, where a crude triumphal arch, probably copied from a genuine Roman survivor at neighbouring Corstopitum, supports the tower. Another link with Imperial Rome as translated by northern English architects is to be seen in the smaller doorway on the south side of the tower at Restennet, where the arch is made out of a single big stone, not unlike the arches still doing service in what remains of the baths at Chesters, half-way along Hadrian's Wall.

Besides Restennet, King Nechtan's Anglian masons may have been busy elsewhere in his domains, indeed Dr James Richardson, in his *Medieval Stone Carver in Scotland* has suggested they began at

Brechin, and that the church dedicated to 'the Prince of Apostles' may have been built there. He bases this idea on some of the sculpture that appears round the tiny first-floor doorway to the round tower at Brechin, a doorway which resembles the smaller one at Restennet both in its narrowness and tallness. It too is arched very simply with a single stone, but the workmanship is definitely superior, and the placing of the doorway above ground level denotes different purposes. The tower had a dual use, that of Christian symbol and place of refuge, its first-floor doorway being reached by a ladder which was taken away in times of siege. Almost everything about the Brechin round tower, except its fifteenth-century cap, put on when the existing cathedral acquired its handsome battlemented campanile, has a Celtic, not to say an Irish look about it, the refinement of the sculpture in particular, which is not rude as at Restennet or its Northumbrian predecessors. So if Dr Richardson's theory is right, and we owe the sculpture, if not the tower itself to master masons sent to the Pictish king from Monkwearmouth, there is certainly a divergence either of workmanship or origins. He arrived at his conclusions after studying a cross-slab at Brechin carved with what he calls 'Hiberno-Saxon characters', including the figure of a saint holding something that looks like a key, that is, representing St Peter. He also makes out the two figures on either side of the narrow first-floor doorway to the round tower as the Saints Peter and Paul; posing the question 'Was this church ordered by Nechtan possibly built at Brechin, and the tower, which is of a later century, (tenth) not the oldest stone-and-lime building in Scotland?'

Brechin Cathedral itself is unrecognizable for what it must have been as late as the beginning of the nineteenth century, when the first of two restorations, and the most disastrous, took place. The building had survived roofed and in partial service until then, while now even the original plan has been lost and the principal remnants of the past, excluding the splendid pre-Norman round tower, are a fifteenth-century tower, which looks older with its round arched windows on the lower storeys, and a fine west doorway, with deeply set early-Gothic features; the wall is thickened to take the numerous pilasters and arches, as was common in Scotland where sculptural elaborations often exceeded functional purpose. Another survival, and perhaps the best-preserved one of all, is Farnell Castle, on the outskirts of Brechin. This was the *palatium nos-*

Brechin Cathedral and Round Tower; detail of towers

trum of the bishops and is still inhabited, privately. I have dealt with Farnell in some detail in my *Scotland's Castles*, and it really is a small castle, the later work resembling a laird's 'tour of fens', or defence; but there are one or two items of ecclesiastical provenance, notably the religious symbolism displayed in a 'crowned Mary' sign, on one of the skew putts, or eaves' corbels, and the design of the whole eastern gable, which instead of being finished with the usual plain crow-steps is much more interesting, each step having its own little gablet, a form seen in Germanic towns and in Flanders and having no special religious significance there, but usually reserved for churches and church buildings in Scotland.

We must now return to St Regulus, or Rule, and the legend of the arrival on our shores of a relic of St Andrew in the fourth century, which if true would mean that the tower, reputedly built by him, and still standing amidst the ruins of the cathedral at St Andrews, would not only pre-date the round tower at Brechin but St Ninian's 'Candida Casa' as the earliest surviving Christian edifice in Scotland. Most authorities, however, seem to agree that the tall square tower in question, together with the small rectangular structure at its foot, was probably part of the first cathedral and dates from the episcopate of Robert, formerly Abbot of Scone, who was elected bishop in 1127, in the reign of Alexander I. In 1144 he brought Austin canons of his order from Scone, when St Andrews became a cathedral-priory. Mr Stewart Cruden, successor to Dr Richardson as Chief Inspector of Ancient Monuments in Scotland, is not quite sure if the little shed and tall tower of St Regulus may not have been a reliquary house, not a cathedral but a stone box and sentinel to mark the site where a possible relic of St Andrew and other precious objects, illuminated manuscripts, plate and vestments, were kept. Surely this cannot have been all? There are marks showing a roof at both ends of the tower, one facing east the other west, which would normally suggest the position of choir and nave with central campanile. MacGibbon and Ross go into this problem fairly thoroughly, quoting Sir George Gilbert Scott's comment that the seals dated 1204 and 1214, preserved at Durham, show both nave and chancel, and that this would relate the building to the church at Jarrow, the choir of which was begun by Abbot Ceolfrid, whom we have already met. At Jarrow one looks from the nave through the arches of the tower to the choir beyond, the difference between the width of the nave and that of

St Andrews: the Romanesque tower of St Regulus

the choir being adjusted elevationally by the placing of false buttresses against the eastern end of the former, exactly as at St Regulus's.

The masonry is ashlar, and as fine as anything to be seen anywhere in Europe for its date. It is certainly unique in Scotland and points to imported workmen, presumably from Durham or York, especially since many of the details recall those of the church at Wharram-le-Street, near Malton, which was attached to the Augustinian priory of Nostell, whence St Andrews' first diocesan bishop. St Regulus's splendid campanile rises to over 100 feet and has brethren at Markinch Kirk in central Fife, and at Dunblane Cathedral in Perthshire, the first now being topped with a Georgian obelisk, the latter with a Gothic upper portion and spire. St Regulus's has lost whatever spire or cap it had, and is finished above a set of twin-arched belfry windows of decidedly Lombardic provenance with a plain battlement. Dr Richardson thinks that four square holes, one at each corner, could either have been provided to support scaffolding or a permanent wooden hoarding, as in medieval castles, capped with a conical roof. It is an intriguing possibility and one worth thinking about, since none of the several tall towers of this date in Scotland have their original roofs.

The Austin canons whom Bishop Robert brought to St Andrews from Scone were responsible for gently ousting a small colony of Culdees that had survived from the days of the Celtic missionaries and established themselves in the town. One mentions this before going on to describe the now ruined but once magnificent cathedral that replaced St Regulus's in the thirteenth century because outside the new sanctuary walls stood the kirk of Our Lady of the Rock, or Kirkheugh, on a cliff overlooking St Andrews Harbour. This has been associated for many years with the last Culdees, who were undoubtedly still there in the twelfth century when Bishop Robert appeared on the scene. The Bishop obtained a royal precept, backed by the authority of the Pope, commanding that on the death of each Culdee his place should be taken by a canon of the cathedral-priory, though it seems to have taken a long time for this process to eliminate all trace of the former Celtic settlement, since in the thirteenth century, when the Kirkheugh was built, the community was still labelled 'Culdee'. In practice this was inaccurate, the proper designation being 'the provost and canons of the Church of the Blessed Mary of the city of St Andrews'. The clergy did, on the other hand, enjoy special privileges; they were often royal nominees with secular rather than purely religious functions, and on at least two occasions took part in the election of bishops.

Bishops in pre-Reformation Scotland were normally elected by the cathedral chapter, the king appointing and the Pope approving, though sometimes there was tension when particular claimants to promotions tried to by-pass chapter and king and appealed directly to the Pope. In 1483, at Dunkeld, the king's appointment was rejected by the Holy See, and an argument began during which the Bishop of Rome was informed that anyone promoted by him without prior and proper election was a rebel and a traitor according to the constitution of the Scottish Parliament. Indeed, such an argument arose over the case of Gavin Douglas, son of that Earl who placed the rope round the neck of Robert Cochrane, Earl of Mar, architect and favourite of James III, in the episode known as 'Belling the Cat', who found himself imprisoned in the archiepiscopal castle at St Andrews for soliciting papal preferment when another nomination had been made by the chapter and monarch. At the Reformation King James VI and I, and his successors on the English throne till Queen Anne, continued to appoint Scottish bishops on advice; but by this time, of course, the Pope was no longer involved. It is interesting to note, however, that even after disestablishment in 1690, and the refusal of the clergy to take the oath to William of Orange, and later to George I, Scottish episcopal appointments were still subject to approval by the exiled James Francis Edward, the Old Pretender, a Papist in Rome. Scottish bishops are now elected by clergy and laity in concert, owing neither their appointments nor spiritual authority to king or Pope, nor yet the Archbishop of Canterbury.

The Augustinian Canons Regular were not monks in the ordinary sense but went out into the world and mixed with the population. They were really precursors of the preaching friars of the thirteenth century, led by the followers of St Francis of Assisi, who worked within an already corrupt church missionizing more like the old Celtic monks, from established centres, owning nothing and professing poverty. The earlier Benedictines and their reformed daughter houses not only held property but worked it, farming and manufacturing, having to justify their existences and pay their way. The Cistercians, founded at Cîteaux, near Cluny, in Burgundy, concentrated on manual labour, while the Tironen-

The entrance to St Fillan's Cave, Pittenweem

The bishop's castle at St Andrews

sians, from Tiron, near Chartres, developed what we would call crafts. The Augustinians come somewhere in between, since although they had to give up all personal possessions and live to a rule, hence the term 'regular', they retained in their abbeys and priories the social status to which they had been accustomed in the world, employing servants and not eschewing the comforts of life. They were not cloistered completely, and their mission was a civilizing one as much as anything. Of their priory at St Andrews even less survives than of the huge cathedral they served, but at Pittenweem, on the Fife coast, quite a lot remains of their house, which itself replaced an older Benedictine foundation, with headquarters on the Isle of May out in the Firth of Forth.

The Austin canons came to Pittenweem from St Andrews in the fourteenth century and part of the existing priory buildings date from that period, notably the lower vaulted floor of the former Prior's Lodge, once the wine cellar. It is expressive of the fact that the canons were renowned for their hospitality, but not only that, for they were also responsible for developing the harbour which is now one of the principal fishing ports in eastern Scotland. Until recently the Prior's Lodge was the episcopal parsonage, the rector's study possibly once the Prior's, with an odd piece of carved masonry behind one wall which may very well have been the support for a preaching pulpit. In the garden is one of two entries to St Fillan's Cave, the other opening towards the harbour. St Fillan was a shadowy figure, sometimes popping up in Fife at other times in Perthshire, who may, like other Celtic holy men, have been more than one person. In any event, his hermitage was here, at Pittenweem, and services are still held in the cave where according to legend he wrote his illuminated gospels, guided by a miraculous light and sustained by a well the water of which is still drinkable, indeed good for one. Smugglers took over the cave later but have since been displaced, as have the rooks and rubbish from the heavily corbelled fifteenth-century gatehouse, which has been made into a novel sort of bothie, or retreat for youthful visitors. The Great House, the former canons' quarters, survives, and has been turned into flats for retired clergy. It boasts oriel windows which may be of the sixteenth century and contemporary with some adorning the archiepiscopal castle in St Andrews, though here they are not eroded away to vacant shells as there.

Pittenweem Priory from the harbour. The Great House is in the centre, the Prior's Lodging on the right

The Great House

Pittenweem Priory is in much better shape than the larger one at St Andrews partly because the latter was sacked at the Reformation and its stones, with most of those of the adjacent cathedral, were used as a quarry by seventeenth-century St Andreans; also partly because a secular commendator, actually a royal bastard of James V, was appointed prior shortly before the Reformation, so that the secular buildings, though not the church which has disappeared almost entirely, were secured and kept in repair. Part was subsequently adapted as the burgh offices, the rest becoming private property until bought back for the church in the eighteenth century by the Jacobite Bishop Low. He tried to revive the priory as a seminary for young priests, and himself lived in the erstwhile Prior's Lodge. He built a new church nearby as well, but unfortunately his quasi-monastic efforts were unsuccessful. One might add that the Austin canons who once lived there had a severer offshoot in the Premonstratensians, whose principal house was at Dryburgh, but had earlier been established at Whithorn Cathedral-priory by Fergus of Galloway. They disapproved of their Augustinian brethren's freer life, and with the Pope's encouragement, and that of the Bishop of Laon, they set up a reformed branch of the order at Prémontré, in Champagne. The buildings still exist, though rebuilt and used today as a psychiatric hospital; but there are still about two thousand Premonstratensians with headquarters in Rome. They wear a white habit to distinguish themselves from the Augustinians, or Black Canons, from whom they sprang.

Of the former cathedral of St Andrews all that remains after the official depredations of the Reformers and the unofficial despoiling by the townsfolk are two giant end pieces, the late Romanesque east end, pierced by a gaunt, no longer traceried Gothic window, and a portion of the west front, rebuilt two bays shorter after a storm at the end of the thirteenth century. The length of this largest of Scottish churches was then reduced from 391 feet to 357, or in modern terms to just over 100 metres. The cathedral was cruciform, with central tower, the collapse of which, as happened at Elgin, completing the ruin of the building. The shrine of St Andrew was behind the high altar, and lining the walls of the sanctuary were the tombs of great men, religious and secular. Only the bases of these have survived, unlike some other churches where the arches above have survived to help support the upper structure. The grandest

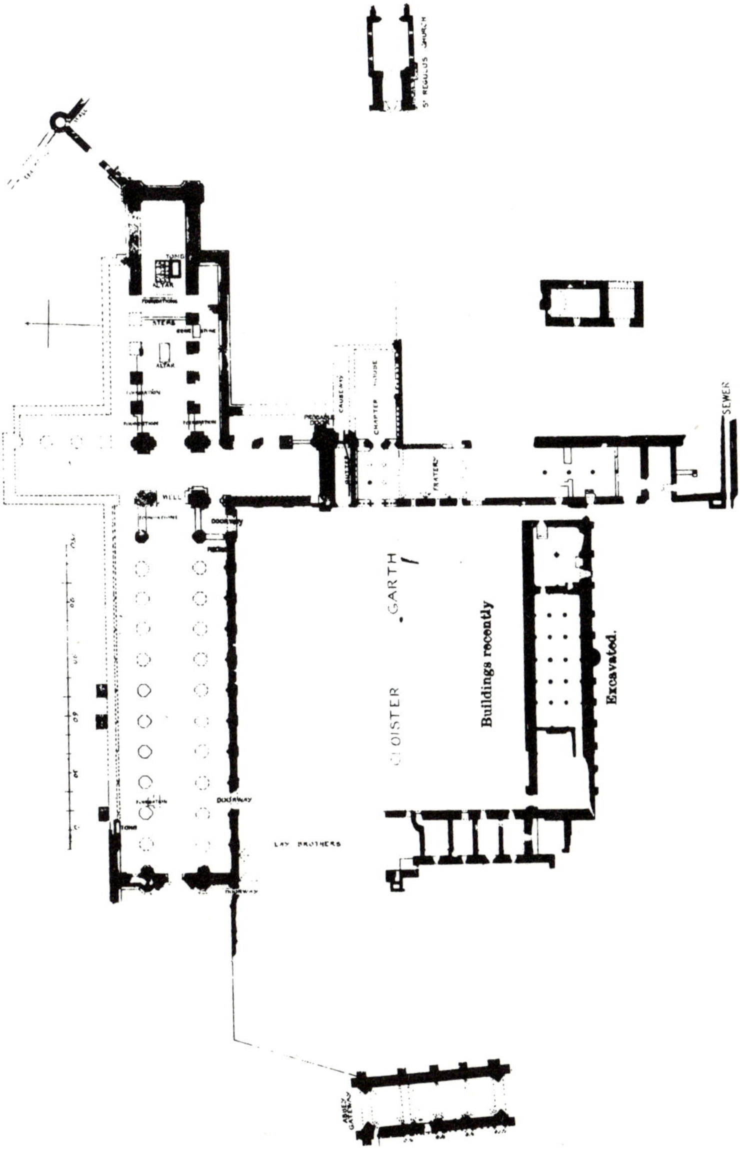

St Andrews Cathedral: plan showing conventual and other buildings

tomb would have been that of Bishop Kennedy had it been placed here as intended and not in the chapel of the College of St Salvator which he founded. Thus it has been preserved, not in its entirety since the pinnacles above the arch have been truncated and the recumbent figure of Kennedy destroyed, but enough to give an idea of what such memorials looked like.

Bishop Kennedy is recorded as having visited Florence and it is presumed that he may have got some notion of what he wanted his tomb to resemble from that visit. He undoubtedly ordered the monument before his demise, and it has some affinities with the grandiose tomb of Cardinal d'Amboise in the cathedral at Rouen. The Cardinal also went to Italy, but a little later on, and the pinnacles that decorate the top of his arched tomb have a decided Renaissance feel about them, whereas Bishop Kennedy's are flamboyant-Gothic, the sculptors probably being Flemish, or northern-French, many of whom were engaged in Scotland at the end of the fifteenth century, when the tomb was made. The sepulchral table, or altar, is of Tournai stone from Belgium, and the elaborations above and around are so intricate and masterful that they must be of Continental workmanship. One is reminded of the so-called Kennedy Mace, which the bishop had made in Paris by the silversmith to the Dauphin in 1461, and which is topped with a similar array of sprockets and niches, albeit in silver and still retaining their figurines.

Besides the rather toothy remains that mark the position and extent of St Andrews Cathedral, arcaded suggestions on the south side of where cloisters once were, a few footings and a reconstructed warming house, now a museum, there is not a lot to show for past grandeur. Yet, dominating a sea of gravestones and an archaeologist's paradise of knee-high masonry, is St Andrews' finest and oldest building, St Rule's or Regulus's Tower, which escaped the attentions of the desecrators and thieves that ruined cathedral and priory, possibly because it had long before ceased to be of any importance and may indeed have been disused. A number of very ancient and significant 'finds' are now housed in the rebuilt warming house-cum-museum, including a sarcophagus which Mr Cruden thinks might have contained the relics of an early Celtic king, St Regulus or perhaps the legendary relic of St Andrew. If the latter, that would explain the separate existence of St Regulus's church, not as a cathedral but, at least in origin, as a relic house.

Bishop Kennedy's mace

Much more impressive than any part of the actual cathedral, however, and certainly better preserved, are its fortified enclosing walls, which, seeming part of a medieval town wall, with ports and towers standing almost to full height as one enters St Andrews from the east, are actually ecclesiastical. These walls, more than half a mile in extent, were largely the work of Prior Hepburn, who raised them in the early sixteenth century. They enclose not only the site of the former cathedral-priory but a famous girls' school, with playing fields, two graveyards and the gas works. No wonder one thinks of them as secular.

The town of St Andrews does boast a genuine entrance gate, its West Port, facing inland, depending otherwise for protection from the high garden walls that ran round the perimeter of the burgh in times past. The ports, or gateways, in the priory wall are Gothic arched, but plain and business-like, and here and there are niches and panels for statuettes and coats of arms. Only the Pends, as they are usually called, are ruined, constituting a double-gated entrance to the priory, once groin-vaulted and very similar to the double entry surviving at Arbroath Abbey, the two being Scotland's only substantial remnants of such features. Within the walls there is also part of the Hospitium Novum, which was built to receive Mary of Lorraine when she came to Scotland as consort of James V and landed near St Andrews at Fifeness. The building subsequently became the 'palace' of the Archbishops after the destruction of St Andrews Castle, and amongst the better-known inmates of the rejuvenated hospice was Archbishop Sharp, as notorious in his day, in extreme Protestant eyes, as Cardinal Beaton, or Bethune, the latter being murdered in the castle, his body salted and thrown into the dungeon. Sharp was brutally stabbed to death by revengeful Covenanters on Magus Muir on his way home one evening from smoking a pipe with one of his clergy. Beaton's principal crime was that he would not play Henry VII's game, and opposed the Reformation, Sharp's that having been a Presbyterian he allowed himself to become a bishop and supported the government of Charles II. His cathedral was the present Holy Trinity Kirk, where his black and white marble tomb is.

The archbishops of St Andrews, pre-Reformation and post, had country retreats which, while not specifically qualifying as ecclesiastical structures, are perhaps worth a brief mention. Monimail Tower to the west of Cupar, county town of Fife, is of some anti-

St Andrews Priory: Patrick Hepburn's harbour port

quity, dating in its older parts from the time of Bishop Lamberton and the reign of Robert Bruce, but mostly from the sixteenth century, when Cardinal Beaton added the existing parapet and Renaissance roundels. These were copied from examples at nearby Falkland Palace and were probably the work of royal masons. It is roofed and in tolerable order and was last occupied by an archbishop immediately before the Reformation storm by John Hamilton, formerly Abbot of Paisley, then Bishop of Dunkeld and finally last Archbishop of St Andrews in the Roman obedience. He was a colourful personality who ended his life on the gallows, at Stirling, having been apprehended for taking up arms on behalf of Mary, Queen of Scots against the Confederate Lords, and being found wearing armour under his clerical garb. He went to Monimail for his health, in the company of a quack Italian doctor, who counselled drinking the water from a spring in the garden, which seems to have cured him. In a nineteenth-century volume of the Edinburgh Architectural Association I found a drawing of a very

Dairsie: Archbishop Spottiswood's castle and tower of kirk

large candlestick which used to be in Monimail Tower, too large for normal domestic use and too grand, which made me wonder if it might not have been the old Paschal Candle-holder from St Andrews Cathedral, and if so the only piece of pre-Reformation furniture left; but where is it now?

Nearer to St Andrews and approached by one of two splendid fifteenth-century arched bridges over the Eden, both built by Bishop Wardlaw, founder of St Andrews University, are the ruins of Dairsie Castle. This was the summer residence of Archbishop Spottiswood, the man who crowned Charles I in Holyrood Abbey in 1633 and wrote his history of the Scottish church and state here. All that remains of the castle are a few lumps of purposeless masonry and one round tower, the base of which is punctured with shot holes for defence, the top lined with compartments for doves. The archbishop was, in common with many others holding archiepiscopal office, also chancellor of Scotland, and primate, and strove hard to restore some sense of decency and order into Scottish religious life. In particular he tried to recreate a species of Gothic architecture which he thought more suitable than the 'God-boxes' that had replaced so many older Scottish churches. He failed in this, as in his other ploys, and was forced into exile during the Civil Wars, dying in the south and being buried at Westminster. Before he went, however, he created the amusing and unique Gothic-revival kirk that still stands crowning the hill at Dairsie, on the north side of the Eden across Bishop Wardlaw's bridge. Dairsie Kirk had no real precedent and no imitators, indeed, everything about it is novel in architectural terms, the traceried windows are not true Gothic, the buttresses are only decoration, and the east end is no more than a slight diminution of the rectangular plan, not a genuine chancel. The tower takes the form of a turreted bellcot supported on heavy corbels, and on it the archbishop's coat of arms appears with the device: JEHOVAH I HAVE LOVED THE BEAUTY OF THY HOUSE. Alas, as with his master Charles I's own inscription over a restored entrance to Holyrood Abbey: HE SHALL BUILD ANE HOISE FOR MY NAME AND I WILL STABLISH THE THRONE OF HIS KINGDOM FOR EVER, which proved premature, fate intervened and the interior of Jehovah's House was gutted by the enemies of beauty, and it has not since been restored. Happily, however, the building itself is roofed and maintained and is the property of St Andrews University, who use it for cultural purposes, chamber music concerts and the like.

The south coast of Fife is noted for its weems, or caves, St Fillan's at Pittenweem we have already mentioned, while at Dysart, further west, was St Serf's 'desert', or place of retreat, hence the modern nomenclature. This saint Serf was the same who had his principal cell at Culross and was the friend and mentor of St Kentigern, the 'loved one'. He belonged, therefore, to the earlier Christian period in Scotland, that immediately following in the wake of St Ninian. St Fillan, on the other hand, was part of the Columban mission, which is interesting since it shows that both missions worked in the same area and after merging had a continuous existence of some sort, Viking raids notwithstanding. In fact the medieval church at St Monans, near Pittenweem, probably stands on the site of a chapel founded by St Ninian himself, the name still being pronounced locally as St Minans. There were actually many ancient Christian settlements hereabouts, one of the oldest being on the island of St Columba, or Inchcolm, where the abbey was refounded by Alexander I and colonized with Augustinian monks from Scone in the twelfth century.

Inchcolm is familiarly called 'The Iona of the East', which it deserves to be, not only on account of its antiquity and probable Columban founding, but curiously enough for its appearance, in which the buildings of Iona, better preserved here but not unlike, would seem in some respects to be repeated. The abbey was included in the huge sprawling diocese of Dunkeld, which, until the slicing off of Argyll and the Isles, also comprehended Iona; and it is worth recalling that several bishops of Dunkeld were buried at Inchcolm, and one, Bishop Richard of Inverkeithing, was responsible for building the thirteenth-century choir there, his heart being set in the north wall. Much older than any part of the medieval abbey, at least according to the late Dr Douglas Simpson, is that tiny stone cell with the beehive roof that may represent the one surviving example we have of a primitive Celtic church or chapel. The site is certainly holy, and the tiny cell, with its simple domed roofing, now mortared but not originally, was undoubtedly in existence when Alexander I, driven onto the island by a storm in the Firth of Forth, sheltered within for three nights with the resident hermit. He refounded Inchcolm as a priory for the Austin canons in thankfulness. Afterwards raised to abbatial status, the conventual buildings on Inchcolm remain for the most part

Inchcolm Abbey: general view

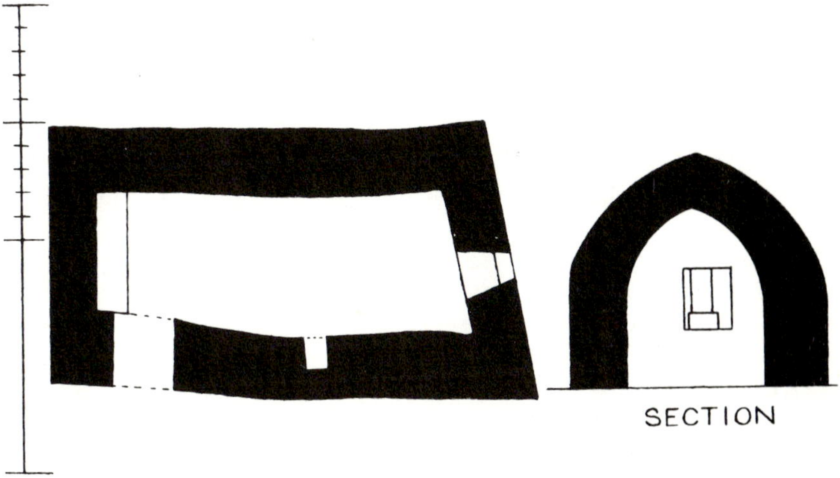

St Colm's Cell, plan and section

roofed, having been used as domestic quarters by the successors to the Regent Moray, half-brother of Mary, Queen of Scots, who obtained possession of them and whose descendants established themselves as secular lords in the neighbourhood. The abbey, but not the church, which has almost entirely disappeared except for the tower and south transept, is the best preserved in Scotland, and was inhabited until placed in the care of the Ministry of Public Works. The tower and south transept have survived because they were made into a house for a latter-day abbot, or commendator, while the church disappeared because its masonry was removed to strengthen the defences of Edinburgh after Flodden!

One arrives at Inchcolm by boat from Aberdour, a modest holiday resort on the north shore of the Firth of Forth, with a fine castle of the Douglas Earls of Morton and the early Norman church of St Fillan, formerly the castle chapel, to whet one's appetite for the more exciting things to be seen over the waves; and there are waves, often quite big ones, which make landing on Inchcolm something of a relief, as well as helping to create an atmosphere of change and remoteness not completely justified by the island's geographical position. In fact, one can see Edinburgh clearly from it, the silhouette of Arthur's Seat, the castle and three tall spires of St Mary's Cathedral, the city still 'reeking' despite the Clean Air Bill, and in the background the Pentland Hills, looking mountainous and wild though nowhere reaching more than two thousand feet in height. To the north Aberdour lies in its sheltered bay, woods coming right down to the water's edge, where small inlets ringed with white sand remind one a little of that other evocative spot made holy by the presence of St Columba.

Before its destruction the church must have resembled that of the abbey of Culross, still further along the coast, for although founded in the early twelfth century most of the buildings are later, and Culross was begun soon afterwards. Both churches were cruciform with central towers, built over the stone pulpitum and screen dividing the nave from the choir, the lay people from the clergy. Culross was, of course, the training ground of the young St Kentigern and the foundations of a church dedicated to him have been exposed at the eastern entrance to the burgh. The newer abbey stands at the top of a hill above the houses and was a Cistercian establishment, the monks coming from Kinloss, in Moray. The Cistercians were the very opposite of the Austin canons, fol-

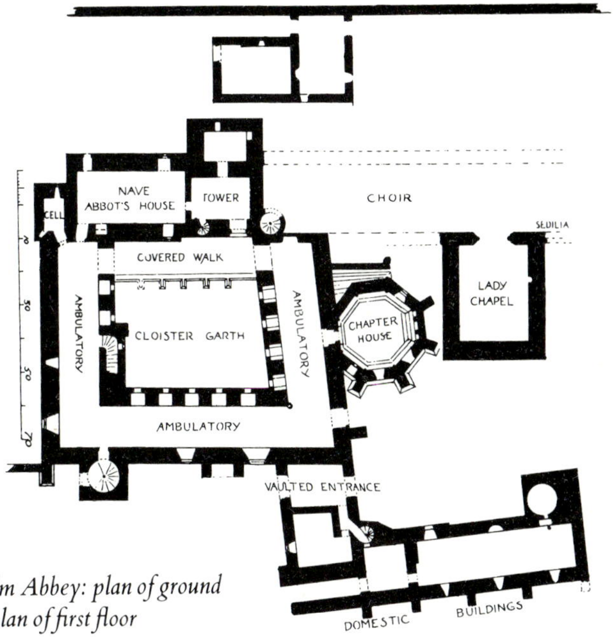

Inchcolm Abbey: plan of ground floor; plan of first floor

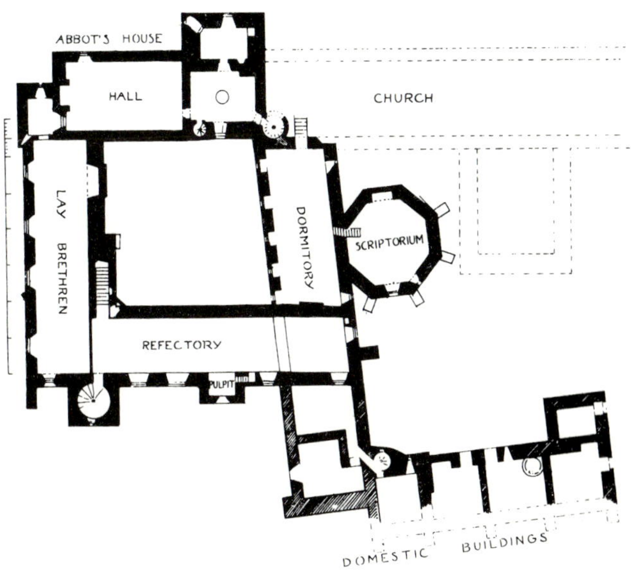

lowing a strict rule, working like beavers and living and worshipping in the plainest of architectural surroundings. Even less of their abbey at Culross remains than most, the nave of the church has gone, as at Inchcolm, the tower has been rebuilt in mock Gothic, and a comparatively modern parish kirk fills most of the choir. However, there is one object worth seeking out in the Jacobean tomb of Sir George Bruce of Carnock, which takes a form well enough known in England, but rare in Scotland, that of reclining parents with mourning offspring lined up in front. There has been a certain amount of spiteful mutilation in the vicinity and the kneeling bairns now face outwards towards the beholder instead of their dead forebears; but generally speaking this monument has survived rather better than many north of the Border, better, for instance, than others in the same kirk, where the despoilers of saintly images have used the opportunity to take a swipe or two with their axes at the noses and other protruding parts of recumbent lairds and dames.

Sir George Bruce, who completed the work of the monks at Culross by extending their coal mines, was the brother of Edward Bruce, first Lord Kinloss. Their father had married the sister of Robert Reid, Abbot of Kinloss, Lord President of the Court of Session, founder of Edinburgh University and last Bishop of Orkney before the Reformation. Thus the nephew fell heir to the commendatorship of the abbeys of Kinloss and Culross, taking his title from the former. He adapted and lived in the old abbot's tower, which is now the most substantial remnant of Kinloss Abbey, and upon which the arms of Robert Reid appear. Other remnants are meagre but include a recessed washing place, or laver, an odd rarity when one considers how many have survived in England and all over the Continent, and odd too that the abbot's fortified tower turned laird's residence should cover a run of the original lavatory drain; but the monks were clean, cleaner than knights and ladies, and at Inchcolm they were able to arrange their lavatory near the sea so that it could be flushed twice a day by the tide.

The ruins of Culross are scanty enough, but show at least one other similarity with Inchcolm, other than the plan of the church, for the abbatial buildings, taking advantage of the fall in the ground, are on two levels, some rudimentary bits of which can be seen in the present manse garden, with vaulted chambers below. The double storeys at Inchcolm derive from different circum-

Remnant of Culross Abbey in the manse garden

stances, the island suffering greatly from raids by marauding ships, and in particular from English pirates, who in the fifteenth century did considerable damage. In order to make themselves more secure from such visitations, therefore, the monks built their cloisters on one level and immediately above were the dormitories; and these cloisters were not of the usual open arcaded variety but tunnel-like and dark, being lit by small, round-headed windows, with seats inside. There is evidence of there having been artificial lighting as well. They are the only surviving vaulted cloisters, albeit barrel-vaulted, in Scotland, and the dormitory still retains its reading pulpit. When there was a raid the inmates fled to the upper floor, shut themselves in and hoped for the best.

Even the chapter house is two-storeyed at Inchcolm, with a reading room and library over connected with the monks' dormitory. It is rib-vaulted in plain, early pointed fashion, without any central supporting column, and is the only one in Scotland so designed. It is also the only octagonal chapter house north of the

Border other than the one at Elgin and the only one attached to an abbey or priory. In common with the rest of the structural details at Inchcolm this building is as plain and good in its architecture as it could be, the simple pointed vaults rising from slender side columns, themselves resting on the stone bench that customarily ran round chapter houses. There is a single step up to the bench, increased to three at one end, where there is a triple sedilia, or seat, with a slightly higher niche in the middle, this being reserved for the abbot, with the prior and sub-prior on either side. The design was probably of English inspiration, if not workmanship, and dates from the thirteenth century and the days when Bishop Richard was at Dunkeld. One or two interesting discoveries have been made since the abbey was taken over by the Ministry, notably the original mensa, or stone altar table, which has been reconstructed, and a fascinating wall painting showing a medieval funeral, with clerics and censors in attendance. This was covered up behind some fifteenth-century plasterwork, and partly preserved, the heads of the participants having gone. Their probable appearance has been suggested by the scholarly Dr Richardson, who considered this one of the most important 'finds' in his term of office and one of the best things of its kind left in Scotland.

TWO

The Legacy of Queen Margaret and Her Sons

PART ONE

TODAY, with the prospect of separate assemblies for Scotland and Wales, it is instructive, and possibly sobering to some, to recall how, in the case of Scotland practically the whole modern history of that kingdom and its recognizable national culture date from the arrival in North Britain of Edgar Atheling and his sister Margaret, who married Malcolm Canmore, King of Scots, in the second half of the eleventh century. They were the descendants of Alfred the Great and the Saxon kings of England and ultimate heirs of Edward the Confessor. It is perhaps also instructive and sobering to recall that the only long period of relative peace and prosperity ever enjoyed by the Scots derives from the same event and lasted for nearly two hundred years, until the untimely demise of Alexander III, last of what might be termed the Westminster line of Scottish kings, in 1286. Then the process of assimilation and union, so far achieved by intermarriage and close cultural contacts, was abruptly ended, when Edward I of England, failing to get his way by peaceful methods, decided to use force. After subjugating the Welsh he proceeded to threaten his fellow Anglo-Normans in Scotland, but without success, instigating a generation of fighting and enmity where none had been before, which ended in the defeat of his son, Edward II, at Bannockburn and a period of intermittent scrapping and racial disharmony.

Thus, I think it is fair to say that Scottish Nationalism, both as we know it today and as it appeared in the fourteenth and fifteenth centuries, derives very largely from the foolish ambitions and delusions of grandeur of 'The Hammer of the Scots', its extreme form being virtually unknown previously. It is important to remember this, especially in the context of the building of Scotland's abbeys and cathedrals, for nearly all of them, certainly the medieval ones, were erected or founded in the two hundred years preceding Edward's invasion, under the aegis of a French-speaking, Anglo-Norman establishment, presided over by the sons and grandsons of a Saxon princess whose piety and determination to bring Scotland into the western religious fold was rewarded by her canonization in 1250. In that year her body was taken from its tomb in the abbey kirk at Dunfermline and placed in a new Lady Chapel beyond the choir, a tiny fragment of which survives. She came to Scotland with her relations and friends as a refugee from William the Conqueror, married Malcolm Canmore, Malcolm III, and began at once her self-appointed task of establishing Roman order in Scottish ecclesiastical life, introducing the feudal system and showing the way for her sons and later descendants to govern through bishops, abbots and knights. Her family founded or refounded between the beginning of the twelfth century and the end of the thirteenth no less than nine out of eleven pre-Reformation Scottish dioceses and over three dozen abbeys and priories.

There are those who consider Margaret, queen and saint, a disaster, and regret she even came to Scotland. These are the believers in a separate and independent Celtic church, which she is accused of destroying, as well as those who would prefer to forget their debt to her and the Anglo-Normans, and decry English influence generally. Such attitudes are understandable but they cannot be maintained for, as Lowland Scots are wont to declare, 'facts are chiels that winna ding', which means more or less that they cannot be denied. This is undoubtedly true when we come to the founding and building of Dunfermline Abbey, though fourteenth-century chroniclers, anxious to re-write history in the wake of the Wars of Independence, went to enormous lengths to try and prove that Queen Margaret did not found the abbey at all but her husband before her arrival. These accounts are easily discounted as false by their late-medieval terminology, but their very existence is symptomatic of post-Bannockburn thinking in Scotland. Queen Margaret did, in fact, found Dunfermline Abbey, as a priory in the first instance in about 1070, as recorded by Turgot, prior of Durham, the Queen's biographer and confessor. It was named after Christ Church, in Canterbury, mother of English Christianity, and traditionally erected on the site of the primitive structure in which she married Malcolm Canmore in 1068.

The base of this eleventh-century foundation, which Archbishop Lanfranc himself sent Benedictine monks to serve, has been traced beneath the floor of the Norman nave of a grander kirk that replaced it in the reign of David I, her second surviving son. This nave, the most exciting and forceful creation of the Durham school of masons in Scotland, has survived intact and roofed, and is today in the care of the Department of the Environment. The choir of the medieval church has completely disappeared, partly as the result of earlier dilapidations, but mostly on account of its rebuilding in 1818 to the designs of William Burn, notorious for his almost simultaneous and equally brutal treatment of St Giles's, in Edinburgh. His understanding of Gothic architecture was decidedly less than that of the neo-classical mode, where there were certain restraints. He lived in the age of the so-called 'Battle of the Styles', when romantic medievalism was accepted as a genuine return to the Middle Ages, and the cult of Greek and Roman motifs was thought to be an authentic reflection of the Antique. One can, of course, ignore the new choir, once one has got over the effect of seeing the letters, KING ROBERT THE BRUCE formed in the balustrading of the tower, and cast a sceptical eye on the possible position of that hero's burial place, marked by a brass plate on the floor of the modern kirk. Queen Margaret rested behind all this, her tomb becoming a national shrine and resort of pilgrims until destroyed at the Reformation. None of the royal tombs that used to be here, including those of seven kings and three queens, have survived, so there is not much point in mentioning them, except to show how prestigious it was to be buried in such holy ground, and to emphasize the presence nearby of a royal palace, one in which not only many Scots kings lived and died, but in which Charles I was born and his sister, Elizabeth of Bohemia, ancestor of our own queen and her proper namesake.

Stewart Cruden gives an intriguing indication as to the probable shape of Queen Margaret's church, having a tall tower and small rectangular west end, to which was later added a tiny choir with a rounded apse. This would suggest affinities with St Regulus's at St Andrews, making it one of several erected about the same time, immediately before and immediately after the setting up of the Anglo-Norman hegemony, and derived from

Northern English examples. These links are confirmed by known history and reinforced by the fact that the Queen's confessor was first prior of the Benedictine cathedral-priory at Durham, at the consecration of which her husband, Malcolm Canmore, was present. There was a wave of anti-English feeling following the death by treachery of Malcolm and his eldest son Edward, at Alnwick, a feeling fanned by Donald Bane, his brother, who usurped the crown until deposed by Edgar, the king's second son by Queen Margaret, when friendly relations with the south, and particularly with Durham, were rejoined. In the fight for supremacy the first abbey naturally suffered and in 1128, under David I, Margaret's fourth son, a new foundation was made and a new building begun.

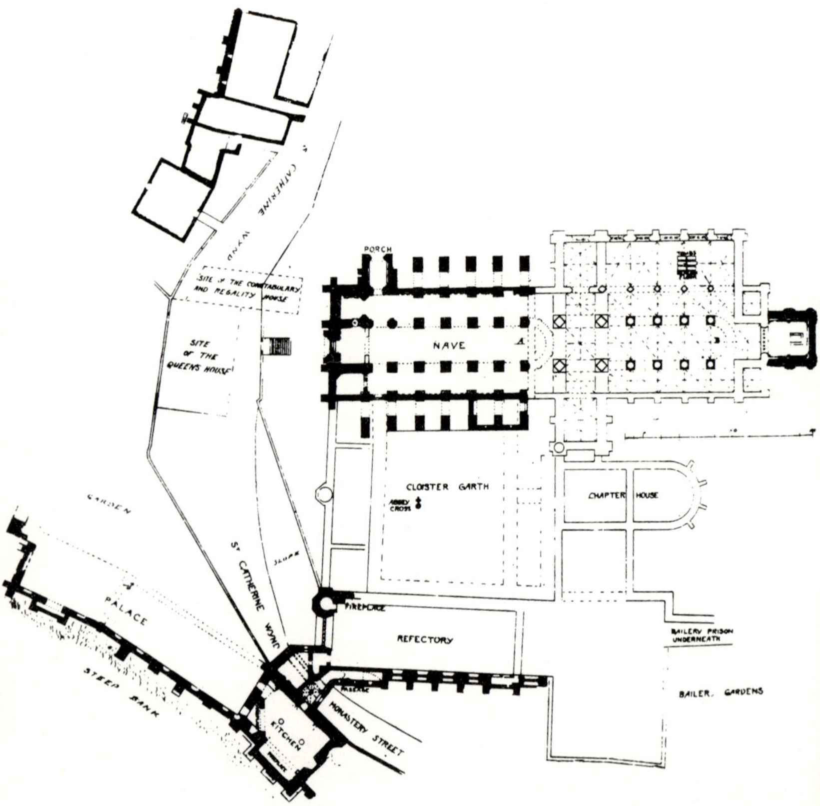

Dunfermline Abbey: plan

Dunfermline Abbey: the nave with columns in the style of Durham Cathedral (R. W. Billings)

Masons from Durham were almost certainly responsible for the great fat round piers of the nave arcade, the deep-set arches of the triforium and complementary clerestory windows. In particular two of the round piers, one showing chevron incisions and the other a continuous twisted band, are direct translations from the mother priory on the banks of the Wear. They create, incidentally, curious optical illusions when seen at different distances, the chevron pier especially, which looks wider at the top than the bottom from one angle and the reverse from another.

The ceiling of the nave is made of timber and flat, while the aisles are stone vaulted, which puts Dunfermline in a lower class than St Magnus's, Kirkwall, which was stone vaulted throughout except for the last two bays of the nave, which have, however, now been so completed. The dates of St Magnus's, Durham and Dunfermline make interesting comparison and are so close as to link all three in a way which has not yet been entirely satisfactorily explained. Could it be that the Durham masons who built the nave at Dunfermline were the same whose marks have been detected at

Coldingham Priory: detail of windows and arcading

Kirkwall, and did this in any way result from the earlier link between Malcolm Canmore and Orkney, when he married for his first wife Ingibjorg, widow of Earl Thorfin? In any event, Kirkwall was begun in 1137 and finished, the original cathedral, by 1152. Dunfermline was begun in 1128 and thought to have been finished, the Norman part, by 1150, when it was re-dedicated. Durham was begun in 1093 and completed by 1140. These dates are so near they cannot be merely coincidental, and they become meaningful in the extreme when one compares their architectural similarity.

There is a fourth Scottish link with Durham in the founding and building of Coldingham Priory, in Berwickshire, where one and a half walls survive of a once extensive monastery and church which may have been re-founded on pre-Norman foundations by King Edgar who, in any case, gave the land to the prior of Durham in 1098. Coldingham differed in some respects from other contemporary Scottish foundations which, although colonized from the south, came under local jurisdiction, whereas here the priory was not only served from Durham but represented a tiny enclave of northern English ecclesiastical territory outwith the authority of the Scottish bishops. Some years before the Reformation this anomalous situation was corrected, and at the Reformation, Coldingham suffered rather more than the average destruction and subsequent use as a quarry. In the nineteenth century its scanty remains were rescued and the two runs of wall still standing incorporated within a new parish kirk, built in a style sympathetic to the old Northumbrian work. My father was actually baptized in this building, but that is by the way. More important in the present context is the refinement and perfection of the surviving portions of the original priory church. No longer do we see the heavy but impressive piers and arches of Dunfermline or Kirkwall, but the first signs of Gothic in the form of delicately conceived lancets above the more usual round-arched arcading of Romanesque; here in the lightest possible relief and far removed in spirit and form from anything seen in Scotland previously. Inside are more interesting variations on a theme in the form of a pointed Gothic arcade around the base of the walls, with a clerestory of more lancets, supported on slender columns and arranged in sets of three, the taller, central lancets, being lit by a window, the others are blank. The sparing but effective use of simple leaf motives, notably the so-called 'water-leaf', sets new standards of sculptural excellence and marks the transition from Romanesque to Gothic detail.

In 1244, at the behest of Alexander III, the Pope gave the Abbot of Dunfermline 'the mitre', which set him above others and second only to a bishop. At that time the number of clergy serving the abbey had risen to over fifty, which is very large indeed, though it no doubt befitted a royal establishment which, much more than Holyrood Abbey was ever to do, represented the Westminster of Scotland. Edward I of England stayed here as a guest and on leaving burnt the abbatial quarters down, leaving only the church slightly damaged. Thus the monastic ruins one sees today are the remnants of a subsequent rebuilding begun by Robert Bruce and continued on and off until the Reformation and the arrival on the scenes of Anne of Denmark, consort of James VI and I. She held the lands and regalities of Dunfermline as part of her dowry, and very lucrative they were too, for the property and its control stretched from Berwickshire to the Highlands; and she was also able to collect the tolls levied on those using the Queensferry over the Firth of Forth, first established by Queen Margaret. Happily, Anne of Denmark was a lady of taste and a notable connoisseur, and she had for chamberlain and master of works a like-minded soul in the form of William Schaw, whom she sent to Denmark, as she later did Inigo Jones, to study Renaissance buildings there at first hand. She employed him on the restoration of the abbey kirk as well as portions of the royal palace, and it is to Schaw that we owe the rebuilt north-western tower, a first-rate example of a late-Gothic structure in the vernacular which perfectly matches the massive simplicity of the Norman nave. He also restored the west front as such, retaining its Gothic features as well as a handsome Norman doorway with five diminishing rings of zigzag patterned arches and supporting columns, protected by a thickening of the wall and a stone lean-to roof.

Two other Norman doorways have survived, with fewer arches and columns but nicely preserved, one to the south is hidden a little from the public gaze between Schaw's enormous buttresses. These are a special feature of the architecture of Dunfermline Abbey, and rise in an arch directly from the ground, being set back in steps as they rise, to end in Gothic gablets against the aisle. The north, or marriage door, where the first part of the nuptials, the espousal and exchange of vows before witnesses took place, was added to by

Dunfermline Abbey: William Schaw's buttresses and towers; the south door

Schaw, who built on a fine vaulted porch, with stone slab roof; and so much in the spirit of the Gothic age that it actually has a niche, though no saint, over the entrance, and stone seat inside. One would scarcely attribute this to the year 1594 in the ordinary way, but the Queen's chamberlain was obviously no ordinary master mason, and his restoration of the west front is equally sensitive and scholarly. A rare achievement for its period, when the destruction of churches was rife and fear of beauty had reached almost paranoiac proportions amongst those enflamed by the preaching of John Knox and his affiliates. William Schaw's tomb is in the nave he restored, it is a typical Jacobean tribute, erected in 1602 at the behest of the Queen herself, and is suitably inscribed with the list of his talents, works and travels. With the royal tribute is another from Alexander Seton, Earl of Dunfermline, the Queen's bailie. He was probably the builder and one of the earliest occupants of the Abbot's House, a tiny angle-turret and crow-steps of which can be seen from the site of Queen Margaret's former burial place beyond the east end of the choir. It is not an ecclesiastical building, nor was the abbot a genuine ecclesiastical figure, representing the secular type of abbot who, with a new breed of semi-secular bishops, sat in the Scottish Parliament under the Reformation settlement of 1560. Sir Robert Pitcairn, for instance, was Abbot of Dunfermline from 1560 to 1584, Archdeacon of St Andrews and Royal Legate and Privy Councillor, but not a cleric in any spiritual sense at all. He lies buried with others in the abbey. The Earl of Dunfermline merely inherited the abbot's secular post and house, he was commendator and an official of the court whose daughter, later Lady Yester, was nanny to the young Prince Charles, the future Charles I.

Today the fragmentary remains of the abbatial quarters at Dunfermline consist largely of two walls of the former refectory or dining-room, and lower vaulted area, joined by an arched tower to the kitchen and former royal palace, in which Elizabeth 'the Winter Queen' and King Charles were born. Curiously enough, Anne of Denmark did not habitually live there since she got her chamberlain-cum-architect to design her a separate, more modern house. This has not survived at all, but a cliff-like line of holed and buttressed masonry does rise dramatically from the trees of Pittencrieff Glen where once the kings and queens of Scotland held court and their bairns grew up. Indeed, so evocative is this ghostly remnant that one cannot help comparing it with what remains of the Schloss at Heidelberg, where Princess Elizabeth Stuart lived as spouse of Frederick of the Rhine, the marriage being celebrated by Shakespeare in *The Tempest*, with James, her father, as Prospero and her husband as Ferdinand, though she teasingly called him her 'Caliban', and she was his Miranda.

That the Scots are no respecters of persons is clear from the eventual treatment the royal palace at Dunfermline received, and the desecration of all the royal tombs, including that of Scotland's hero king, Robert I, in the abbey kirk. The same fate befell those at Holyrood as we shall see. The despoilers descended upon Dunfermline as soon as the last Stuart king to stay there, Charles II, departed. That was in the days when the 'Merry Monarch' was the unwilling guest of the Covenanters in his father's kingdom. Later, after his Restoration, the central tower of the abbey kirk collapsed and put paid to the choir. This, plus the terrible fate meted out to the abbatial quarters and royal shrines must make one doubly

The ruins of Dunfermline Palace

grateful for the efforts of Anne of Denmark and her chamberlain in preserving for us the splendid nave and west front. Perhaps the very solidarity of the Norman masonry did not lend itself to amateur quarrying and carting way as softer stone did at St Andrews and Holyrood? At any rate, the nave is still there, only rivalled by St Magnus's at Kirkwall, to which grand building practically the only serious threat has come from over-zealous restorers, rather than from the axes and pikes of the 'deformers'. In fact, St Magnus's was saved by the townspeople of Kirkwall themselves, who resisted orders coming from Edinburgh to give their cathedral what we would probably term 'the treatment'; and thus the building has come down to us more or less intact.

Orkney only officially became part of the Scottish kingdom in 1472, when it was annexed by James III in lieu of his wife's dowry, of which only 2000 florins out of the 60,000 promised by her father, Christian I of Denmark, were paid. Pleading lack of funds the king, who was also ruler of Norway, placed first Orkney, and then Shetland, in pawn in 1468, but made no attempt to redeem them, though perhaps in international law this could still be done if the Norwegians or Danes wished to. The subject interests me because I have inherited a copy of the fresco painted on the courtyard wall of the Castello di Malpaga, near Bergamo, which shows Christian I out hawking with the retired Venetian *condottiere*, Colleoni. Apparently he had enough funds to visit Italy and pay his respects to the Pope, but not to provide for his daughter Margaret when she married James III. In 1486 the King of Scots granted Kirkwall its Royal Charter when he made over the fabric of St Magnus's to the burgh, in whose care it has been ever since, except for a brief period in the first half of the nineteenth century, when the government in London claimed the cathedral as crown property. They set the newly created Board of Works to restore it, and did some good work clearing out unsightly galleries and repairing the roof, but when the mistake was found out, and they were forced to vacate, a great deal of this was undone; the town council showed a rare thrawnness, put all the galleries back and did what they could to restore the earlier *status quo*. In fact, the attitude of some of those concerned definitely left much to be desired, as witness the sweeping up of and throwing out as rubbish of the bones of Bishop Tulloch, and the picking out from the rubbish of anything that glistened, taking it away for the Museum of Antiquities.

One suspects that a greater sense of propriety pertains amongst most Orcadians nowadays than many folk living further south, more pride in local traditions and their remarkable architectural heritage. One is reminded of a similar state in Norway, particularly in respect of religious buildings, which were not destroyed or irrevocably damaged by iconoclasts at the Reformation, and in which church life continued much as it had always done. Something of the same spirit seems to have survived in Orkney and Shetland at the time of the Reformation, for the line of bishops continued unbroken until the first years of the eighteenth century. It was then that St Magnus's, almost for the first time since the days of Patrick, bastard royal earl in Jacobean times, was subject to minor desecration. Earl Patrick had tried to set himself up independently of the Scottish crown, for which treasonable act the Earl of Caithness was sent to arrest him and bring him to trial. In a vain attempt to evade this he tried to turn the tower of St Magnus into a refuge and strongpoint, but fortunately Bishop Law talked him out of it.

Interestingly enough, in R. W. Billings's *Baronial and Ecclesiastical Antiquities of Scotland*, from which we illustrate certain features showing the condition of several abbeys and cathedrals as they were before restoration or further dilapidation in the nineteenth century, there appears a detail of woodwork from Kirkwall Cathedral together with a drawing of what the author describes as 'Earl Patrick's pew'. It seems unlikely that the earl ever darkened the doors of St Magnus's, except for the purpose mentioned above, as when he was taken to Edinburgh for execution he could not recite the Lord's Prayer, and his departure for the next world had to be postponed until he could do so. MacGibbon and Ross are probably correct when they describe the canopied seat illustrated by Billings as the bishop's throne, but they are incorrect in saying that this and all the other woodwork has disappeared, since the screen in St Olaf's Episcopal Church in Kirkwall is made up of old woodwork coming from the cathedral. Evidently the 'pew' and panels escaped the attentions of the Town Guard in 1702, when St Magnus's was again in some danger of despoliation, the Guard making use of it as their headquarters and having to be evicted for smoking and swearing and generally committing a nuisance. Thus Kirkwall Cathedral remained little altered and the structure undamaged until the partial restoration and attempt to undo it in the

St Magnus's Cathedral: the nave, looking east (R. W. Billings)

nineteenth century, and the replacement of the low-pitched, Norman style-roof by an inappropriate Gothic spire. At some future date the Friends of St Magnus's hope to raise sufficient funds to have this taken down and a proper one substituted; meantime what money they have has had to be spent on strengthening the vaulting and walls of the nave, and supporting the west front, work necessitated by faulty repair work following an earth tremor in 1927.

MacGibbon and Ross say St Magnus's Cathedral is 'practically a Norwegian edifice', having been commissioned by a Norwegian jarl, or earl, designed and supervised by a Norwegian master mason and built as the seat of a Norwegian bishop suffragan to Trondheim. John Harvey in his *Gothic World* goes even further and places Kirkwall Cathedral firmly alongside Trondheim, which he actually likens in some respects to St Magnus's, not the other way round. In fact, he includes Iona in the same Norse context. Certainly the dioceses of Orkney, and the Isles, which these buildings respectively served, were both Norwegian, but much of Trondheim is English in feeling, as is curiously enough St Magnus's. While the former shows English Gothic feeling, the latter is predominantly Norman in character and in what Gothic features it has more closely follows French precedent, a fact that has suggested another link with Uppsala Cathedral in Sweden, which is wholly French, with rounded chevet and ring of chapels about the apse. The date of this Gothic work, English at Trondheim and French at Uppsala, is 1232 in the first instance and 1273 to 1315 in the second; the bulk of Kirkwall dates from the first half of the twelfth century, that is a considerable time before either of the previously mentioned influences could have been at work there. One does not discount the French influence via Uppsala as representing later work at St Magnus's, but this is chiefly to be seen in additions and decorative detail, not in the main building itself. What does go without saying is that this splendid little cathedral is a European church, as opposed to a Scots or English one, an amalgam of styles which merge so well that unity is produced in diversity to a degree not often found anywhere so complete, and remarkable in so relatively remote an area.

The story of the founding and building of this Scandinavian bishop's seat is itself worthy of a true Norse saga, for St Magnus, before his canonization, shared with his cousin Haakon, the earl-

St Magnus's Cathedral: under restoration in the nineteenth century (R. W. Billings); vaulting over the choir showing cracks

dom of Orkney until Haakon had him murdered. The two quarrelled and it was arranged that they should come together in a neutral spot, each in two ships and with a specified entourage, and there settle their differences peacefully. Magnus came as agreed, but his cousin arrived with eight galleys and many men. After various propositions had been made by both sides it was decided that only one could remain earl, and Magnus, being pacific by nature and no warrior, was executed at Haakon's command, his head being spliced in two by the stroke of an axe. In due course Magnus's nephew, Rongvald, succeeded where he had failed, and became sole ruler of Orkney, building 'a stone minster' in thankfulness and in memory of his martyred uncle. Both were subsequently buried within one of two separate piers on either side of the high altar in the new cathedral, and the amazing thing is that when repairs were being undertaken in the vicinity in 1916 a skull with a split across it was accidentally discovered in the appropriate place.

The cathedral was begun in 1137 and finished in its original form in less than twenty years, an extraordinary result when one considers not only the work involved but the transport of materials by land and sea, mostly by sea since Orkney has, to begin with, no timber. In the thirteenth century the choir, which had a round apse, was extended and given a flat east end, and the nave enlarged, when the first weakening of the structure took place and the masons, taking fright at what they had done, left the new bays in the nave unvaulted. The tower was altered a century later, and again after that, but St Magnus's remained very largely the Norwegian church it began life as, with its Northern English and French touches giving it an inimitable flavour all its own. Masons' marks from Durham have been detected, and the design of the sturdy piers in the choir and nave bear witness to their presence anyway. In fact, the total effect of the interior is slightly more that of Durham than the restricted Norman nave at Dunfermline, principally on account of its very diversity, and despite the lack of imitative chevron and twisted forms in the piers. Merging of transitional features with older Norman work is also very similar in effect. The triforium arches are less tunnel-like than at Dunfermline, and several are double with central columned supports, as at Durham; and there is more lightness in the clerestory, where some of the windows are pointed arches instead of round. All this

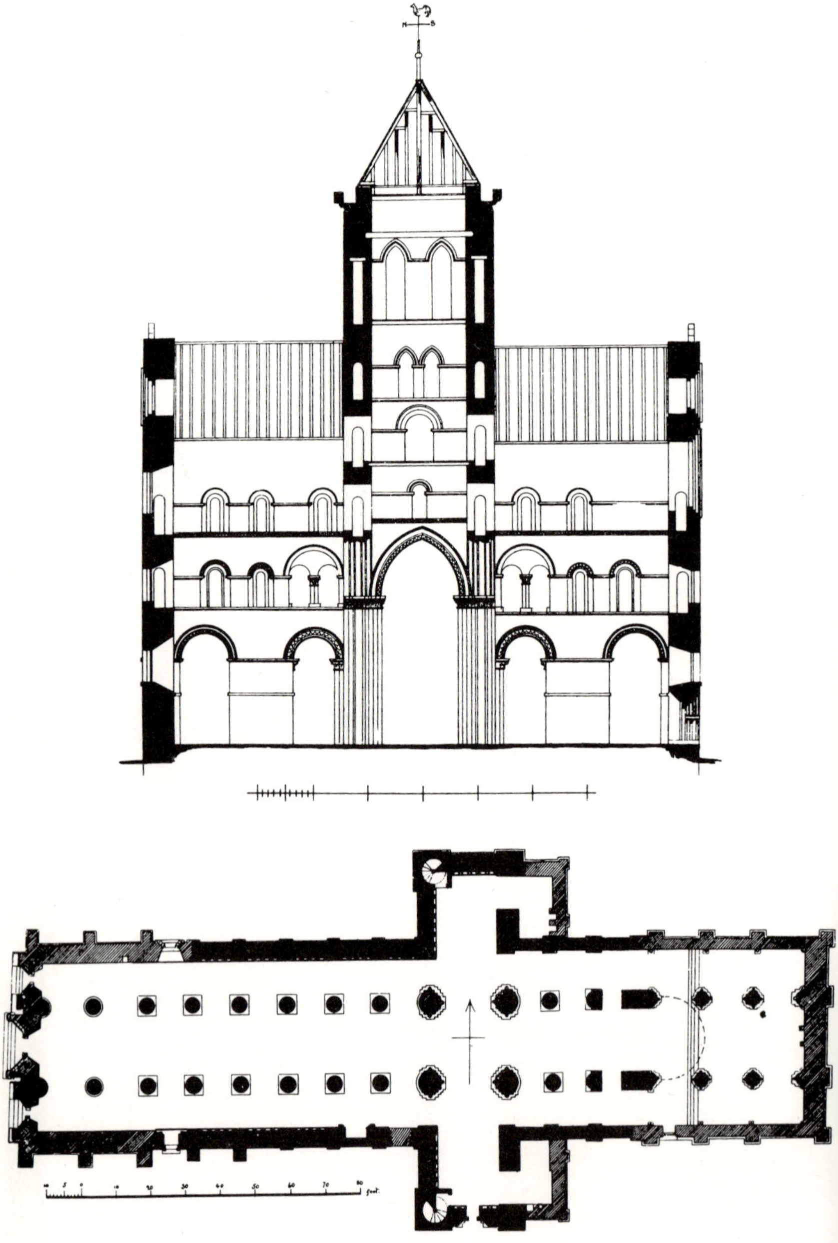

St Magnus's Cathedral: section through transept from north to south; ground plan

helps to create a strong but less heavy impression, while smaller decorative details, such as the jolly Romanesque arcading with stylized head corbels that runs around three sides of the transepts and most of the nave, have no counterpart at Dunfermline.

As already mentioned the first church built by Earl Rongvald was shorter at both choir and nave ends by three bays each, and the work then done was probably the original cause of the weakening of the structure, especially the rebuilding of the west front, which led to various attempts at different times to correct the faults as they appeared. It was usual in medieval times when enlarging a church to do so from the outside, encasing the old work so that services could go on uninterrupted as long as possible, and it seems that it was the final taking down and rebuilding that did much of the harm in the thirteenth century, the west front becoming immediately subject to pressures that have been slowly pushing it outwards ever since. To correct this Mr Alexander Heward, the Glasgow architect in charge, devised a scheme whereby the weight could be transferred almost totally onto newly constructed concrete beams running the full length of the clerestory, and transmitted onto a steel frame above the vaulting to take the strain there. At the same time faulty work carried out in 1927 when the end vaults of the nave, finished in timber by the Board of Works in the nineteenth century, were vaulted in breeze concrete with heavy infilling between the ribs, was removed, and replaced by new or rebuilt ribs from which the weight was transferred to the concrete beams behind, the infilling now being made of fibreglass. This was done between 1970 and 1973 without altering the essential appearance of the cathedral but making it safe for the first time in centuries and for many years to come.

I have referred to St Magnus's unity in diversity, and to the fact that it stands more in a European tradition than any particularly national one. Even some of its Norman work may have been influenced by churches built in Normandy by a branch of the same race which ruled Orkney. They excelled in Gothic architecture as well as Romanesque and most of the Gothic work at Kirkwall predates the annexation of Orkney by the Scottish crown by two hundred years. It has been suggested that since English craftsmen were engaged at Trondheim and French at Uppsala masons of both persuasions crossed the North Sea and worked at St Magnus's. It is quite possible, even probable, but it does not explain everything, for instance, the multi-coloured stonework around three west doorways, and one on the south transept, which have no counterparts in the British Isles, at least not until the days of the pre-Raphaelites and the Oxford Movement, and none in Scandinavia. One is tempted to relate them to another Norman territory at that time, Sicily, or to Siena, which would be my first choice, though Siena Cathedral is in black and white whereas here we have red and yellow. This is arranged chequerwise across the arches of the doorway in the south transept, radially above the most southerly doorway on the west front, and with the arches over the main doorway and the most northerly. The pilasters supporting these were also once coloured, but have been rebuilt in plain masonry, which is a pity because the effect is unique, and is carried on inside the church as well, giving it an almost exotic appearance at the west end. The central doorway is very grand, being set within the usual thickening of the wall, in this case almost porch-like with a high, pointed gable, lacking its balancing pinnacles, but effective just the same. It reminds one of Bourges, only on a very much smaller scale. The whole cathedral is built of red sandstone with a whiter stone here and there showing where additions and heightenings have taken place, and the total result is very striking.

In 1486, as we have seen, James III gave the burgh of Kirkwall possession of the cathedral, when Orkney and Shetland finally became part of the Scottish kingdom and passed from Norwegian suzerainty altogether. Even before this, however, Scoticisms had begun to appear in the structure, notably latter-day round arches were built over the three Gothic-transitional ones on either side of the extended choir. This is a sure sign of out-of-date mainland workmanship as opposed to more able work done earlier by foreign craftsmen. One will also find a curious side door on the south side of the nave inserted by Bishop Robert Reid, formerly abbot of Beauly and Kinloss, whose mitred arms appear above the three-sided arch. Then there are the bells, three of them, cast by Robert Borthwick, who with his brother James was master-gunner and blacksmith to James IV and James V. They were given by Bishop Maxwell in 1528; one shows the episcopal and royal arms, another the effigy of St Magnus, and all are dated and named as having been made in Edinburgh Castle by Master Borthwick. Better known for their canon, one of the Borthwicks probably made 'Mons Meg', which still stands on a platform on the Castle

Rock near Queen Margaret's Chapel. It is said to have fired its first shot to announce the birth of James V, and its last in salute to the departing James, Duke of York, brother of Charles II.

If the building of the Norse cathedral of St Magnus at Kirkwall seems almost an intrusion into the story of Queen Margaret and her son's foundation of Scottish abbeys and cathedrals, except possibly where the work of the Durham masons is concerned, it is not wholly so, for during the comparatively peaceful two centuries of Anglo-Norman penetration practically the only real threat to the system came from the kings of Norway and from their unruly vassals, the West Highland chiefs. In the end the question of who ruled Argyll and the Isles was officially settled by the Battle of Largs, in 1263, when Haakon of Norway retired defeated to die in the Earl's Palace at Kirkwall. It was to be another two centuries before Orkney and Shetland also passed to the Scottish crown, and meantime the chiefs in the west, led by the Lord of the Isles, went on disobeying whoever was set over them, Norse or Scots. Alexander I, more Scottish in outlook than his brother Edgar, ruled mainland Scotland north of the Scottish Sea, as the Firth of Forth was then called, leaving the southern half of his kingdom and northern England to his young brother David, who governed as Earl of Lothian and Northumberland and Prince of Cumbria. He was that 'sair sanct for the croun' who had already, before his brother's death, invited Tironensian monks from northern France to settle at Selkirk, in 1113, later transferring them to Kelso, the abbey of which was formally founded by him, as king, in 1128. This was in the same year as he founded Holyrood Abbey, with Austin canons, apparently from Merton in Surrey, and fulfilled his father's scheme for rebuilding their mother's damaged church at Dunfermline, re-colonizing the abbey with an abbot and monks from Canterbury.

Still Prince of Cumbria and Lord of Northumberland and Lothian, the future David I brought Austin canons to Jedburgh, not from Scone or St Andrews but direct from Beauvais, in France, in 1118, and in 1142 he raised the new priory to abbatial status. The list of his foundations might be continued almost indefinitely, with Melrose, in 1136, served by Cistercians from Rievaulx, in Yorkshire; and Cambuskenneth in 1140, with a return to the Augustinians, who seem to have been preferred for specifically royal establishments. In the same year Newbottle, or Newbattle, was founded for a colony of Cistercians from Melrose, while more monks of the same order, from Rievaulx, were settled at Dundrennan, in Galloway, in 1142. Kinloss, in Moray, he founded in 1150, towards the end of his reign, again with Cistercians, who were obviously the 'sair sanct's' favourites, from Melrose. Besides these numerous foundations David I established the Scottish diocesan system as it pertained for many centuries, attended the dedication of the medieval cathedral of St Mungo in Glasgow in 1136, the sixtieth anniversary of the original founding by St Kentigern, and created anew the diocese of Dunblane, in 1150. His successors continued in the good work, aided by highly placed servants of the crown, such as Hugh de Morville, Constable of Scotland, who founded Dryburgh Abbey, and the High Stewards who founded Paisley, until a network of abbeys and cathedrals covered the country. They survived almost intact until the advent of the Reformation, which was heralded by two devastating invasions from England, both led by the same man, 'wearing a different hat', first as Earl of Hertford and secondly as Duke of Somerset. The outcome was that Melrose and the other border abbeys were sacked and burned at least twice and made almost untenable. What remained there, and further north, for Hertford reached Dundee in his march of destruction, was further reduced by Knoxian visitations and by the Covenanters.

Until a sixteenth-century document turned up in the Vatican to disprove it, most authorities assumed that the present ruins of Kelso Abbey represented the original shape of the church, or as near as could be ascertained. Thus, Billings assumed an east-to-west orientation, with the existing one-bayed projection to the west of the tower as the choir, and the three-bayed eastern extension as the nave. Messrs MacGibbon and Ross, equally mystified by the layout but better versed in the vagaries of Scottish ecclesiastical architecture, reverted to the more normal orientation and assumed that the short western bay must have been the nave and the longer eastern one the choir. This, of course, made sense in a purely monastic context, where the monks would be accommodated in the presbytery, or choir, with the lay brothers housed in the smaller nave, but it would have been very small indeed. What has now been established is that Kelso's towering remnant of damaged masonry, so enigmatic in its form and purpose, is only one end of an even larger building, only one crossing

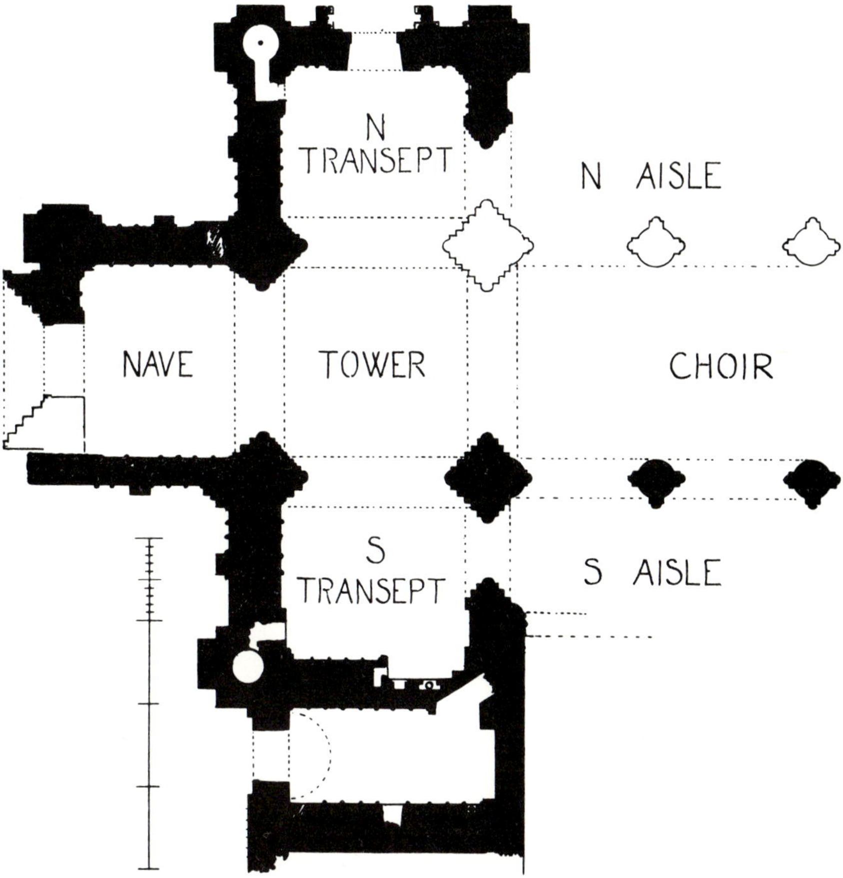

Kelso Abbey: plan

of the two it formerly boasted, the tiny nave being a repeat of an eastern apse. It is, in fact, a narthex, or atrium, often called in this country a Galilee Porch. There was one at Durham, only not so high and later made into a Lady Chapel and site for the tomb of the Venerable Bede. The Galilee here rises to the full height of the nave, and presumably of the long-lost choir, and had octagonal turrets at each corner, one of which survives. There are round turrets on the corners of the transepts, which gives the abbey a decid-

(left) *Kelso Abbey* (right) *Detail inside the narthex*

edly castellated appearance, and not without reason, since in the sixteenth century it was fortified and stoutly defended by the burgesses of the town and the monks against Hertford, who massacred those whom he captured.

The abbey was founded in 1128 after the initial failure of the Tironensian experiment at Selkirk, the monks going to Roxburgh Castle until their new quarters nearby were ready; and for a while the abbey was called Roxburgh not Kelso. Architecturally this is the last great Romanesque church built in Scotland, not Norman for it has distinct Continental affinities, with transitional features in the tower arches and in the upper part of the narthex. It is almost honeycombed with round-arched openings from ground level to the clerestory, which, with the triforium, forms a continuous arcade, a most unusual feature and weakening to the structure. The usual arrangement is to have vertical supports between the arches and a regular system of solids and voids, thus maintaining the solidarity of the walls. Attractive Romanesque blind arcades exist at the foot of the transepts, while a novel feature is the design of the porchlike doorway to the north transept, which is complete with a first-floor look-out, the narrow slits of windows being camouflaged behind by blind arcading. The pointed gable above is decorated in a rare criss-cross pattern, which, with other details, not to mention the very original plan of a large church with double transepts and tower over each, would seem to suggest Rhineland precedents.

Kelso Abbey: section through transept from north to south

The principal characteristic of Rhineland Romanesque is its following of the Lombardic tradition rather than that of Northern Europe, a direct result of the River Rhine's function as a principal trade route between north and south. This tradition was further strengthened by the existence of the Holy Roman Empire, whose centre was in Italy but whose head was either a Frank or a German, Frederick II, for instance, *stupor mundi*, was born in Palermo, in Sicily, and held court most of the time amongst the Norman knights of Apulia. Thus if there is a positive cultural link between the abbey at Kelso and any German or Lombardic contemporary it could have come through the Normans, or via David I himself. The king's sister Matilda was married to Henry I of England, and he spent many years with her at the English court, where, amongst other people, he met St Bernard, the Benedictine monk from Poitiers, who founded the Tironensian order. He seems to have had a personal attachment to that good man, and later, after the first abortive settling of the Tironensians in Scotland, he went to the Continent to meet his abbot friend and seek reinforcements; but this is not all, David Prince of Scotland was also Earl of Huntingdon, which is not far from Ely and Bury St Edmunds, where there are architectural similarities.

The abbey at Edmundsbury, which is its older name, has largely disappeared, but the Romanesque tower survives with deeply recessed and richly carved doorway and pointed hood almost identical with the remaining portion of the west door at Kelso, while at Ely we have a church with double transepts and two towers, as at Kelso, plus a Galilee Porch. There is nothing to prove the building of one provoked that of the other, and Ely itself has Rhineland connotations, particularly its west end, where the plan closely follows that of Worms Cathedral. So perhaps Kelso derives from the Rhineland Romanesque either through Ely and Bury St Edmunds or through another interesting link. David I's niece, also Matilda, daughter of Henry I, was none other than the Empress Matilda, spouse of the Holy Roman Emperor Henry V, before she married Geoffrey Plantagenet. Can one suppose, therefore, that David witnessed either or both her marriage and coronation, and thus saw for himself the architecture of the Empire, or was his knowledge of it second hand from Ely? We do not know, but Kelso undoubtedly derives in many of its particulars and especially its plan from the same sources. Other details, such as the pilaster, or flat buttresses, which rise to the full height of the building, are more local in inspiration, and can be seen at Lindisfarne and Coldingham, as well as St Magnus's Cathedral, Kirkwall.

Kelso itself is a pleasant place, retaining something of the air of a small provincial town in Central France, with the huge protecting *château* of the Dukes of Roxburghe, big square *place,* cobbled and only recently spoilt by the intrusion of red brick banks and other architectural aberrations, the whole set down beside a wide and placid Tweed between grassy banks and parkland. It has been suggested that had someone tried to start the Reformation here they would have made little progress, yet three of the first Reformed ministers at Kelso were members of the Knox family; and that marvellous old abbey, dedicated to the Virgin Mary and St John, was earlier attacked by soldiers fighting under the banner of the mother of Jesus, completely unaware of the incongruity of their actions. In fact, they sacked the place, removing the lead from the roof, destroying the east end of the church totally, hence its present enigmatic condition, and reduced the monks to beggars. Hardly had this happened than a second, and a third attack came, the last being that to which we have already referred in which the remaining tower was used as a strongpoint by a handful of clergy aided by the burghers. All but a dozen who escaped under cover of darkness were slaughtered, and those monks that survived were soon turned upon by the very burghers who had fought beside them, once the Knoxian message had got through.

Today it is difficult to believe that the chunky, embattled ruins of Kelso Abbey represent only a third of what was originally there, that within these walls Prince Henry, heir to David I and like him Earl of Huntingdon, was buried with pomp in 1152 and that by the end of the twelfth century the abbey had become so rich and powerful that Pope Alexander III conferred the mitre upon its abbot and placed him above all others in Scotland. His successors lost this exalted position in the fifteenth century and by the time of the English invasions in the sixteenth the revenues had already passed into secular hands, into those of the Ker ancestors of the present Duke of Roxburghe. In 1220 the abbey obtained a new charter, one of the signatories being Robert de Fenwic, which seems to indicate that the Fenwicks had not yet acquired the description 'fierce'. Of course, Kelso was not in the front line of Border warfare then, and did not become so until the days of

Edward I and the Wars of Independence, when it received its full measure of attack, sharing with Jedburgh, Melrose and Dryburgh in this respect, the wonder being that so much remained to become the prey of local philistines once the English had done their worst.

The presence of a royal castle in the immediate vicinity naturally gave Kelso Abbey a certain prominence, and in 1239 Alexander II married his second wife, Marie de Coucy, there. His first, Johanna, daughter of King John, had died a year earlier and was buried at Melrose. Two centuries later, in 1460, when the English were temporarily in charge of the castle, James II mounted a powerful siege, bringing up his favourite canon. Unfortunately for him one of the wedges keeping the barrel hoops tight flew off and killed the king instantly. His body was taken to Edinburgh for interment in the abbey at Holyrood, while his Flemish queen, Mary of Gueldres, carried on the siege until the enemy was ousted. Two days afterwards she had her eight-year-old son crowned as James III in Kelso Abbey. This was the last grand occasion and probably the finest in the abbey's history. Soon came destruction and disuse until in the mid-seventeenth century the space under the western tower was roofed-in to become the parish kirk, which it remained for just over a hundred years, when a piece of masonry fell down and so alarmed the congregation they vacated the building in a hurry and never returned. In 1715 Jacobites from southern Scotland and northern England met for worship in the makeshift kirk, after proclaiming the Chevalier de St Georges as James VIII and III. Since these mildly exciting incidents Kelso has settled down into the modest Border town it is, and after the First World War the then Duke of Roxburghe presented the abbey ruins to the nation, a few arches of the erstwhile cloister being rebuilt as a war memorial and the Duke retaining his own family burial 'aisle'.

The Tironensians flourished in Scotland and four Scottish abbeys, as opposed to only one in England, were successfully established: Kelso, of course; Kilwinning, in Ayrshire, which was founded by Hugh de Morville; Arbroath, which William the Lion founded in honour of St Thomas à Becket; and Lindores, in northern Fife, which we might as well deal with here because its monks came from Kelso and the foundation was by David, Earl of Huntingdon, son of Henry Prince of Scotland, who was buried at Kelso in 1152. There is very little left of Lindores, only a few picturesque lumps of masonry dotted about the fields near Newporton-Tay, and one recognizable doorway, probably the entrance to the monks' parlour, on the far side of the cloisters. This was one of the most celebrated abbeys in Scotland, it was the place where the founder's three sons, Robert, Henry and John, were laid to rest, their deaths without offspring precipitating problems of succession which ended in the Wars of Independence, for of their four sisters the eldest married Alan, Lord of Galloway, grandfather of John Baliol, the second Robert de Bruis, grandfather of Robert I, the third died unmarried, and the fourth wedded Henry de Hastings, grandfather of the third claimant to the Scottish throne at the end of the thirteenth century, John, Baron de Hastings. As if this was not enough by way of royal and noble connections, the young Duke of Rothesay, eldest son and heir of James I, who was murdered by his uncle, the Duke of Albany in Falkland Palace, was also laid to rest in the abbey kirk. Edward I visited Lindores but did not burn it down as he did Dunfermline, probably because he was well satisfied with the fealty swearing session he attended there. Not long afterwards Sir William Wallace gave thanks at Lindores for his victory over Edward's forces at nearby Black Earnside.

The abbey had a complement of twenty-six monks and an abbot, and retained this number until the Reformation, escaping Hertford's attack on Balmerino, only a few miles to the north-east, and only coming to grief in 1559, when members of Knox's 'Godly Congregation' descended on the place, ruining it almost in a single day. It then became the usual quarry, and thus it is no surprise to see Gothic doorways and windows incorporated in cottages and farms in the vicinity, and the one remaining recognizable archway bearing a notice which says 'Beware of the Bull'. Lindores supported nine mills one of which has survived with its wheel and adjacent building, though rebuilt and not medieval in style or date. The monks played a significant part in Scottish history, one was actually Grand Inquisitor, and it was to Lindores that 'Bell the Cat', the Douglas Earl whose main occupation was leading revolts against James III, retired and spent his last days as a Black Monk. The site is excellent and typical of the best royal and ecclesiastical foundations, and the inmates made full use of its privileged position to establish a number of industries some of which persist to this day. Thatching, for instance, has only recently died out, the reeds from Lindores Loch and from the Firth of Tay being used until Norfolk thatch supplanted them. More significant still is the prevalence of fruit growing on both sides of the Firth, which the monks introduced and which, changing from pear and apple orchards to raspberry farms covers the hillsides like vineyards.

There seems to be some dispute as to the precise date of the founding of Jedburgh Abbey, which began life as a priory. It certainly had some sort of existence, as Kelso had done, while David I was still Prince of Cumbria, the date usually being given as 1118. At that time he had just returned from France with reinforcements for his Tironensian settlement at Selkirk, prior to their settling at Roxburgh and his founding of an abbey there in more favourable surroundings. The monks he encouraged to come to Jedburgh were also French, but of the Augustinian Order, which choice must surely be related to the Prince's sojourn on the Continent, since well-established Augustinian priories existed at Scone, St Andrews and Inchcolm, from whom the new settlement could easily have been colonized. It is thought that as David I was well up in current ecclesiastical attitudes he wished to introduce into his Kingdom, 'of French, Angles, Scots, Picts and Galwegians', as wide a variety of religious thought and practice as possible. Besides this he was a close associate of Bishop John of Glasgow, who was consecrated in 1118 and who subsequently fell out with the Holy See and took refuge with Tironensians near Beauvais, before returning to Scotland in 1138. Two years previously he and the King had attended the dedication ceremony in Glasgow of a new cathedral, and it was the same Bishop who in 1128 had given his permission for the re-establishment of the Tironensians at Roxburgh. His new cathedral in Glasgow, incidentally, was destroyed by fire, and the one we see today was begun by Bishop Jocelin, formerly Abbot of Melrose, at the end of the twelfth century. It was continued by Bishop Bondington, who built the choir in the thirteenth century, William Turnbull and Robert Blacader, who between them completed the building in the fifteenth century.

Jedburgh was raised from a priory to an abbey in 1147, the year in which the king's episcopal friend died, Bishop John being buried in the new church. There were few other notable events in its history, apart from the usual quota of sackings and one grand occasion, in 1285, when Alexander III, who was born in Roxburgh Castle, married his second wife, Iolanda, daughter of Count Robert IV of Dreux, there, which must have enlivened the neigh-

Jedburgh Abbey: detail of the west front; view from the south

bourhood no end. The ruins of the abbey kirk are amongst the most substantial of their period in Scotland, the town being better protected from Border raids, and indeed so strong that the Earl of Hertford himself had the idea of turning it into a fortress. In the event he was content to ravage the abbey on two occasions, on the last leaving it in such a sorry state that it never recovered. Still, the walls remained fairly hale, standing to eaves' height, and the principal damage was to the abbatial quarters, which were carted away as building material by the local people until the Kerr family, with two *r*s this time, stepped in and prevented further depredation. As Marquises of Lothian they looked after the ruins, before handing them over to the Ministry of Works. The remnants of the choir, the smallest part of the church, were fitted up as a parish kirk, the tower re-roofed and provided with a suitable bellcot. All that has gone now, the congregation has since built a fancy new kirk, leaving the apsidal transepts and east end to fall down, and only a late-Gothic side chapel for the use of the Lothian family as its burial aisle. In the process of making themselves comfortable an earlier

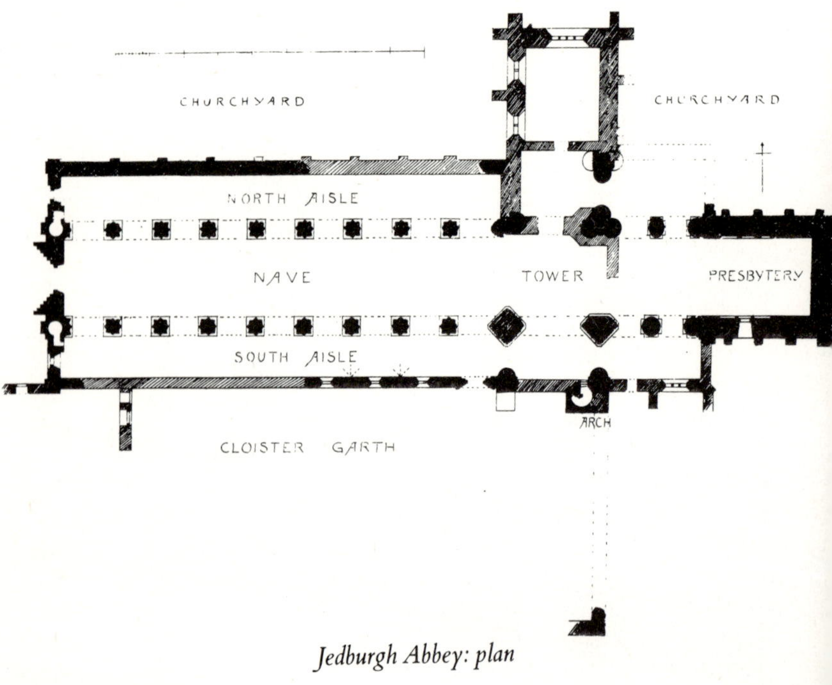

Jedburgh Abbey: plan

congregation removed the north aisle of the choir, and today little of the vaulting in the aisles remains. In the rest of the church the vaulting had been of timber, so would not have escaped burning by the English.

Jedburgh Abbey-church does not present the same architectural enigmas as Kelso, it was planned in Norman times and completed within a single century, becoming transitional in style by the time it was finished. There is a distinct break beyond the crossing, where the nave arcade is pointed, in contrast to the predominantly round-arched choir, but the general rhythm of the design and overall unity is not spoilt thereby, and the original west front survives. One only has to close one's eyes slightly to forget the lack of a roof and see Jedburgh as it might have been hundreds of years ago. The crumbling dog-tooth motif of the richly decorated and recessed west doorway may be a little the worse for wear, its three pointed gablets chipped and vacant, but later traceries remain in the wheel window above, creating a silhouette in which the colour of the sky provides a suggestion of stained glass. There is another very fine but equally corroded Norman doorway on the south side of the nave, formerly leading into the now non-existent cloisters; but the most interesting feature in Jedburgh's architecture is the arrangement of the lower arches *vis-à-vis* the triforium in the choir. These fat round Norman piers rise to the full height of the triforium to reach the base of the clerestory, and this is the only example of such a daring exercise in Scotland. South of the Border one finds two precedents in St Fridewide's in Oxford, made into a cathedral by Henry VIII and better known as Christ Church, and the Norman abbey at Romsey, in Hampshire. Neither is exactly the same and curiously enough Jedburgh derives from both. For instance, on the south side of the choir the lower arches supporting the triforium spring from supplementary pilasters attached to the main piers, as at Oxford, while on the north side a more elegant procedure similar to that at Romsey Abbey pertains, whereby the supporting arches for the triforium spring directly from corbels projecting from the piers.

The clerestory is in pointed lancets, deep set with slender clustered columns on the inside, not unlike Coldingham, and a feature clearly copied by Sir George Gilbert Scott for the clerestory in the choir of St Mary's Cathedral in Edinburgh. This was the first large Gothic cathedral erected in Britain after the Reformation and celebrates its centenary in 1979. I will have more to say about St Mary's in another chapter, meantime it is worth mentioning that the celebrated architect, whose forte was a proper use of the authentic medieval style, based his design on what he considered to be the finest period in medieval Scottish architecture, namely that beginning with David I and ending with his grandsons, the period which saw abbeys such as Jedburgh and cathedrals like Dunblane built in the purest Early English. The nave at Jedburgh, though lacking a roof, is its most perfect portion, variety in form being provided by an imaginative interchange between pointed and rounded arches in the triforium. The lower arcade is in the usual transitional style, with a handsome triforium above in which the main arches are round-headed and wide, with a pointed double inset, each supported by a delicate central column and pierced by a small decorative circle in the infilling. It is this very simplicity, without any display of elaborate carving, that gives early Gothic its charm and structural propriety, which obviously appealed to architects like Scott, and to William Butterfield, who also worked in Scotland in the nineteenth century. Pointed and arranged in quartets, the clerestory arcade in the nave appears at first sight to run continuously as at Kelso, but there is actually a definite gap between the sets of openings, coming exactly where it should, immediately over the centre of both triforium and base piers. In the century before Henry VIII sent his generals north as part of the so-called 'rough wooing', as an encouragement to the Scots to give their infant queen in marriage to his ailing son, Jedburgh was repaired and embellished by, amongst others, Robert Blacader, when he was still abbot and not yet bishop of Glasgow. He was responsible for completing the squat square tower with its amusing top gallery, as witness his shield, charged with a chevron between three roses upon it.

David I's next foundation after becoming king was the Abbey of the Holy Rood, which he established in 1128, and colonized with Austin canons, traditionally from St Andrews but more probably from Merton, in Surrey. The history of this famous sanctuary is both well and incorrectly known, no doubt as a result of its close association with the over-romanticized royal palace alongside. It has had a continuous existence for more than eight centuries, it is older than Edinburgh Castle, and four hundred years older than the palace itself, the latter growing from it, not the other way round. Architecturally both turreted royal residence and grimly empty abbey kirk contain some of the best work of their respective eras in Scotland and in Britain. We are not so much concerned with the palace, though it is the principal mecca of tourists, suffice to say it was begun by a French master mason, with one of the Mylne family in attendance, in the reign of James IV, left unfinished by him and not finished until 1672, when Sir William Bruce, architect to Charles II, completed the original sixteenth-century plan in an intriguing and successful mixture of Gothic on the front and Palladianism behind. By that time the old abbey had already been reduced to its nave, and was devoid of internal interest. Bruce arranged it as a Chapel Royal for Charles II in the chaste but dull manner of such places in the second half of the seventeenth century, and in the event no monarch, 'merry' or otherwise, ever worshipped in it. Indeed, masking what remained of the west front was the commendator's house, a contemporary structure which was not removed until some years later, when the roof of the abbey kirk collapsed and was not restored.

What one sees of the Abbey of Holyrood, therefore, is a rectangular building, with a Gothic-revival east window inserted by Charles I for his coronation in 1633, three-quarters of the west front, now reduced to the entrance and the most northerly, spireless tower; plus the vacant nave, blackened with soot and corroded with age but still displaying considerable refinement of detail. It is decidedly worth a visit provided one can get over the fact that this, the burial place of the Stewarts and hallowed since the twelfth century, has become a graveyard and lapidary museum shown to visitors by a hatted government official. The royal tombs were actually desecrated and their contents strewn around on two occasions, the first when the church, made into the chapel of a reconstituted Order of the Thistle by James VII and II, was attacked and sacked by an Edinburgh mob, which broke open the coffins and made merry with the bones of their kings and queens. The second occasion followed the collapse of the roof, when a repeat performance of earlier acts of sacrilege occurred, and eye witnesses have described such sights as the thigh bone of Darnley being taken home as a souvenir by morbid vandals. Queen Victoria, to her credit, saw that what could be rescued was gathered together and decently re-interred in a common sepulchre, which may be viewed by visitors, a black and gloomy stone box in the same

The gaunt remains of Holyrood Abbey today; plan

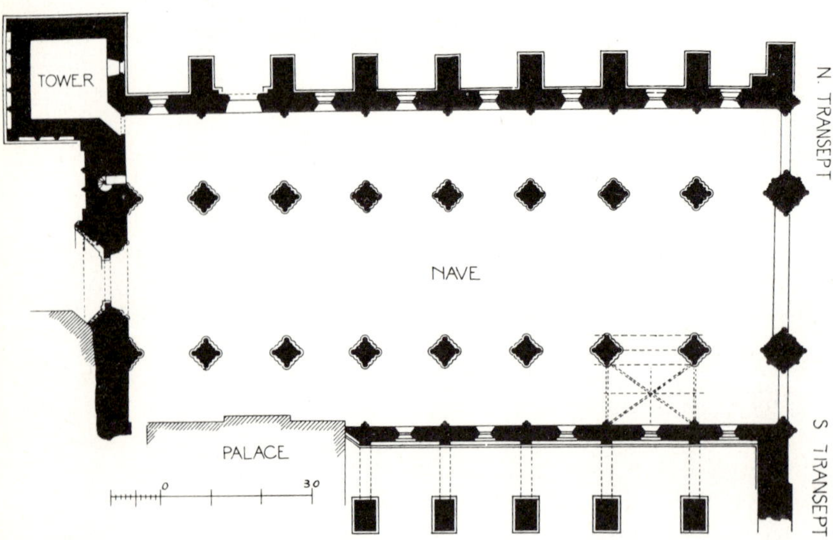

corner where the royal dust had previously lain unprotected.

The interior of the abbey kirk as it may have appeared in the reign of James VII and II, before the mob wreaked its vengeance on it in 1689, is amongst the engravings in William Adam's *vitruvius scoticus,* and depicts not only the very fine thirteenth-century vaulting that had survived till then, the only such in Scotland since the ruination of Melrose, but the classically designed knights' pews, with banners above and throne under the east window. An earlier view, made before the restorations of Charles I and his second son, forms the background to the Darnley 'Revenge Picture', painted by Lieven de Vogeleer in 1567 after the murder of 'Henry, King of Scots' in the notorious Kirk o'Field episode. It shows Darnley's family, including the infant James VI, wearing his crown, praying beside the victim's tomb, with appropriate banners and testimonies displayed behind and in front. The windows of the church are leaded lights, as they would have been, and the altar, except for a large half-life-size representation of

Holyrood Abbey set up as the Chapel of the Order of the Thistle (from William Adam's Vitruvius Scoticus*)*

Christ holding His cross at the centre, is a typically Anglican one, with plain frontal, dorsal and hangings, symptomatic of the fact that the Catholic Church to which Darnley and his family belonged bore few outward semblances to modern Roman Catholicism, far less to the rococo cults of the Counter-Reformation. The original picture, which also depicts the Battle of Carberry Hill in the left foreground, in which Mary, Queen of Scots was defeated by Darnley's associates, belongs to H.M. The Queen and is in the Royal Apartments at Holyroodhouse.

The legend of the Holy Rood, or crucifix, in honour of which David I founded the abbey which became a palace, has two variations, both widely differing. Perhaps it would be best to dispose of the better-known version first, since it bears very little, if any, relationship to fact. According to it King David is linked with the almost identical legends of St Eustace and St Hubert, the latter being the patron saint of hunting, who, profaning the Lord's Day, found himself confronted in the middle of a forest by a mysterious white stag, between whose antlers was a crucifix. This vision brought the beholders to repentance, and has since become a favourite subject for pictorial and armorial representation. In the case of Holyrood it was made, in the fourteenth century, the supposed reason for the abbey's very existence, a myth perpetuated right down to the present day in a number of ways, notably in the placing of stags' antlers above the façade of the Kirk of the Canongate, which edifice replaced Holyrood Abbey as the local parish church at the end of the seventeenth century. Latter-day antlers came from the Balmoral estate and were presented by the late King George VI, who as Duke of York, served as Lord High Commissioner to the Assembly of the Church of Scotland; which role his Stuart predecessor, James, Duke of York, afterwards James VII and II, also played, before evicting the congregation from Holyrood Abbey Kirk.

The real Holy Rood was a piece of the true cross, contained within a gold casket, with an ebony and ivory crucifix on the top, which belonged to the sainted Queen Margaret and which her third son honoured by the foundation of an abbey. This object became in time a sort of talisman for the Scottish people and was carried about in procession on grand occasions and in times of trouble until it was lost by David II, son of Robert Bruce. He invaded England in the second half of the fourteenth century, was defeated and came back without it, when the much venerated Holy Rood was taken to Durham Cathedral, where it remained until destroyed at the Reformation. Thus the Austin canons in Edinburgh, like their confrères in St Andrews on another occasion, showed their ingenuity by inventing a new story, one that has stuck and which no amount of debunking or denunciation seems able to eradicate; but it is not authentic, however picturesque or plausible. Of the building erected under David I not much remains, and the gaunt ruins one sees today mostly date from the thirteenth century and later, when foreign craftsmen, including Flemish and French masons, helped in the construction, hence so much fine and unusually sophisticated detail. The original aisleless church was incorporated in the enlarged nave, the walls being built around it first and then removed as the work proceeded, the normal practice. That this reconstruction took a generation at least to accomplish is proved by the attractive blank interlacing Romanesque arcading that runs round the base of the new north aisle, contrasting, not unfavourably, with the plain Gothic repeat on the south side. More arcading enlivens the west front, that on the remaining north-west tower being especially good. The spaces between the arches on the lower run are graced with roundel portraits of a very high sculptural quality, one of which was so nicely replaced during the restoration of 1633 that one would not know the difference.

The west door, extremely corroded with the atmosphere of smoky, beery Edinburgh, not to mention the destructiveness of malevolent men, is still worthy of the best Ile de France Gothic, and has a particularly entrancing lintel carved with ten winged angels, which feature was borrowed by Sir George Gilbert Scott for the cathedral of the diocese founded by Charles I in 1637, St Mary's, and used by him in a similar position. Above this beautiful but cramped entrance, the south side of the arch being hemmed in by a wall of the palace, is a much-altered double west window, full of tracery, not all of it medieval, for it was recast by the architect to the Martyr King, probably not Inigo Jones, as has been suggested, but John Mylne, who redesigned the palace façade and restored the abbey. There is, in fact, a handsome sundial in the garden just near this western portal bearing the initials of Charles I, Henrietta Maria and Charles, Prince of Wales, the future Charles II, which is known to have been carved by Mylne himself. The windows once lit a tribune at the rear, where on special occasions, the patronal festival, a royal wedding, a coronation or funeral, the choir stood, with trumpeters in attendance, heralds and all the welcoming panoply necessary to such an event. There is another such tribune at Arbroath, composed of a pillared loggia, but opening outwards as well as inwards; and both these must have been very impressive in action, more so one imagines than the forward-standing Galilee, at ground level, that existed at Kelso. One can imagine the scene at the last crowning of a Scottish-born king at Holyrood, organized meticulously by a fastidious monarch who intended that everything should be done as it had been in times past, notably at the coronation of James IV in 1488. Between the windows is that Baroque framed panel on which King Charles's somewhat over-optimistic quotation about stablishing God's House for ever appears; only the tablet and the wording having survived to tell the tale.

Of the numerous other royal events that took place in the abbey it is perhaps worth recalling that James II of the Fiery Face, whose spouse so dutifully had his body returned here after his unexpected death at the siege of Roxburgh Castle, was actually born in the monastery, not yet a palace, and crowned in the church in 1437, marrying Mary of Gueldres there two years later. James IV wed Margaret Tudor, wayward sister of a wayward Henry VIII at Holyrood in 1503, and Madeleine de Valois, daughter of François I of France, was buried in the kirk within a couple of months of her marriage to James V. Darnley, as we have seen, had his tomb here, and his widow married Bothwell in the same year as he was blown up at Kirk o' Field. As it turned out Mary, Queen of Scots need not have worried about having a father for her child since it was still-born, and she and her turbulent partner fled, he dying a pauper in Denmark, she spending the next twenty years a prisoner before being beheaded at the behest of her cousin, Elizabeth Tudor. The abbey soon fell into disuse or improper use, and despite the efforts of James VI, when still king of Scotland, to tidy it up, even organize sacred concerts in it, and his son's restoration and brilliant coronation of 1633, it reverted first to a local parish kirk and finally became a ruin.

Holyrood Abbey did not escape the Earl of Hertford's attentions, and it was he who did so much damage that only the nave remained serviceable after his visitation of 1544, when the choir was burned and the royal corpses had their first taste of barbarous disrespect. A certain amount of looting accompanied this treatment and two items from the abbey subsequently appeared in churches in St Albans; a brass font, presented to Holyrood by the late fifteenth-century abbot, Robert Bellenden, became part of the furniture of St Albans Abbey, while the brass eagle lectern, the gift of Abbot George Crichton, went to St Stephen's Church in the same town, where it still is, bearing the arms of the donor and the words 'Georgius Episcopus Dunkeldensis', which he became in 1522. More recently other items have turned up dating from the end of the seventeenth century when the Kirk was restored as the Chapel of the Order of the Thistle for James VII and II. They consist of the bulk of the altar furniture, minus the candlesticks which have disappeared, and include the silver communion plate, thurible, incense boat and spoon, sanctus bell and monstrance, as supplied by silversmiths in Edinburgh and London. They were bundled into a sack and raced away by a quick-witted priest at the approach of the mob; and he did not stop until he had reached the safety of a papist enclave in Banffshire.

These objects are unique in Britain, there being no others made for use with the liturgy of what John Evelyn called 'The New Religion of Trent' in any Chapel Royal surviving, the monstrance in particular having no rival. Their saving from destruction almost coincides with the beginnings of modern Roman Catholicism in Scotland, for it was in 1695 that the first bishop was appointed, and the country placed under the direct protection of the Papacy. Throughout the eighteenth century tiny, almost miniscule pockets of supporters weathered the Jacobite rebellion to become the nucleus of the present Scottish Roman Catholic population which, swelled by adherents of Irish extraction, is second only to the Established church itself, and is the majority in some western parts of the country. The altar silver from Holyrood was used in church-houses, literally a house with a meeting room-cum-church at one end, until dispersed, the monstrance coming back to the Palace of Holyroodhouse and being made available to the exiled Charles X of France during the French Revolution. He arrived in an impecunious and distraught condition but benefited from the fact that the right of sanctuary still applied within the old abbey bounds, so that he could take his daily constitutional without the embarrassment of meeting creditors, and on Sundays could even sally forth into the streets of Edinburgh in perfect safety, since on that day no debts could be collected.

The idea of restoring the abbey kirk was made earlier this century, when money was left in order to make it once more the Chapel of the Order of the Thistle, as the last Stuart king had made it. A body was set up to explore the possibility, but decided against proceeding on the grounds that no authentic restoration could be undertaken with the funds provided, and anything short of that would be wrong. An odd comment when one remembers just how much the building had suffered already; surely a slightly less than genuine medieval finish would not have been worse than leaving it as it is? In any event, it was not done and obviously will not be now, which seems to confirm J. S. Coltart's remark in his *Scottish Church Architecture* that 'the present dismal state of the abbey church, the Chapel Royal, the burying-place of the Kings of Scotland, and the most important church in the capital of the kingdom, is a vital piece of evidence in estimating the Scottish appreciation of art, and the pride of Scotsmen in their country and its past'. It is extremely difficult to disagree with this assessment, and pointless to get hot under the collar, for the proof is in the eating; and the proof is there for all to see, and not only at Holyrood. Hertford and his predecessors may have done great damage to Scottish abbeys, and indeed to many secular buildings, but it was repairable, and much more damage was done later by way of official policy and deliberate vandalism. The truth cannot, therefore, be gainsaid, and no amount of blaming the other fellow, or shouting nationalistic slogans will alter it. What has to be done is to try and redress the balance where and how we can, and demonstrate our appreciation of what artistic treasures are left to us, while they are still there.

After Holyrood the next royal foundation was Melrose, in 1136, to which the 'sair Sanct' brought monks of the Cistercian order north of the Border for the first time. They came from Rievaulx, in the Yorkshire Dales, and when one realizes that the English mother-house itself had only been settled since 1131, one begins to appreciate how up-to-date and *avant garde* David I was in religious matters. The white monks, a reformed branch of the Benedictine order, spread rapidly to Galloway, where they established themselves at Dundrennan, Glenluce and Sweetheart Abbeys, to Newbottle, near Edinburgh, Balmerino and Culross in Fife, and north, Kinloss to Moray. Dundrennan was another of King

David's foundations, probably jointly with Fergus, Lord of Galloway, the same who in 1128 refounded Whithorn Cathedral-priory, and subsequently invited there canons of the Premonstratensian order. The Dundrennan monks came also from Rievaulx in Yorkshire and made for themselves daughter houses at Glenluce and Dulci Corde, or Sweetheart, while most of the other Cistercian colonies were settled from Melrose. It is unfortunate that this famous abbey should have lain in the direct path of southern invaders, and that the twelfth-century founding from Rievaulx should have been partially wiped out during the Wars of Independence. The existing beautiful ruins, which to be seen aright must be visited in the 'pale moonlight', a thing Scott himself admitted to never having done, almost entirely date from after the middle of the fourteenth century and much of them from the fifteenth. Only the base of David I's church survives, at the west end, where a run of wall was left standing instead of being removed in the course of the last rebuilding of the nave.

Melrose was first rebuilt with funds provided by Robert Bruce, who intended his heart to lie before the high altar, and again in the same century after the devastation wrought by the army of Richard II, who, surprisingly, seems to have suffered some remorse for his actions and sent craftsmen from northern England to assist in the work of reconstruction. Henry VIII's generals of course passed this way, including Hertford, more than once, and afterwards Melrose was never wholly restored again. In the seventeenth century part of the nave was roofed over with heavy, ungainly stone slabs supported by ugly pillars that clash horribly with the delicate and refined remnants of previous ages, particularly the high-Gothic sculpture for which Melrose is celebrated. Long before any of this, however, there had been a Celtic monastery at Melrose, in the days of St Cuthbert and Abbot Eata, each of whom became Bishop of Lindisfarne, with their cathedral at Hexham; and Melrose was one of the stopping places for St Cuthbert's body, as the monks sought refuge from the Danes and a permanent resting-place for his hallowed remains. There is nothing to be seen from that era and what we are presented with today is a remarkable show of medieval masonry in which the Ile de France style is perfectly matched by English Perpendicular, a foreign-built abbey church to all intents and purposes. The huge east window, miraculously preserved, together with adjacent late-

Gothic vaulting, immediately recalls contemporary work in York and Beverley Minsters; the flamboyant south transept, with its curvaceous expression, not only recalls French precedents, but actually was the work of Jean Moreau, French master mason whose epitaph can still be seen in the ruins. It states that he was born in Paris and 'HAD IN KEPYNG AL MASON WERK OF SANTANDROYS, YE HYE KIRK OF GLASGW, MELROS AND PASLAY, OF NYDDYSDAYLL AND OF GALWAY'. These references are fairly clear, the High Kirk of Glasgow being St Mungo's Cathedral, where Moreau was responsible for the elaborately conceived stone pulpitum, or choir screen, which has a smaller twin in the college at Lincluden, in Nithsdale; and his work in Galloway probably took in Glen Luce, which has several fifteenth-century features.

Discussion of the late-Gothic niceties of Melrose takes us well past the days of David I and his family to the post-War of Independence period, and further comment must logically wait its turn. In 1140 the king founded the abbey of Cambuskenneth, near Stirling, for Augustinian canons, again from France and a particularly stern variety, more like Premonstratensians. The site is unusual for Scotland, being extremely flat and on one of a series of gigantic loops in the River Forth, so rich in alluvial deposit that one loop was traditionally said to be worth an earldom elsewhere. The feel would be more of East Anglia than mid-Scotland but for the Highland hills to the north, and Stirling town and castle rising from the plain to the south against a background of the Campsie Fells. Of the once wealthy and powerful abbey nothing remains of any substance except the twelfth-century bell-tower, which was built free-standing, in common with a number of others in south-eastern Perthshire, notably at Muthill and Dunning, both now attached to later churches but originally campaniles, as at Dunblane, just round the corner from Cambuskenneth. Dunblane now has a rebuilt top portion, and a small spire to finish it off, but Muthill and Dunning still retain their saddle-back roofs which Cambuskenneth must also once have had, though it now has stepped battlements and a polygonal stair turret, capped with a stone roof sporting individual gablets at each angle. Double lancets light the upper storeys of the nearly 70-feet-high tower, which has early Gothic blank arcading half-way down and is entered through a pointed Gothic entrance, the lower chamber being rib vaulted.

The campanile of Cambuskenneth Abbey

Cambuskenneth has witnessed a number of significant events in Scotland's history. On a commanding rocky craig in the immediate vicinity is Wallace's statue, symbol of his victory at Stirling Brig, and on the opposite horizon is the Field of Bannockburn, where Bruce defeated Edward II's vast host; but the buildings suffered comparatively little damage in these wars, more in the aftermath of David II's foolish invasion of England, when he got his fingers badly burned and returned home, minus the Holy Rood of Queen Margaret, minus his army and with minimal prestige. Probably in an attempt to gain wider support for the crown, and himself personally, he called a parliament at Cambuskenneth to which he invited bourgeois and civic representatives, who joined the feudal establishment for the first time. This was the beginning of the Three Estates, of church, barons and people, that subsisted in varying forms until the union with Westminster in 1707. The choice of Cambuskenneth was fairly natural, since it was central and guarded by the royal castle of Stirling. Its abbots were also of a very high calibre, several of them being statesmen of note, ambassadors to foreign parts, scholars, historians, royal tutors, and in the case of Alexander Miln, whom we met as Canon of Dunkeld, Master Mason and first President of the Court of Session under James V.

Margaret of Denmark, Queen of James III and the Scandinavian Princess who brought Orkney and Shetland finally into the Scottish Kingdom, was buried before the high altar at Cambuskenneth, and the body of her husband is thought to lie beside her, though there is some doubt as to the exact details of his death, in 1488, just off the battlefield at Sauchieburn, near Bannockburn. Contemporary accounts speak merely of the 'unhappy field in which the King our sovereign lord happened to be slain', and Billings, somewhat facetiously, talks of a body found in a field nearby 'faintly attested as that of James III'. The king was the victim of a baronial revolt which, with a little more firmness, he could probably have put down as he did others, but he seems to have lost his nerve, and before his supporters had actually been defeated fled the battlefield on the great grey charger with the Earl of Lindsay had given him either for this purpose or to pursue his enemies. He had girded himself with the sword of Bruce, realizing the association with Bannockburn, but it availed him nothing, the sword was dropped in flight, and the king was thrown by his horse as it leapt a burn near a farm cottage. He was taken into the cottage where he called for a priest, thinking himself dying. Apparently someone passing heard the call, came in and stabbed him to death, presumably one of his enemies.

James III, or the corpse of someone thought to be him, was buried with Queen Margaret of Denmark in a Tournai marble-topped tomb in the abbey church, and in 1864 part of a similar blue marble slab, plus some bones, was discovered near the site of the high altar. The bones were then reverently re-interred in a newly constituted tomb, using part of the broken Tournai marble top, at the command and expense of Queen Victoria. What modern Scotland would have done without that good lady one scarcely knows, for it was she, almost as much as Burns or Scott, who put the country on the map, indeed, in the matter of royal bones and general restriction of the honour of 'We Stuarts' she was indispensable. It might be added that the desecration of the royal tomb and the effectual disappearance of kirk and monastic buildings, except for the merest remnants of a western entrance and the tall campanile, the latter useful for defence, owes nothing to English ill-will but was entirely the work of the Reformers. They descended upon Cambuskenneth in 1560 and were so thorough in their destruction that hardly anything was left, even to be picked up by freestone pilferers or made particularly profitable by the Earl of Mar who obtained possession of the abbey at the time. Its geographical position probably prevented too much unofficial looting, not being connected to the town by any bridge; and it was the subject of surveillance from the castle. The Earl of Mar was himself Keeper of that royal residence in which Henry, Prince of Wales was born and christened, and where James VI, 'The Wisest Fool in Christendom' or 'The Scottish Solomon', depending on one's predilections, established his court when not in Edinburgh.

THREE

The Legacy of Queen Margaret and Her Sons

PART TWO

ONLY FOUR YEARS after the founding of Melrose for Cistercian monks from Rievaulx, King David and his eldest son, Prince Henry, were jointly responsible for a daughter-house being established at Newbottle, in Midlothian, quite near Edinburgh. It is now called Newbattle but has no connection with any battle, though in the vicinity is the curiously named 'Justinlees', a pub and cross-roads marking the scene of erstwhile jousting on the lea. Originally spelt Newbotil, which merely meant new dwelling, the abbey quickly became one of the largest and richest in Scotland, until the Reformation, when its abbot, Mark Ker, succeeded as secular commendator, and the monastic buildings were converted into a private house. Newbottle suffered from the usual English invasions, including that of Richard II in the late fourteenth century, after which, in emulation of those at the mother house, the monks rebuilt their abbey with loving care and in more elaborate form than before. Hertford then proceeded to burn it down in the sixteenth century, and today practically nothing remains above ground of Newbottle's former grandeur. The calefactory, or monks' warming house, was made into a chapel in the nineteenth century, when some fine medieval glazed tiles were discovered and copied; and a lower floor of the existing William and Mary mansion retains a ceiling of ribbed vaulting.

The transition from ecclesiastical to secular use at Newbottle, or Newbattle as it then became, is more typical of what happened in England than in Scotland, with the adaptation and eventual absorption of monastic quarters into an eighteenth-century house, and its continued use as the seat of a local noble family. The same applies to the church and manse just down the road. James Smith, successor to Sir William Bruce as surveyor to the king in Scotland, and architect for James VII and II of the new Kirk of the Canongate in Edinburgh, designed Newbattle Abbey as it is now, a patrician seat with handsome classical gates and Palladian proportions. The kirk was designed by his partner, Alexander McGill, architect to the City of Edinburgh and restorer of the Kirk of the Greyfriars in that burgh. It contains the laird's pew, or elevated gallery, filling the short arm of a typical T-shaped Protestant church, facing the pulpit, which is reputed to have been used by Robert Leighton, then minister of Newbattle but later Bishop of Dunblane and Archbishop of Glasgow. Leighton's good name and works are remembered throughout the country, he being the principal protagonist of religious harmony in Caroline Scotland and dying, disheartened at his failure to produce peace, in an inn in the south of England. It is doubtful if the pulpit in question was ever mounted by that saintly man, as the kirk was not built until after his death but next to it is the old crow-stepped manse which was certainly his.

In modern times the Marquis of Lothian presented Newbattle Abbey and its contents to the nation and it is used as an adult education centre. Amongst the pictures was a remarkable set of Scottish kings and heroes, Bruce and Wallace, and all the Jameses, painted by George Jamesone, the 'Scottish Van Dyck', for the coronation of Charles I at Holyrood in 1633; together with other royal portraits, mostly of the Martyr King's contemporaries, Louis XIII, Marie de Medicis, Henry IV, all dated before 1650 and never removed from the walls since first hung. Suddenly they appeared in a saleroom in Edinburgh in 1971, without advertisement and incorrectly catalogued, the sellers probably having no idea what they were, far less knowing that Jamesone's Scottish kings served as the models for those by de Wet presently gracing the walls of the Long Gallery at Holyroodhouse. Both sets, foreign and Scottish, were thus wantonly broken up and dispersed, and one wonders with what authority, for they were included in Lord Lothian's gift 'to the nation'. As a group the Jamesones, at least, were part of our national cultural heritage, yet no voice was raised to try and save them or keep them together in one place, preferably in the Scottish National Portrait Gallery.

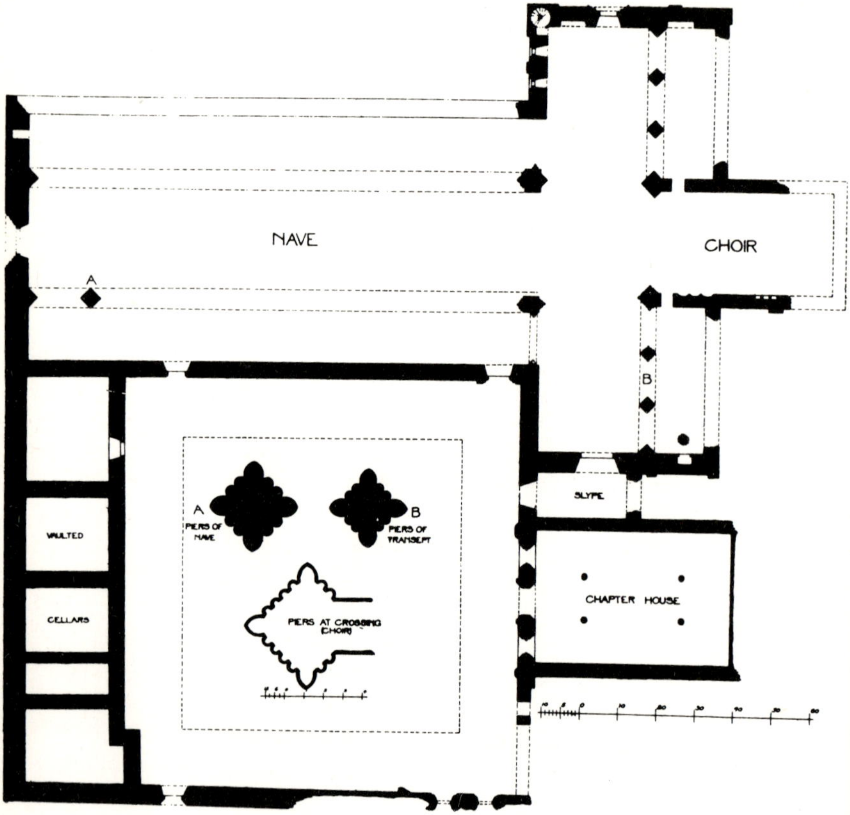

Plan of Dundrennan Abbey

Kinloss Abbey, in Moray, was also founded by David I for Cistercians from Melrose, and has been mentioned before. Little of it survives and the best part, as we have seen, is the Abbot's Tower, really the Commendator's House and seat of the first Lord Kinloss. He was ancestor of the Earls of Elgin and Kincardine, whose modern seat is at Culross, in Fife, where there was another Cistercian abbey, founded by Malcolm, Earl of Fife, and settled from Kinloss. Dundrennan, in Galloway, has much more to show than either of these two, and since it was not the subject of Border raids nor of English malevolence its remains are very much those of an original early medieval Cistercian establishment. Though greatly ruined the overall plan is well exposed and the surviving masonry gives a much better idea of the Cistercian ethos than Melrose, which has been damaged and altered almost beyond recognition. The fact is that the White Monks were extremely strict both in their habits and outlook, and in particular they were anti-art, literally so, considering sculpture, pictures, even books, as irrelevant and distracting to the monastic life. They concerned themselves wholly with contemplation and work; no original Cistercian church displayed any religious imagery or aids to devotion, no stained glass, no statues, no colour, walls were white and unadorned, glazing absolutely plain. Functional simplicity was the keynote externally as well as internally; towers for instance were frowned upon, they were not allowed over the crossing and no spires were tolerated. In view of this it is odd to see how far from the stated ideal the architecture of Melrose departed, for no other church in Scotland, except Rosslyn Chapel, which is proverbially extravagant in its decoration, is so elaborately conceived and finished, its figure sculpture being uniquely splendid. Dundrennan is quite the opposite, conforming to the Cistercian rule of abstinence in decoration and display, and never having been too rich or too damaged to have been rebuilt, is essentially as first intended. Its only substantial improvement since the middle of the twelfth century was the enlarging and remodelling of the chapter house in the thirteenth century, on account of an increase in personnel.

The Cistercians arrived in Scotland partly through the intimate association between David I's son Henry and the companion chosen for him by his father, one Ailred, who subsequently became a novice at Rievaulx and afterwards abbot. Besides this the King had a stepson, Waldef, who also went to Rievaulx before returning to Scotland in 1148 as Abbot of Melrose. There was thus not only a close link between the Scottish court and the Yorkshire abbey but between the Cistercians of Ryedale and those settled in the valley of the Tweed; and later between them and those in that delectable spot in the Stewartry of Kirkcudbright which goes by the name of Dundrennan, or Hill of Thorns in Gaelic. The foundation of this abbey has been variously attributed to both David I and Fergus, Lord of Galloway, and probably both had a hand in it, the king suggesting the Cistercians and Fergus giving his approval, for at that time Galloway, though nominally part of Scotland, was really an attached province and loosely held, like Cumbria and

Dundrennan Abbey: the north transept from the west door; the chapter house

Northumberland; and it was not until the reign of David's grandson, Malcolm IV, that it became integral to the Scottish kingdom. Even then it remained under the supremacy of York in respect of ecclesiastical affairs almost till the Reformation, which is interesting when one considers how the Galwegians, or Gallovidians, marched with the King of Scots when he invaded northern England in support of his niece Matilda, against the claims of her husband Stephen. They engaged the forces of the Archbishop of York, who defended his patrimony with such vigour that the Scots were obliged to retreat in disorder; and the Galwegians, their backs bristling with arrows, like herries, or hedgehogs, were decimated. They prided themselves on not wearing armour, and fought with spears and swords as well as bows and arrows, relying, like the Highlanders in the Forty-five, on their fierce appearance and wild charges for victory in battle.

Dundrennan has a remarkable resemblance to Dryburgh, a resemblance slightly more noticeable in photographs than in real life, since it is actually built of a sturdy grey stone while Dryburgh is pink and soft. The architecture is nevertheless much the same, being transitional and contemporary in date, while the highest standing parts of their respective churches are almost the same. Both are entered through west doors in a wall that has largely disappeared and via a nave marked only by foundations, to reach transepts and the remnants of a choir; and it is the transepts that recall each together, especially the north-eastern transepts, of which almost equal parts survive. Oddly enough too these transepts have been used as burial aisles, Dryburgh being the best known, for beneath its vaulted eastern chapels lie Earl Haig of Bemersyde and many of the Scott family, Sir Walter, his wife Charlotte, his son, Charles, and Lockhart, his chief biographer and son-in-law. Dundrennan boasts a medieval tomb *in situ*; it dates from the thirteenth century, is recessed under an arch and bears the effigy of a recumbent knight on it. The figure is thought to represent Alan, last Lord of Galloway, husband of Margaret, daughter of David, Earl of Huntingdon, and father of Dervorguilla, Lady of Galloway and spouse of John de Baliol, of whom more anon.

As with most comparisons when explored in detail the differences begin to appear, and Dryburgh's west door, although round-arched like Dundrennan's, is not Norman at all, but dates from a rebuilding in the fifteenth century. It is a clever Scottish

Dryburgh Abbey: the north transept; viewed in its parklike setting

reversion to ancient practice within the late-Gothic period, having neither pilasters nor capitals or any authentic Romanesque sculpture, consisting of continuous mouldings running right round from base to base, over the arch. Again the north-east transept, so alike at first glance in both churches, is at Dryburgh composed of pointed transitional arches supporting a decorative band of masonry, not a true triforium, pierced by six-fold openings, one above each arch, with a pointed clerestory above. The latter is particularly delicately conceived, with a gallery behind each set of three lancets, the central lancet being larger than the others and supported by slender columns. At Dundrennan there is a nearly continuous run of pointed arcading at triforium level, with a passageway hidden behind, and above, the clerestory is lit by large round-headed windows. A variation of this occurs on the south transepts, where instead of the continuous arcading of the triforium three sets of pairs of pointed openings reveal the passageway behind. The mixture of round and pointed architecture has puzzled some observers, including MacGibbon and Ross, who seem to think this denotes a rebuilding of Norman work or an enlargement at a later stage, but in practice both Dryburgh and Dundrennan are essentially transitional buildings, and Dundrennan is a daughter Rievaulx, which has Norman transepts and an Early English choir, all built consecutively.

The founder of Dryburgh Abbey was Hugh de Morville, a Norman baron who, with the active assistance of David I in the form of a Royal Charter and a large donation, brought Premonstratensian canons regular from Alnwick in Northumberland to settle on the banks of the Tweed in 1150. Twelve years later the monastic quarters were finished, though not the church, which took another half century to be completed, when the founder was buried below the chapter house together with his wife, Beatrix de Beaumont. He was Constable to David I and his wife was related to the king. Earlier in the same year, 1162, Hugh de Morville had made another monastic foundation, this time entirely on his own account, at Kilwinning, in Ayrshire, colonizing it with Tironensian monks from Kelso. In fact the unusual plan of that abbey, with its double transepts and immensely tall gables is repeated. Unhappily even less of Kilwinning survives than of Kelso, and it is extremely difficult to appreciate in the ugly little town which its grisly remains still dominate the grandeur that once was there.

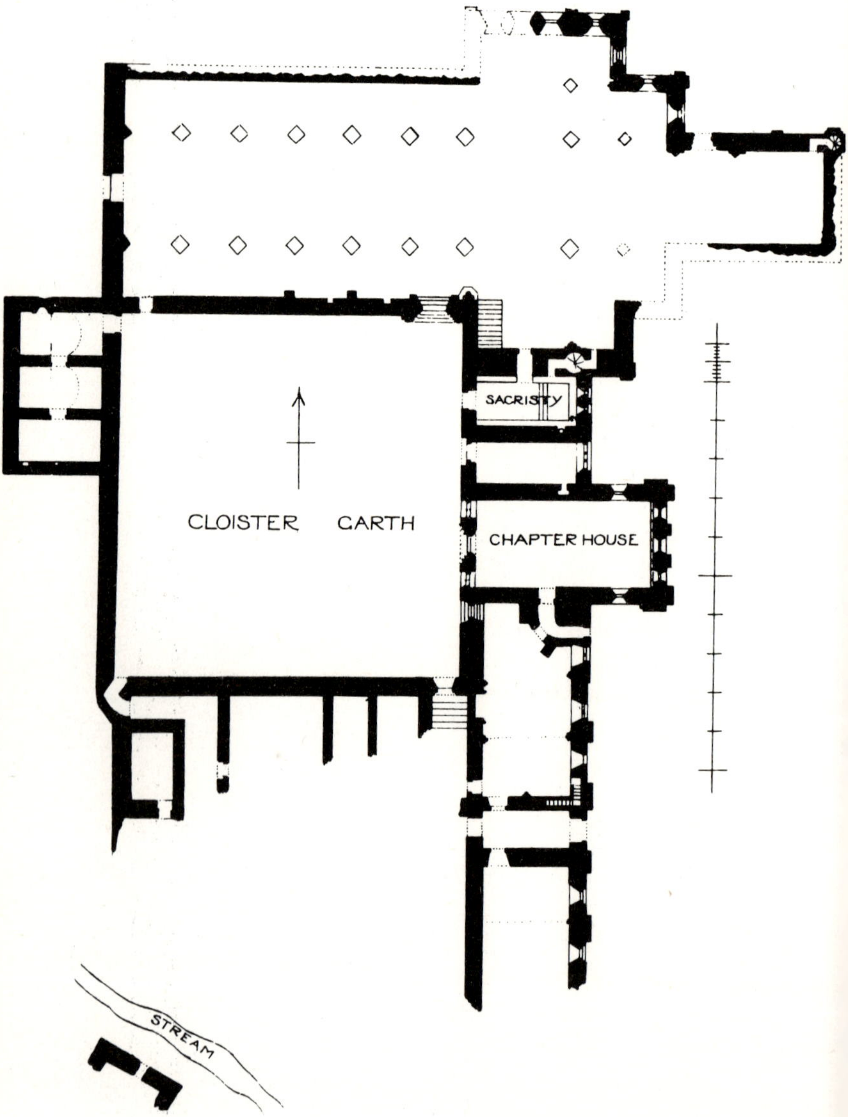

Plan of Dryburgh Abbey

Blackened and uncared for, allowed to remain standing merely on sufferance, surrounded by hideous memorials and with an uncompromisingly rectangular 'God-box' built on the site of the former choir, Kilwinning Abbey presents one of the most dismal prospects of any erstwhile Scottish monastery extant. A ninety-foot-high gable-end, pierced with three long lancets and oval above, represents what is left of the south transept, presaging in its form the south transept gable of Arbroath, founded by William the Lion in 1178 in honour of St Thomas à Becket and similarly colonized with Tironensians from Kelso.

It is said that the masons employed at Kilwinning came from several countries on the Continent and formed the nucleus of one of the first international masonic lodges. What is meant is that they belonged to a guild, and their marks, since they were nearly all illiterate, appear as signatures on the walls. The standard of workmanship is very high, and apart from the towering south gable the east processional doorway survives plus part of the chapter house, arranged as at Dryburgh, with central round-arched doorway and divided side windows. The Tironensians, unlike the Cistercians, were lovers of art and would almost certainly have been engaged themselves in the building and beautifying of their splendid new abbey.

There is a theory that the existence of a large number of ancient yew trees at Dryburgh means the site was sacred to the Druids, while the naming of a chapel in the twelfth century abbey after St Modan suggests Celtic origins, as at Melrose. Neither theory finds much favour with modern scholars, however, and it is probable that this particular loop of the Tweed was first surveyed as the site for a suitable religious settlement by the canons regular from Alnwick in 1150, coming here for that purpose expressly at the behest of Hugh de Morville. The naming of a chapel after St Modan could not have occurred until comparatively modern times since the chapel in question, now used as a burial place by a noble family, was formerly the slype, or parlour, where the canons were permitted free conversation, in fact the only place in which they were. One would scarcely expect to find holy relics deposited there. This slype or parlour came between the chapter house and the sacristy, or vestry, which at Dryburgh was also the library, something denied the Cistercians at Dundrennan. Indeed, there was also a book cupboard, or aumbry in the wall between the vestry door and the east processional doorway into the cloister from the church, and the place is still clearly visible though no longer protected by the cloister roof. It is the best-preserved part of the abbey, this cloistral portion, having been adapted as a private residence at the Reformation, perhaps before, the revenues of Dryburgh falling to a series of abbots *in commendam* and post-papist squatters. They found the southern facing wall of the church useful as a windbreak and ideal to grow fruit trees against, made the cloisters into a pleasant courtyard and lived in the two-storeyed monastic wing on the east side, allowing the rest of the abbey to fall down or be carted away as building materials.

The Premonstratensians did not flourish north of the Border as the Tironensians and Cistercians did, and besides Dryburgh, and Whithorn, which was revived as a cathedral-priory for them in 1154, the only other notable Premonstratensian establishment was at Fearn, up in Ross-shire. This was settled from Whithorn in the early thirteenth century and until the end of the fifteenth the links remained close. Fearn is today represented by the parish kirk which boasts four tall lancet windows at its easternmost end and several other pre-Reformation features, a side chapel with the tomb of an abbot who died in 1485 and a curious place in history, the penultimate abbot being none other than a boy, Patrick Hamilton, illegitimate offspring of the Earl of Arran and grandson of Princess Mary, sister of James III. He is known in Scottish history as the first Protestant martyr, having been burned as a Lutheran heretic in front of St Salvator's College in St Andrews at the age of twenty-six, largely at the instigation of his kinsman, another bastard of the Arran family, John Hamilton, last Archbishop of St Andrews in the Roman obedience. The third of this extraordinary trio of bastards was Sir James Hamilton of Fynnart, architect to James V of Scots and the murderer of John Stewart, Earl of Lennox, grandfather of Lord Darnley and father of the last abbot of Dryburgh, John Stewart, whose coat of arms appears in the south-western corner of the cloister near a now vacant tomb recess. Pluralities were, of course, the order of the day in this corrupt period, the most notorious example being another abbot of Dryburgh, one Andrew Forman, who combined the offices of commendator here with those of prior of Pittenweem and Coldingham, bishop of Moray, archbishop of Bourges in France and archbishop of St Andrews, which office he acquired through mild blackmail and on the excuse of preventing an Italian from obtaining it. In fact, no Italian ever held the see. The tombstone of this unlearned and ignorant man, who was unable to speak or understand Latin, is in the little Episcopal Church of St John at Pittenweem, in Fife, which proves one thing at least, he stayed in the priory there long enough to die in it.

Despite the divergence of the orders settled at Dryburgh and those at Dundrennan their plans are similar and typical of early monastic layouts, with cruciform churches on the north side of the cloisters and monastic quarters. At Dryburgh there are night stairs to and from the dormitories into the church, and the southernmost gable of the south transept is stepped up into the window tracery to accommodate the roof of the adjacent buildings. In the midst of these, and the best-preserved feature in both, is the chapter house, which at Dundrennan is the one important building or part of a building ever to have been enlarged or rebuilt, but in the thirteenth century, not later. It is extremely fine in its conception and details; one hesitates to say beautiful in view of the Cistercians' professed aversion to beauty, but they have produced here an exquisite piece of Gothic architecture worthy of the best in northern England, and the Cistercian abbeys of France. Rectangular in shape, the roof was formerly vaulted and supported on four slender pillars, the entrance being divided into three almost equal arched openings, the central arch being slightly larger and cusped, or broken to form three segmental archlets, the design is the same inside as out. The side arches are subdivided by smaller, unglazed windows; this being normal since it allowed the monks to hear what was being discussed in the chapter house without going in; and each side window is again divided into two, the central supporting columns unfortunately being missing.

The chapter house at Dryburgh has not been rebuilt or enlarged and retains its original Romanesque doorway with deeply recessed arches and contemporary detail, plus a transitional touch in the waterleaf motif carved on the capitals of the side columns. As at Dundrennan there are two smaller open windows for the canons to listen at, and these have round heads, the smaller openings within them being pointed and retaining their supporting colonnades. Inside the barrel-vaulted roof is intact, the eastern end is lit by three early Gothic windows below which is a run of blind Romanesque arcading rising directly from the customary stone seat, and on the walls there are traces of decorative colour work in the form of red-jointing against white masonry and other simple devices. The chapter house floor is well below the level of the cloister garth, which is well below the floor of the church, so that the whole site is terraced, which gives it a particular cachet, the final fall towards the river, and the edge of the loop on which the abbey is built, reaching to the stream that once washed out the drains and ending at the gatehouse. The surroundings have long since been made into parkland planted with trees, cedars of Lebanon, splendid beeches and the celebrated yews, so that Dryburgh Abbey, as well as being the mausoleum of gentry, heroes, and wizards of the pen has become one of the most distinguished follies in the country.

The present setting was the inspiration of David Steuart Erskine, eleventh Earl of Buchan, the flamboyant character who wrote Scott's funeral service and arranged suitably theatrical obsequies when the Bard was ill in 1819, but himself died first, in 1829. He was an amateur artist and historian, relative and friend of the great, originator of the Society of Antiquaries in Scotland and claimed descent from the Kings of Scots, though he could only do so in the illegitimate line. In furtherance of these pretensions the Earl erected in the abbey grounds an amusing memorial to his supposed ancestors, namely James I and James II, in the form of a standing stone. On one side is the figure of James I, only dressed and looking like James II of the Fiery Face. It is evidently copied from an old German print in which the monarch who lost his life at the Siege of Roxburgh is shown wearing tights and short tunic, turned-up boots and wide-brimmed hat, his hand on his dagger, with rampant lion shield beside him. The second figure, meant to be James II, might be James III, though he is shown with emblematic canon at his feet and dressed in what can only be described as Cromwellian armour, replete with gay flutter of feathers from his helmet! The stone has weathered nicely and probably deceives more by its false appearance of antiquity than it did when newer. It is lichened, like the old abbey, which is built of local pinky-grey stone, not so red as Melrose, and harmonizes well with its environment.

Dryburgh suffered the usual number of raids and sackings, the repetition of which is almost too boring to proceed with, though it was spared a burning by Edward I as a result of the abbot swearing fealty to him, and would have escaped Edward II's bad temper on the way home from defeat at Bannockburn if the canons had not appeared to be jubilant at his and his troops' humiliation. Richard II visited the place with his displeasure in 1385, but neither his nor earlier burnings seem to have been so thorough as that of Melrose, and no great rebuilding was necessary, indeed, by the beginning of the sixteenth century and long before the arrival on the scenes of the inevitable Hertford, Dryburgh was already in a state of decay, both as regards its appurtenances and inmates. The poor-to-average quality of its later abbots bears testimony to this: and one suspects that the library and wall book-case by the door into the cloister was not much used after 1503, when Andrew Forman was nominal superior of the place. He could neither read nor write the language of the church and could hardly speak English, except in the broadest of accents. One of the canons, Ralph Strode, is reputed to have travelled to Rome and reached the Holy Land, and in England become the friend of Chaucer and the enemy of John Wycliffe, but that, of course, was in the fourteenth century; and the Cistercians, whose learning and knowledge of anything other than practical work was supposed to be minimal, made a pretty good showing by comparison with these Premonstratensians, who despised their Augustinian brothers for their assumed worldliness but did no better, in fact worse, themselves. As for the Cistercians, one has only to look at neighbouring Melrose, which in its early days provided refuge for the aged philosopher-confessor of Queen Margaret, and in its heyday, the mid-fifteenth century, had for superior Abbot Hunter, Lord High Treasurer of Scotland and ambassador to France of James II of the Fiery Face.

Dundrennan was lucky in the matter of English raids since it did not suffer from any, though its remains are even scantier than those of Dryburgh, its stonework was removed stage by stage by local builders and those desirous of enlarging their dykes or otherwise improving their property. This did not happen at first, however, indeed not until the eighteenth century to any marked degree, as the abbey kirk was spared, having become a place of Protestant worship. It may seem surprising, but it is certainly the case, that the entire abbey, church and monks' quarters was standing and functioning, with its full complement of abbot and monks, the same number it ever had, as late as 1568, when Mary, Queen of Scots was received there by Abbot Edward Maxwell, whose brother, Lord Maxwell, was the local laird and a prominent supporter of the old religion. It was with him, or possibly another brother, Lord Herries, who fought with her at Langside and escorted her south after her defeat, that the Queen may have spent her last night in Scotland. Legend will have it she was a guest of the monks at Dundrennan, which she certainly visited, and from which she departed for England, sailing from the mouth of the abbey burn in a small fishing boat that took her across the Solway Firth to 'cousinly' custody.

Twenty years later the abbey was appropriated by James VI and attached to the Chapel Royal at Stirling, while the Maxwells became hereditary bailies, or sheriffs, in place of the abbots. Dundrennan suffered from no secular commendators, its church continued in use by another denomination, and only the domestic buildings were used as a convenient quarry until the early nineteenth century, and a visit by Henry Cockburn, the great preservationist and public-spirited citizen of Edinburgh, a law lord and originator of the idea of the modern amenity society. He made protests in the proper quarters about the appalling state of the ruins of Dundrennan, the abbey being reduced to nothing better than a 'rubbish heap'; and in due course the quarrying was stopped and the remains tidied up and partly repaired by the Commissioners of Woods and Forests, today represented by the Department of the Environment.

The church was originally entered through a narthex, or porch, with lean-to roof, as was usual in Cistercian abbeys, and the corbels supporting this are still visible. Other items of special interest that have survived the years of pillage and misuse are the tomb of Alan, Lord of Galloway, who died in 1124, and which has already been mentioned, and a number of slab tombs of abbots, in the chapter house. More intriguing are three memorials inside the west wall of the church, one dating from 1607 and commemorating Sir William Livingstoun of Culter 'ane richt honorable man', another a monk's cellarer, one of the *conversi*, or lay brothers, who died in 1480, and more particularly, the upturned slab gravestone of an abbot who was murdered by a Galwegian, perhaps another of the *conversi*. The abbot is shown holding his crook, with a dagger piercing his heart, standing on top of the diminutive figure of his short-tunicked Celtic murderer, at whose head the base of the crook points and from whose stomach intestines ooze. A rose carved to the right of the abbot's head shows his Tweedside origins. There can be few such memorials anywhere, and this one is unique in Scotland. The lay brothers were fairly numerous, many being employed by the monks on their various agricultural ploys, and they had their own living quarters in the abbey. At Melrose they were so numerous they had their own cloisters as well as dormitory, refectory, kitchen, cellar, parlour, and warming-room, but at Dundrennan were quite adequately accommodated on the western side of the monks' cloister, having their separate enclosed choir in the middle of the nave, which they entered at the south-western end. This was divided from the monks' choir, which spread down from the presbytery into the nave, by a screen and a passage, the so-called retro-choir, and a stone pulpitum, as at Fountains Abbey in Yorkshire.

So far we have dealt mostly with abbeys because they were the speciality of David I, and the question of cathedrals has had to take second place. In fact, the diocesan system in Scotland was largely created before his reign in the course of the overall introduction of feudalism, in which bishops played their part, together with barons and the king. Thus, when David I came to the throne, Aberdeen, Dunkeld, Galloway, Glasgow, Moray, Ross and St Andrews all had cathedrals, as well as the two Scandinavian sees of Orkney and the Isles; and by the time of his death in 1153 only Argyll and Edinburgh remained without separate bishops, the first being created in 1200, with the division of Dunkeld, the second in 1633, with the division of St Andrews. Caithness acquired its cathedral in 1146, the architect being one of its first bishops, Gilbert de Moravia, of the same family whose descendants now include the Dukes of Atholl and Sutherland. Gilbert himself combined ecclesiastical and secular occupations in a manner not uncommon in the Middle Ages, serving both as bishop and Lord High Treasurer to Alexander II, and practising the art of architecture in his spare time. He built Kildrummie Castle, in Aberdeenshire, with its beautiful chapel lit by slender lancet windows. Dornoch Cathedral and his own palace. Of the latter the base of the present Castle Hotel in Dornoch may be a remnant, while of the Norman cathedral there is virtually nothing authentic to be seen, what does exist is a twice-rebuilt, and much-restored parish kirk. More substantial remains survive in the erstwhile Cathedral Close at Elgin, and in the ruined Bishop's Palace at nearby Spynie, in Moray, of which diocese Gilbert de Moravia was formerly Archdeacon,

Dunblane Cathedral from the east

while his kinsmen filled other posts in the neighbourhood, one being the builder of Duffus Castle, the other Bishop of Moray.

The diocese of Brechin was founded, or perhaps in view of past history, refounded by David I in 1150, with a new cathedral on the probable site of the Pictish King Nechtan's church. His tenth century Round Tower was matched to the north with a new medieval campanile, with a good early Gothic west front between. The 'Pictish' tower served both as Christian symbol and as a place of refuge, round but otherwise similar in arrangement to that at Dunblane, which the king founded *de novo*, in the same year. Dunblane's square campanile, now attached to the cathedral, was originally free-standing like Brechin and rose to four storeys, still discernible by their deep crimson masonry, twin round-headed windows and Norman doorway, today opening inside the nave, but above ground level, recalling that in times of trouble it could only be reached by removable ladder. The tower was probably finished with a saddle-back roof with crow-stepped gables, as at Muthill and Dunning, in the same district. In the fifteenth century the height was increased by two more storeys with Gothic windows and a short spire, while a hundred years later the top was battlemented as we see it today, with open bartisans at each corner. The fifteenth century work is in a different stone from the earlier, grey with streaks of yellow, while the battlements are again red, verging on madder, as is the base. Thus the different ages are expressed architecturally and masonically, and the history of the tower too, for is it not interesting to see how it began life half-defensively and ended it almost wholly so, the top imitating that of a contemporary 'tour of' fens', and demonstrating how history does repeat itself, despite the doubts of some twentieth-century observers?

Unlike Brechin, which boasted an authentic previous existence as an important Christian settlement, Dunblane has for antecedent little more than a legendary association with the sixth-century St Blane of Bute, a holy man of presumed Irish origin who performed his most celebrated miracle somewhere in the vicinity of the present cathedral. The Celtic monks were famous for their miracles, the range of them and their efficacy, so that St Blane, returning through England on his way home from a pilgrimage to Rome, restored a blind boy's sight, cured him of his sins and restored him to a state of grace, in three separate stages. The boy eventually died and was buried in what is now Dunblane, and although there is nothing to substantiate this story all the signs are that the place is of greater antiquity than the existing Norman and Early English cathedral proclaims; and this is half-confirmed by the survival in this building of a fine eighth-century Celtic cross. Otherwise the oldest masonry dates from King David's foundation of 1150 and is represented by the first four floors of the formerly detached campanile, and in the Lady Chapel, which takes the form of an aisle to the north of the choir and may have been that of the first cathedral, pre-dating as it does the completion of choir and nave.

The architecture of this former Lady Chapel is severe and sturdy to a degree, its most notable features being the flattish buttresses which support it and the unusual fenestration whereby a series of tiny pointed windows, each diminishing from the centre, are encompassed within larger segmental openings, a form that is repeated in the clerestory of the choir on the north side, and is obviously part of the original design. The same device clearly

Dunblane Cathedral: west end; plan

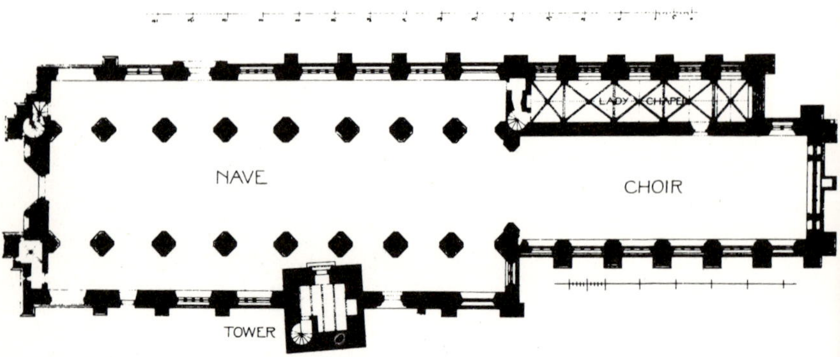

appealed to William Butterfield when he adopted it for the small Cathedral of the Isles at Millport, on Great Cumbrae, in Buteshire, which he undertook for the Hon. George Frederick Boyle, afterwards sixth Earl of Glasgow, in the nineteenth century. Butterfield's detailing of the porched clergy entry to that cathedral, the smallest in Britain, is almost identical to work at Dunblane. Indeed, there are other details he may have consciously copied, such as the clerestory-cum-triforium windows as they appear on the exterior of the nave, which re-appear at Cumbrae in the guise of traceried openings in the cloisters; but then Dunblane is an excellent model, being the most perfect expression in little of Early English architecture in Scotland, and so simply inspiring that even Ruskin's admiration was assured, his comment, 'that it was no common man who designed the cathedral of Dunblane', merely revealing the truth. The ex-Lady Chapel is now used as a vestry and store, and has two floors, the upper being partly in the roof but lit by three steeply pointed arches at its west end and tiny twin arches between the buttresses to the north. A spiral stair, leading from the existing vestry and the restored nave, climbs to a lavatory and broom cupboard and to the attic which was once probably a reading-room and library. This particular building may be the oldest bit of the cathedral, apart from the tower, and may have monastic connotations, suggesting Inchcolm in function.

Between its royal founding, and the election of Bishop Clement to the new see in 1233, progress seems to have been slow at Dunblane, in fact, the diocese was not at all flourishing and Clement had to the new see in 1233, progress seems to have been slow at Dunblane, in fact, the diocese was not at all flourishing and Clement had second-to-last in the Roman obedience, and Robert Leighton, who ruled in the reign of Charles II and loved the place dearly. Bishop Edmund Chisholm was succeeded by his half-brother and by their nephew of the same name, who retired shortly after the Reformation and died a monk in France. Leighton, of course, was that saintly divine to whom we have referred before, he hated being translated from Dunblane to the archdiocese of Glasgow, and when he died left his library to the cathedral clergy. It is still there in a special house built for it, set amongst others of a similarly discreet nature suitable to stand around this modest but attractive church. Dunblane is one of the very few (Old Aberdeen is perhaps the only other comparably sited cathedral) in which the proverbial precinctual atmosphere pertains in Scotland, with old houses decently complementing the Gothic church, not too much traffic and the clock telling the hours, the relentless passage of time being audibly marked by unhurried, mellow-toned bells.

Though the choir may be older than the nave it is by no means the most beautiful part of the church, it has been more altered, not always to its benefit, and used as parish kirk and Reformed Episcopal cathedral since the seventeenth century; while the marvellous nave was allowed to fall into ruin. In the nineteenth century Sir Rowand Anderson was commissioned to restore and repair the whole building, and no better man could possibly have been chosen. He was that rare architect who saved his clients' money and whose plans were often less ambitious than theirs. Having saved them money he refused to spend what was left on extraneous decoration or unnecessary additions, and instead, if his client insisted on spending every penny, he either made a stronger building or improved some functional detail, such as the drains. His masculine devotion to simplicity and solid qualities, plus a scholarly understanding of the Gothic style, makes his restoration and practical rebuilding of Dunblane Cathedral one of the most satisfactory exercises of its kind in recent Scottish cultural history, one's chief regret being that after he had finished the framework another, less fastidious architect, with a love of elaborate carving and sheer whimsy, was given free rein in the choir and on the pews and in the nave. Sir Robert Lorimer, who here followed Sir Rowand Anderson, as indeed he did in the rebuilding of Paisley Abbey, had just finished the Thistle Chapel in Edinburgh, his most exhaustive and jewel-like design in recreative flamboyant Gothic, and unfortunately he employed the same style at Dunblane. The angels in the choir have a distinct femininity not usually given to such personages, and a playfulness not in keeping with the more grotesque humour of the Middle Ages, but nearer to the spirit of *Peter Pan*. The decor of the haffits or pew ends in the nave can only be described as Beatrix Potter interpreted in oak, with rabbits and squirrels, mice and dicky birds, conceived in a thoroughly unmedieval manner. Oddly enough, six canopied choir stalls surviving from the time of Bishop Edmund Chisholm were not used as models, instead they were futiley placed at the bottom end of the rebuilt nave, three on either side of the west door. They were probably made in Flanders and should have been studied as the basis for any restitution of the cathedral's woodwork, but they were not. Some others, lacking canopies, do remain in the choir, beyond the Lorimeresque furnishings. They are virtually unique in Scotland, so far as any cathedral is concerned, the most remarkable assembly of medieval church furniture remaining *in situ* in Scotland actually being in the chapel of King's College, Aberdeen, where the old bishop's throne was brought from the half-demolished cathedral of St Machar.

There are several novelties in the design of the nave at Dunblane, for example, of the six transitional arched bays on either side, the four westernmost are wider than the others, while some of the windows in the triforium-cum-clerestory (the two are combined in one gallery), are subdivided with supporting colonnettes and quatrefoil insets, while the rest are not. Some of these variations may be intentional as they are about equal in proportion, and it is quite clear that the two separated walls in the triforium are intentional, one on the inside line of the nave, the other on the line of the exterior, with a clear space between them. This peculiarity is also carried on across the west end, where the three, simply traceried external lancets have repeats inside, supported over the tribune. I mentioned the possible influence of such features on William Butterfield, but it was not only he who looked to Dunblane for inspiration, Sir George Gilbert Scott studied its architecture pretty thoroughly, devising an intriguing new version of the double window form in the triforium for the choir of St Mary's Cathedral in Edinburgh. He used the windows inside, keeping the passage behind, but omitted the external openings altogether. The west front at Dunblane is perhaps the most refined and appealing part of the whole design, the top vesica, or symbolic fish-shaped window, was a special favourite of Ruskin; but the entire masonic conception is excellent, with its handsome triple windows rising above a deeply recessed early pointed doorway, not unlike that at Paisley, with which it is contemporaneous, and a similar arrangement at nearby Inchmahome Priory, on Lake Menteith. The recesses are accounted for in the masonry by the usual thickening of the wall, and on either side narrow, much more sharply pointed blank openings occur, with smaller, cusped arched features within. The stone is the most attractive mixture of soft grey merging with vermilion; imagination and strength are given to the architecture by the shape of the side buttresses, which contain a turnpike stair in one case and a little vaulted room and steps leading up to the tribune in the other.

The cathedral has no stone vaulting in the choir or nave, or even aisles, but the vestry, or former Lady Chapel, is nicely ceiled with stone groins and ribs, the latter springing from very plain pilasters, without any figurative sculpture, to meet under bosses decorated with simply carved leaf motifs. One might add that a number of monuments have survived at Dunblane, which was not ravaged at the Reformation and has, throughout its history, had a fairly peaceful existence, decay and a certain amount of dubious restoration being the real enemies. In the choir may be seen a recumbent bishop vested, wearing his mitre, and another in the nave, likewise in his pontificals, recumbent under an arch; while nearby is the double monument to the eighth Earl of Strathearn and his lady, who lived in the thirteenth century. He is shown lying beside the Countess, clad in armour, though not with his legs crossed in the crusader manner, half-covered by his shield, she, her face gone, dressed in a long flowing gown, her hands held together in prayer. Bishop Clement has his memorial in the refinement of the early pointed architecture all around, Bishop Chisholm in the splendid canopied stall and misericords, one of which bears his coat of arms, while Bishop Leighton is remembered not only in the continued use of the choir, the smallest portion of the building, throughout the seventeenth century, but in his library and the Scottish Churches House in the Cathedral Close, where churchmen of all persuasions can and do meet in the spirit of charity so devoutly desired by the Caroline prelate.

With the death of David I the founding of abbeys slowed down, and with the notable exceptions of Arbroath and Balmerino passed from a predominantly royal exercise to one also performed by the greater servants of the crown and other important personages. There was still more than a century to go before the end of the 'Golden Age' in Scottish History, which found its culmination in the reign of Alexander III, last of the Anglo-Norman sovereigns, whose death without a male heir in 1286 led inevitably to a conflict of claims by the three principal descendants of David, Earl of Huntingdon, and to the War of Independence and the accession of Robert Bruce in 1306. The last abbey to be founded was Sweetheart, or Dulci Corde, in Galloway, a labour of love on the part of the Lady Dervorguilla, mother of one of these claimants, John

Baliol, and this was not completed until the following century, its workmanship suffering from the ending of peace during the course of its building. Glasgow Cathedral was half-finished in the thirteenth century, Melrose was destroyed in the early fourteenth, and both were begun again later, with the aid of a French master mason, though in the case of Melrose with craftsmen from Yorkshire as well, thus creating a remarkable and lively comparison between the two influences at work in Scotland at that time. The mixture changed in the fifteenth century to one of Flemish and French, reflecting closer links with the Continent, and it was from this merging that a national style in ecclesiastical architecture evolved, having its climax in the years immediately preceding the Reformation.

We have seen how King David's High Constable, Hugh de Morville, emulated his master and founded Dryburgh in 1152, followed by Kilwinning ten years later. In 1163 Walter FitzAlan, Dapifer, or Steward to the King and ancestor of the Royal Stewarts, founded Paisley Abbey for Cluniac monks from Much Wenlock, in Shropshire. It was in this part of England, near the Welsh border, that his family had settled in the wake of the Norman Conquest and become local sheriffs, though it is likely the future Steward met the future David I at the court of Henry I when the Scottish prince resided there. For centuries Walter FitzAlan's forebears had controlled the households of others, of the Dukes of Brittany in particular, and it would appear they had an hereditary gift for stewardship which commended itself to successive employers, ordering things justly and firmly for two centuries in Scotland. Their misfortune seems to have been to marry into royalty, for almost at once the fatal flaws in the proverbial Stewart character emerge, at least in the early Jameses, and stayed with them till the end, when Cardinal York died in Rome in 1807. The switch in character is so marked it cannot be overlooked, and is present straightaway in the offspring of Walter, sixth High Steward, and Marjery Bruce, afterwards Robert II, who was prematurely born as the result of his mother being thrown from her horse, herself expiring shortly afterwards. At this time Robert Bruce had an heir, and the idea of the Stewards, made High and Hereditary and Justiciaries of the realm by William the Lion in the latter half of the twelfth century, inheriting his crown was not considered; nor did anyone have the remotest idea of what was in store for the descendants of these Breton dapifers and Scots stewards in the course of the next few centuries.

The monks of Cluny were the first to turn the older Benedictine rule into a formal order, and became the largest and most powerful body of their kind in medieval Europe. Like such bodies they had their rise, triumph and decline, breaking up in due course into splinter and reforming groups of which the best known were the Carthusians, who had their Charterhouse, or Chartreuse, near Grenoble, and are known today mainly for their liqueur. In fact they are extremely strict and their Charterhouse has never been open to visitors. More numerous and less restricted in their mission were the Cistercians, based on the abbey at Cîteaux, or Cistercium, near Dijon and not very far from Cluny. This order, which set up many colonies in Britain, had for its first abbot an Englishman, Stephen Harding, and its first English house at Waverley, in Surrey, was established only two years before Rievaulx and scarcely more than six before Melrose, which shows how quickly the order spread and how up-to-date David I was. It is purely fortuitous but amusing that Sir Walter Scott should have visited the remains of Waverley Abbey whilst staying with friends in the south of England and decided to use the name for his celebrated novels. It is almost a commonplace name now in Scotland for all sorts of things, from shortbread to a railway station, pens to suburban villas, and few have any idea of its origin.

The chief reasons for the Cistercians breaking away from their mother house at Cluny have been mentioned previously: they considered the older establishment had got into a rut, and more than that had become positively corrupt and in need of drastic reform. The codification of St Benedict's ancient rule had been one thing, wealth and power and love of ritual another, indeed, the order's patronage of Romanesque art was renowned and significant, and one of the things that set the Cistercians against all art. These forms, with Lombardic inspiration, developed in Burgundy, as did the diverse religious movements associated with them, but whether or not this could be related to the climate of the country or some other natural cause is difficult to say, except perhaps that being in the centre of the richest and biggest kingdom in Europe, and half way between the north and Italy, Cluny was ideally placed for control of land and people in many directions. Of the original abbey only the tower and adjacent portions of the church have survived to tell the tale of past glories, rather like some Scottish abbeys, for the French attitude to ecclesiastical buildings has on occasions shown a remarkable similarity to the Scottish, especially in the days of the Huguenots and again during the Revolution. At that time all religion was at a discount, papal and Protestant, monastic or parochial, and churches and abbeys became, as in Scotland, suitable places for the display of physical violence, of getting things off one's chest; and were then made use of as ready-made quarries. The only real difference is that while the stonework was mostly free for all to take in Scotland, it was usually requisitioned in France and sold by the authorities!

Revolutionaries are rarely respecters of persons and only of property if it is of use to them, and just as Cluny was not spared and its monks dispersed, so Cîteaux, home of the puritan Cistercians, was confiscated and reduced to its sectarian, functional essentials, a barn and outbuildings remaining to this day. La Grande Chartreuse fared better on account of its remote position in a deep fold of the Savoyard Mountains on the borders of France and in a quasi-independent state. Today the Carthusians are still there, selling Green Chartreuse, but only at the gate, a mile or so from the actual Charterhouse. The fate of abbeys obviously took different forms in different countries, in Italy and Spain most have survived unharmed, at least by anti-clerical marauders, while Monte Casino itself, St Benedict's haunt in the days before the Goths and Vandals, was expensively and laboriously rebuilt for the third time after the last war. The bones of the saint whose rule formed the basis of all monastic orders in the Middle Ages, reformed and unreformed, were brought to France to the valley of the Loire, in the eighth century, and laid to rest in the abbey of St Benoît-sur-Loire, where they have remained ever since. Probably from this results the initial French monopoly in the matter of monastic influence, and it may explain why once the revolutionary outburst had subsided the monks were able to come back and are today re-established in so many of their old abbeys as well as new ones. In this respect France is different from either England or Scotland, for although a dozen Benedictines have resettled at Pluscarden, in Moray, coming, curiously enough, from a new English abbey at Prinknash and composed almost wholly of Anglican converts, in general the older monastic sites in Britain have not been revived, even where the disabilities pertaining have largely disappeared and the public antipathy towards monks and nuns has receded.

Henry VIII set a bad example by handing church property over to his friends as bribes and rewards, but it did mean in some cases that the conventual buildings survived, and that many churches were preserved for public use and were not seriously damaged until the seventeenth century, when Cromwell's men, armed with the authority of Parliament, went round systematically destroying all ornament, stained glass, sculpture or other works of art. The Yorkshire abbeys, which had such close links with Scotland, suffered rather more from vandalism and deliberate sacking than those further south, first during the Reformation, when the North rose against Henry VIII's edicts, and later in support of Mary, Queen of Scots; this revolt was put down with undue severity by Queen Elizabeth, when Durham Cathedral, for instance was desecrated and emptied of its treasures. These probably included the Holy Rood of Queen Margaret of Scotland lost by David II at Northallerton, and certainly the tomb and shrine of St Cuthbert, which was defiled and mutilated. The vacant ruins of Rievaulx, Byland and Jervaulx are in no better state than their contemporaries at Melrose, Dryburgh and Jedburgh and were partly rendered so by the Scottish Covenanters, who invaded northern England in support of Cromwell, during the Civil War, when they burned the nave of Carlisle Cathedral and generally laid waste to that part of the country which in the twelfth century had belonged to David I and his successors, the Bruces and Baliols. The former came from Guisborough, in the North Riding, the latter from Barnard Castle in County Durham. Fountains Abbey is extraordinarily intact, because it was already protected within the park walls of a Jacobean mansion and not, therefore, so easy a prey to vindictive Scottish soldiers seeking to get their own back for past English misdeeds.

The abbey at Paisley, which Walter the Steward founded in 1163, was a typical Norman structure, having architectural connections with the Cluniac abbey at Cérisy-la-Forêt, near Bayeux, which lost half its nave in later centuries but is otherwise entire, including a chevet of little chapels around the apse and tower, all of which resembled the mother church at Cluny. Unfortunately, the steward's kirk, founded originally to serve a priory, and in which both he and his son Alan, the first hereditary steward, were buried, is no more. No part of it has been left standing and the building we

St Mirin's Chapel, Paisley Abbey, showing false rib vaulting (R. W. Billings)

see today dates, except for the west entrance and lower courses around it, form a series of restorations and rebuildings. The first of these took place after the abbey's burning by the English in 1307, presumably because James, fifth High Steward, and his brother John, took the national side in the War of Independence and fought under the banner of Sir William Wallace, their feudal inferior, Sir John losing his life at the Battle of Falkirk in 1298. This would have been thought improper by many of the other nobles but the great patriot himself probably had territorial links with the Stewarts and may have come from the Welsh Marches (his name suggests it), the same region in which the Stewarts had been sheriffs. In the fifteenth century, under Abbot Thomas, the abbey was again burned, when the nave was rebuilt and the central tower, which afterwards collapsed, was completed. The choir was at first apsidal, like Cérisy and Cluny, but the tower fell down and ruined it and not until modern times was there any attempt to recreate it, with a flat end, in the seventh restoration-cum-rebuilding in the abbey's history, and the fourth since the Reformation.

The nave continued in use, being much smaller than the choir, and it is the nave which really interests us here, especially the masonic curiosity it displays in the form of small corbelled-out galleries at clerestory level, which provide a complete walk around without weakening the structure by cutting through the arches. This is said to have its origins in the cathedrals of Angers and Rouen. In these, however, the projections are at triforium level, not higher up; at Angers iron balustrades are included for protection, while at Rouen the outcoming polygonal platforms only occur on the aisle side of the arcading, not in the nave proper, and are supported by delicate columns, not clumsy corbels, and are not at such a dangerous height. The triforium arches at Paisley remind one both of Jedburgh and Dunkeld, Jedburgh for their detail and Dunkeld for their half-moon shape, with very short supporting pillars. The architecture is pointed and sturdy rather than fine, but not lacking in dignity, and we are lucky so much of it has survived. When one comes to the transepts and choir, practically the only authentic part is the chapel of St Mirin, a Celtic personage to whom the early church is said to have been dedicated and after whom a football team is now named. The chapel sports false ribs on its barrel vaulting, and two vaults, just in case. In it is a tomb traditionally thought to be that of the Princess Marjery, who mar-

Paisley Abbey and 'Place'

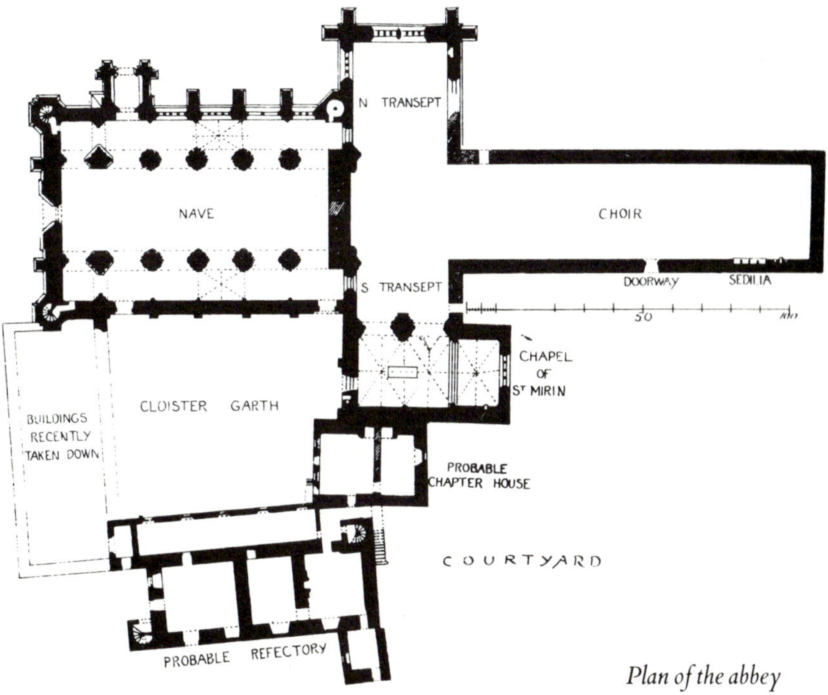

Plan of the abbey

ried Walter the High Steward, thus bringing royal and fateful blood into the family. Experts disagree as to whether this really is her tomb or not, the problem being complicated by the existence of a number of conflicting armorial items on the side panels, including the insignia of a bishop and an abbot of different dates. The whole thing may be a composite arrangement of collected remnants, indeed, this is very probable.

The Reformers did their worst to the fitments at Paisley, but no doubt they left a few items of carving lying around without taking it all away and destroying it, hence, possibly, the odd make-up of the supposed royal tomb. Queen Victoria with her usual attention to such matters had it restored, and in 1963, on the occasion of the 800th anniversary of the founding of the abbey by her ancestor, Her Majesty the Queen paid a visit to the scene. Actually, with the Scots, penchant for accepting legend unsupported by proof it was suggested that St Mirin's Chapel should become some sort of national shrine, and a red light placed in it to signify the fact. The proposal inspired one of the late Dr James Richardson's more telling stories; and since the chapel was a Cluniac foundation, the product of men devoted to the maintenance of correct liturgical practice, perhaps one may be permitted to repeat it here. What the learned architectural historian and ecclesiologist said was: 'When I see a red light in a Roman Catholic church I know what it means; when I see one in an Episcopalian church I think I know what it means; but when I see a red light in a Presbyterian kirk I should jolly well like to know what it means!' The fact is that a red light, or tended light of some sort, does have a liturgical meaning, it marks the place where the Sacrament is Reserved for the Sick, and this would have been understood by the Cluniac monks. What is commonly and loosely called a 'Sanctuary Light' might be anything, even electrically controlled; the whole point is that the light should be manually tended and only lit when the Sacrament is actually there.

Paisley retained part of its monastic buildings alongside the abbey kirk because the last incumbent had the good sense to see that his nephew became commendator while the chance existed. The abbot who did this was none other than John Hamilton, who came to Paisley as a mere youth, rose to become archbishop of St Andrews and last Roman Catholic primate in Scotland. He survived the first wave of the Reformation and supported Mary,

Queen of Scots in her final bid to keep the crown at Langside, wearing armour and fighting like a warrior. He was captured in the siege of Dumbarton Castle and hanged at the mercat cross in Stirling in 1571, being subsequently buried in the abbey over which he had presided in the days of his youth. The abbots of Paisley were very powerful indeed, almost as powerful and rich as their patrons, the Royal House, and emulators in their own way of the abbots of Cluny, in Burgundy. They stood up to the bishops and archbishops of Glasgow, who periodically tried to bend them to the diocesan will, as they did the abbots of Jedburgh, Kelso and Melrose, who at one time came under their jurisdiction. These ones, however, rarely gave way, relying finally on the king's support, which was usually forthcoming. After all they had under their roof the bones of the daughter and heir of Robert Bruce, seven Stewards, Lord High Stewards and Justiciaries of Scotland, two Queens and a King, Robert III, and saw that due respect was paid to their descendants.

In 1897 a local Improvements Committee was set up to do something about the building and its surroundings. The abbey was crowded round with houses and virtually hidden by them, some belonging to what is called the 'Place of Paisley', which included a portion of the erstwhile cloisters and the commendator's house, plus a seventeenth-century mansion in which 'Bonnie Dundee' was reputed to have been married in 1684. Much of this was demolished in the clearance, but the best part was saved and that is now open to the public. As for the church, and especially the very long choir which replaced the apsidal one ruined by the collapse of the tower, it was heavily restored and in parts rebuilt from the ground upwards. The first architect was Sir Rowand Anderson, whose excellent work was continued by Dr MacGregor Chalmers, and completed by Sir Robert Lorimer in 1928, the year before his death, thus making two thirds of the abbey kirk practically a new structure. The original intention had been to reconstruct it from old prints and records more or less as it had been before the tower fell in the fifteenth century, and both Sir Rowand Anderson and MacGregor Chalmers planned for this. Unfortunately the First World War intervened and when Lorimer came to take over alterations were made, including a new design for the tower.

Central towers had a habit of being weak and of falling down, damaging adjacent buildings, the most notorious disaster of the kind being at Ely, which was not reconstructed of stone or to its full height but lower and with an oak ceiling in place of vaulting, as is well known; and when Sir George Gilbert Scott came to design St Mary's Cathedral in Edinburgh, in the second half of the nineteenth century, he carefully studied what occurred at Ely before proceeding with the central tower there, which he finished with a magnificent spire, using a number of clever structural devices to make sure it did not fall down. Sir Robert Lorimer seems to have combined a certain amount of experience with discretion and omitted the spire altogether at Paisley, designing the flat-roofed, squattish tower we see today, which does not resemble what was there before but at least has some architectural affinities with the tower at Jedburgh. What Paisley should have got was a tower and moderately tall spire similar to that of St Mungo's in Glasgow. Lorimer filled the choir with furnishings not dissimilar from those at Dunblane, the organ case being almost the same, but here his rather florid designs and rich carvings are more in keeping with the recreated late-Gothic interior, and his new stone vaulting really is first rate, with its bosses boldly sculptured, robust and not whimsical, as good as the fifteenth-century vaulting of the choir of St Giles's High Kirk in Edinburgh, on which he almost certainly based it. The medieval spirit is perhaps better captured here than at Dunblane, for amongst the stone caricatures to be seen in the new work is the face of William II of Germany, matching older figures in the nave, such as two of the corbel supports of the clerestory gallery, one showing a human being on all fours, another a humanized dog; both are illustrated in Dr Richardson's book on the medieval stone carver in Scotland.

Associated with Paisley and colonized with Cluniac monks from it was Crossraguel Abbey, in Ayrshire, which was founded by Duncan, Earl of Carrick, towards the end of the twelfth century, though not settled until about 1214, the Paisley monks being glad enough to take the revenues offered but not so ready to do the hard work or move out into the country. Robert de Bruis, father of Robert I, inherited the earldom of Carrick through marriage and became in the process patron of Crossraguel, the superiority falling in due course to the House of Stewart, hence the abbey owes its principal charter to Robert III, who gave the abbot sweeping powers, secular as well as ecclesiastical, plus royal exemption from the customary visitation by the Bishop of St Andrews. This had

Crossraguel Abbey: the gatehouse and hospice; the church showing the central bellcot

been instituted by the Pope in an attempt to control corruption and error and normally covered all religious establishments in Scotland. The abbots of Crossraguel ruled Carrick, or southern Ayrshire, practically without let or hindrance, much as their brothers did their part of Burgundy; the monks had the right to coin their own money and regulate the fishing, they administered the law and ran their own breweries and mills, holding these rights 'for ever in free regality'. This may explain why at the Reformation everything worth having was returned to the crown for its disposal, notwithstanding the efforts of the local Kennedy Earl of Cassillis to gain the property for himself by roasting alive the secular abbot, or commendator. He did extract from his victim the title deeds to the property, but was taken to court and his misappropriation reduced, while being forced to pay the broken abbot an annual pension. Soon afterwards James VI took back what was left, though the monks remained *in situ* until 1592, which is probably the latest date of any pre-Reformation establishment in Scotland. In 1617 all was made over to assist the Bishop of Dunblane, who, as on previous occasions, was finding difficulty in running a small and monetarily unproductive diocese.

With such a remarkable history and legacy of continuing power – even the last papal Archbishop of Glasgow, James Bethune, deposited his library, plate and vestments at Crossraguel before leaving for exile on the Continent – it is surprising how modest the ruins of the abbey appear. One comes across them suddenly, standing in the fields, surrounded by black and white Ayrshire cattle munching the rich grass and buttercups that make Carrick a rival to Devon or Somerset for dairy products, the single-storeyed aisleless kirk, with simple bellcot and gable between choir and nave, seeming more like a private chapel than the remnant of some mighty abbey whose antecedents lay at the great monastery of Cluny. Indeed, the tallest and most substantial remains are those of the Abbot's Tower, or 'keep' and the well-preserved gatehouse, which is in essence another defensive tower, and much resembling the gatehouse to any fifteenth- or sixteenth-century Scottish castle. It was, in fact, the guest house as well as fortified entrance, and behind it can be seen the round, domed beehive doocot, or dovecot, facing the rolling hills and a typical white Ayrshire farm and steadings. It is all so rural and placid and domestic one scarcely feels the breath of history or religious contention, far less senses the greed

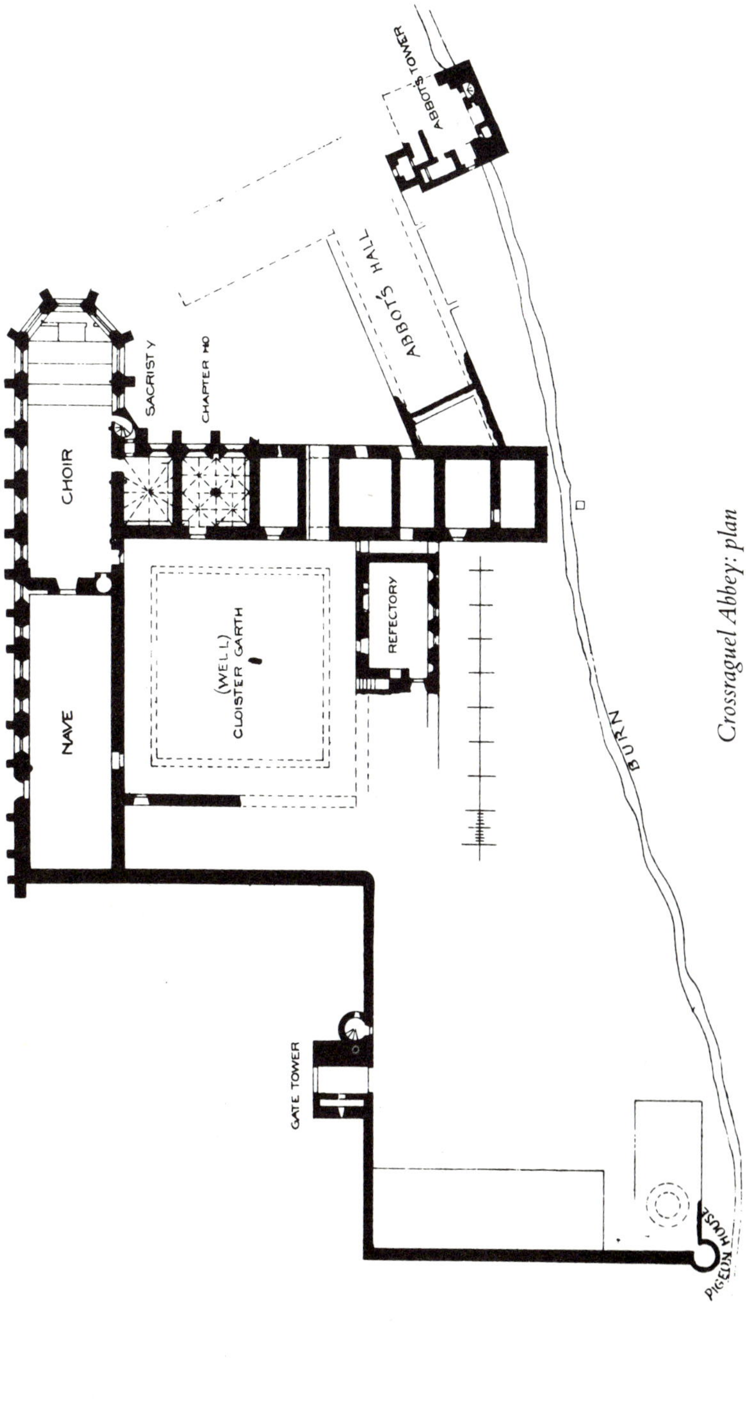

Crossraguel Abbey: plan

leading to torture that characterized the last stages of the last abbot's tenure.

There is little to show for the first, thirteenth-century abbey, which suffered like its mother in Paisley from the malevolence of Edward I and was rebuilt in the fifteenth century, witness the decorated windows in the church and other late features, such as the richly carved canopies to the sedilia, and the aumbry, or wall cupboard for sacred vessels, in the choir. The sacristy and chapter house are both nicely rib-vaulted, the former having once served as the latter, which is larger, and above part of the library and writing room have survived, lit by a flat-arched mullioned window. This is very late indeed, presaging the Renaissance. There are very few such windows in Scotland at all, the most conspicuous being in the Royal Palace at Dunfermline, probably dating from the early sixteenth century. More French than most abbey kirks, and reflecting direct Burgundian influence, is the polygonal apse, as well as some of the ornate sculpture, which is flamboyant rather than perpendicular. In this respect the architecture is closer to contemporary Scottish town kirks, particularly those large collegiate churches like St Giles's in Edinburgh, Holy Rude in Stirling and St Michael's at Linlithgow, which rivalled cathedrals and abbey kirks in their size and wealth and were the burghers' answer to the diversion of funds from the cathedrals and abbeys into prelatorial pockets or to Rome, which so weakened religious life in Scotland in the fifteenth and sixteenth centuries.

The corbels that formerly supported the cloister roof still project from the walls around the cloister garth on two sides, and in the middle is the old well. The oddly simple shape of the bellcot and the reason for its being between the nave and choir can probably be explained by the reduction in the number of monks in the sixteenth century and the closing off of the nave altogether, for the dividing wall is neither a screen nor pulpitum. It is perhaps interesting, even instructive, to note too that the cross on the bellcot gable bears a striking resemblance to the heraldic cross of the Kennedys, who provided the penultimate abbot in the Roman obedience, a man made famous in Scottish history by his defence of the church's teaching against John Knox, whom he took on single-handed in debate in the Kennedy town house in nearby Maybole. His stance compares with that of James Bethune, the archbishop who went into exile voluntarily, thinking thereby to weather the

Crossraguel Abbey: the abbot's doocot

storm of the Reformation and at the same time retain his freedom of action should he return. Bethune subsequently revived the Scots College in Paris, where he acted as ambassador for Mary, Queen of Scots, but he never came back to Glasgow, despite the fact that James VI offered to keep him in his bishopric; and he lived on in exile into the first years of the seventeenth century. The Kennedy abbot with whom he left his treasures occupied, if he did not actually build, the 'keep' at Crossraguel, and it seems strange after all this to find his kinsman taking the opposite side and behaving in so barbarous a manner to Andrew Stewart, his successor *in commendam*.

The priory of Inchmahome on one of two islands on the Lake of Menteith, in Perthshire, the other island being occupied by the ruins of the Earl of Menteith's castle, never acquired either the riches or power of Crossraguel, though in common with it and Paisley it enjoyed Stewart patronage and gifts from other magnates. The site is amongst the most picturesque and romantic in

Inchmahome Priory: the entrance to the cloisters from the church; the chapter house, looking across the ruined cloister

Scotland, much more so than Loch Leven, and with much happier reminders of Mary, Queen of Scots. Here the infant daughter of James V and Mary of Guise came as a child of four, with her Maries and her little half-brother, James Stewart, afterwards Regent but a not very sympathetic member of the family, before being taken to Dumbarton onto a French ship for her journey to France to be reared as a Frenchwoman and the promised bride of the Dauphin. Sentimental legend has made of some overgrown box-hedges 'Queen Mary's Bower', the implication being that the young queen, who certainly loved gardens, planted at Inchmahome a tiny formal garden of low hedges and paths which has now become the wilderness we see today. As she and her childhood companions were only on the island for a month or so it seems hardly likely, but not entirely impossible. The priory was founded by Walter Comyn, fourth Earl of Menteith, whose sister was married to Sir Walter Stewart, brother of Alexander the High Steward, who led the Scottish knights to the Crusades. There was said to have been a Celtic monastery on the same site earlier, and this, like Queen Mary's garden, is not wholly without possibility, especially since the foundation documents speak of 'confirming' an existing settlement of monks.

Whatever was there before, Augustinian canons regular, presumably from Cambuskenneth, were set up on the island by the Comyn Earl, and the church and ancillary buildings, apart from a later tower, almost all date from the thirteenth century. They closely resemble in many details contemporary work at Dunblane, this being particularly noticeable in the design of the west door, though here, in place of one steeply pointed blank arch on either side, there are pairs of them. The church had a single aisle, on the north, containing three chapels, each one divided from the nave by wooden screens, while tacked on to the same side of the choir is a largish sacristy as at Dunblane, but lacking an upper floor. Of the conventual buildings little remains, no commendator lived here. The local baron had his own castle, and the Earl of Mar, who filled the post of secular abbot, also held Cambuskenneth and Dryburgh, besides possessing a handsome town house in Stirling, where he resided as keeper of the castle for the king. The Austin canons remained at Inchmahome until they all died sometime shortly before the end of the sixteenth century, and thenceforth the place simply became a private ruin, but not a very easy prey to itinerant

Inchmahome Priory: the west end of the church

free-quarriers. No doubt buildings on the lakeside – Menteith is Scotland's only lake to be called such – benefited, but few further afield.

The site became in effect a burial place for different lairds including Lord Kilpont, who was murdered by an adversary in Montrose's camp in 1644, and Sir John Drummond, whose memorial Dr Richardson links aesthetically with warrior monuments in the West Highlands since it portrays the deceased knight holding a spear and bearing his shield. The latter displays the three wavy bars which are said to recall the fact that the first Drummond was captain of the ship that brought Queen Margaret to Scotland from the Continent. A Celtic saint is also thought to be represented on the same grave slab, which is still in the roofless church, most of the others having been removed into the chapter house, under cover. The best of these is probably unique in Christendom, though not much attention is paid to it in the guide-books. It shows Sir Walter Stewart and his Dame, the sister and heir of William Comyn, lying facing one another, on their sides and not on their backs, their arms locked in a loving embrace. Such a naturalistic pose is not recorded as existing anywhere else at this date, the knight died in 1294, so that it can only hark back to an earlier period, perhaps Celtic, preceding the formalized feudal era.

Walter Stewart, who became fifth Earl of Menteith in his wife's right and ancestor of successive earls, also fought in the Crusades under the banner of St Louis. He was lucky in a way to die before the War of Independence, spared the fate of many of the rest of his race, but he took part in the Battle of Largs, again with his brother, Alexander, the High Steward, when the power of Norway was finally broken in Scotland and Argyll and the Western Isles passed to the Scottish Crown. Later he was a witness to the marriage of Alexander III's daughter and heir, Margaret, to Eric of Norway, the child of which union, the so-called 'Maid of Norway', died shortly after landing at Kirkwall following a terrible voyage to Scotland made at the age of eight. Earlier the little girl had been promised to the first Prince of Wales, the future Edward II, and the growing closeness of England and Scotland seemed to portend happy times ahead for both kingdoms, but her death prevented it. Walter Stewart is shown in his armour, with headpiece, his back almost covered by his huge shield with the Stewart fesse-chequey on it; his legs are crossed for a crusader, and his feet rest upon a lion, symbol of fortitude. His countess lies half-turned towards him, her left arm under his head, below the pillow, coming out on the far side, her right hand clasped in his as he bends to take it. At her feet is a dog, symbol of fidelity. The pair of figures are carved from a single stone and neither is mutilated.

The priors of Inchmahome were protected by the earls, whose castle was on the neighbouring island of Tall, and they were well used to receiving the great and the mighty as guests in this peaceful haven amidst the Perthshire hills between Loch Lomond and Strathern. They paid lip service to Edward I's claims in 1296, thereby preserving their patrimony, but made peace with Robert Bruce later, that king visiting them thrice. Robert II, who was of course a Stewart, came to Inchmahome in 1358; his son Robert, Duke of Albany, later Regent of Scotland and the probable murderer of David, Duke of Rothesay, son and heir of his brother James I, married the several times widowed Countess of Menteith; previous husbands having been Sir John Murray, the thirteenth Earl of Mar, and Sir John Drummond. She herself was the daughter of Sir John Graham, all of which helps to explain the varied gravestones in the church and elsewhere, and also the ultimate fate of the property, as after the Drummonds and Erskines of Mar had superseded the Stewarts and Comyns the Grahams appeared on the scene in the person of the great Marquis of Montrose; and it was the sixth Duke of Montrose who put the priory in the care of the Ministry of Works in 1926.

There are a number of remarkable things about St Mungo's Cathedral in Glasgow, not the least being that it is there at all. I mean standing, roofed and used, the only example of its kind on the mainland of Scotland, and, apart from Sir George Gilbert Scott's St Mary's Cathedral in Edinburgh, the largest Gothic building in the country. Traditionally founded in the seventh century and named after St Kentigern, the gentle Mungo, above whose tomb the present mainly Early English structure rises, the church displays a rare homogeneity which disguises the fact that it took more than three hundred years to complete and was actually rebuilt on two occasions. Happily successive bishops carried on much in the manner of their predecessors, one of the few notable differences in the architecture occurring in Bishop Blacader's Aisle, as it is called, which represents the crypt of a big new transept which was projected but never got on with, possibly fortunately, since it would have broken the existing elevational pattern and been in a more flamboyant style. Blacader was the first Archbishop of Glasgow, the see being raised to that status in 1491. We have met him before, as Abbot of Jedburgh, his arms being on the top of the tower there; similar arms, with an archbishop's mitre in place of an abbot's, appear on the side altars of the pulpitum in Glasgow Cathedral.

When looking at St Mungo's one has to try and envisage its original setting on a sloping site above the Molendinar Burn, with woods not far away, the Clyde flowing gently and cleanly between green meadows, a pleasant city of old crow-stepped houses, medieval churches, and in the fifteenth century, a splendid new university, founded by Bishop William Turnbull. A strong episcopal castle and adjacent canon's house complemented the cathedral, of which an ancillary building, Provand's Lordship, still survives amidst the stour and stink of the modern industrial city. To compare the site with Jedburgh would not be entirely inappropriate, only Jedburgh has remained green and welcoming while

Glasgow Cathedral before 1850, showing north-west tower since demolished (R. W. Billings)

John Knox's view of the cathedral. The chapter house is on the bottom right

Glasgow has destroyed itself to become what it is now, a large and pompous Victorian town, pockmarked with inelegant skyscrapers and cut across by nasty roof-level urban motorways. Perhaps a better comparison might be with Dunblane, though the cathedral there is even more modest than the town, smaller than Jedburgh or any of the Border abbeys, and about half the size of Glasgow Cathedral. On the other hand, the architecture of both is contemporary in essentials and 'English', indeed Glasgow appears amongst the English cathedrals in many professional volumes. This Englishness is expressed in its slender pointed windows and doors, the magnificent early Gothic vaulting in the crypt and aisles and in much of the detail, though there are also Scoticisms, these increasing in number after the War of Independence and the severance of links with the south at the end of the thirteenth century, when the choir and nave were completed but not the central and west towers, the chapter house and sacristy. These latter all display local features and the tower has a typical top gallery reminiscent of Jedburgh and Paisley as it appeared in old prints, with an octagonal spire sporting late-Gothic lucarnes and ringed twice with masonic circlets.

The two western towers were demolished in the nineteenth century. The consistory tower, the lower of the two, which scarcely exceeded the roof of the nave in height and contained legal and other documents pertaining to the consistory court, was demolished in 1846 at the behest of the Corporation and on the advice of the Master of Works employed by the Government to deal with such matters. The old Butter Tower, taller and built with money saved in Lent from not eating butter, came down two years later on the same advice and at the behest of the same vandalistic Civic body. The excuse in both cases was that their disparate designs and shapes spoilt the appearance of the west front, which it was intended, with the usual Victorian insenstiveness, to tidy up; and so thorough and barbarous was this process that the very documents were burnt on the site, consumed by the flames except for a handful snatched from the embers by curious onlookers! The towers had a notably native look, with their sturdy supporting buttresses perfectly matching the contiguous range that runs round the nave and choir to the back of the cathedral to support the two-storeyed chapter house and sacristy, which incidentally resembled the Consistory Tower closely and dates from the same period. They were

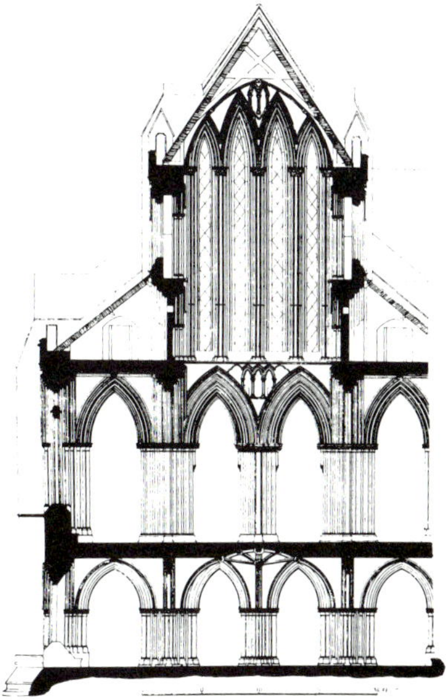

Glasgow Cathedral: the south door to the crypt; transverse section through choir and lower church, looking east; Jean Moreau's choir screen and entrance to the crypt (R. W. Billings)

both finished with saddle-back roofs and crow-steps, and were once ceiled with stone slabs, the chapter house now being slated. The Butter Tower, which rose to the north of the west front, contained the bells and had a single broach-shaped spire.

The result of the removal of these distinctive features, which it was proposed to replace with new towers of equal size and design by goodness knows who (for it was after the demolition of the Bishop's Castle, to make room for Robert Adam's decent but unmannerly Royal Infirmary), is to render the initial view of the cathedral not only disappointing but positively off-putting. It seems so ordinary, insignificant and isolated in its miserable setting of tombstones stretching to infinity, beyond the tunnelled-in Molendinar Burn, the horizon on the summit of a hill dominated by a giant statue of John Knox! It is the Scottish necropolis *par excellence*, rivalled only by similar features in, say, Italy, behind Genoa, where, however, the vast monumental acres do not encroach upon the city itself, do not prejudice the character of its principal architectural treasure. In fact, if one wants to see Glasgow Cathedral at all properly one must go over to that awful hill and look down upon it as Knox does, and thus appreciate the medieval craftsman's conception and the clever use of contours, there being two churches, the first, in the crypt, being repeated above in its constructional details, even to the central pillar behind the altar, as at Rosslyn and Exeter.

One has seen many crypts in Europe, nearly all performing two complementary functions, enshrining the tomb of a saint and supporting a church above, but few are anything like Glasgow, most representing an early phase in the building, usually Romanesque as opposed to Gothic, and often crude by comparison with the rest of the structure. There is nothing crude about Glasgow's crypt, or lower church, it is one of the most delicate and refined constructions in early pointed vaulting that exists, and far from enshrining an original tomb is a thirteenth-century re-edification. The remains of St Kentigern were temporarily moved while the operation was carried out, and then put back in their much more sophisticated setting of four clustered columns rising from a podium immediately under the high altar. The new tomb was desecrated at the Reformation, but the splendid vaulting is intact, boasting the most comprehensive and best-preserved assembly of carved ceiling bosses in Scotland. All is so simple and beautiful, re-

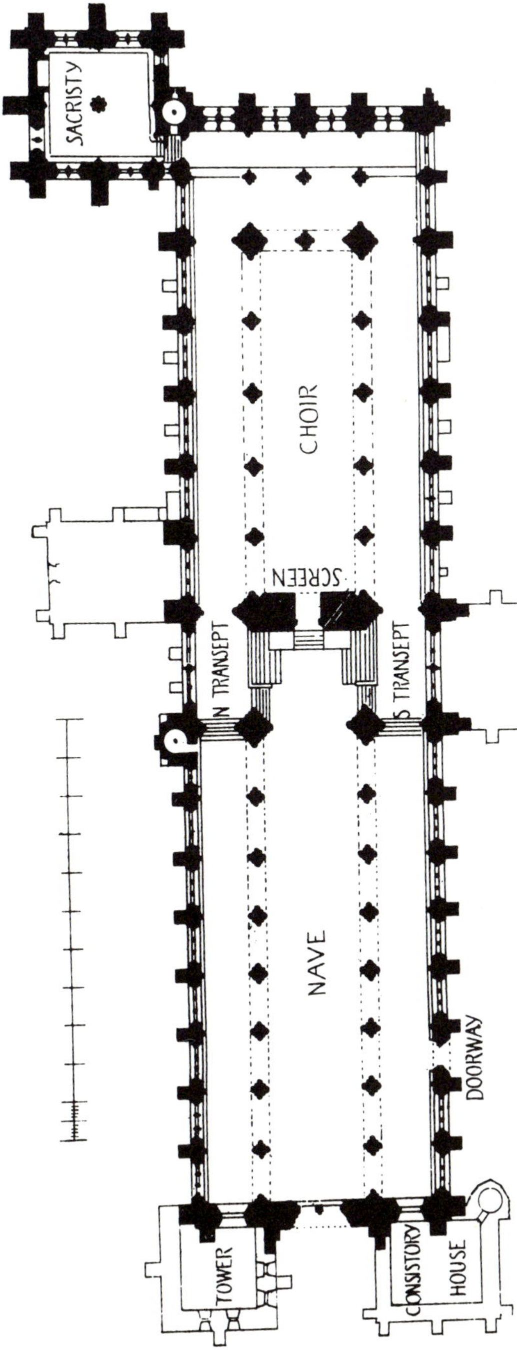

Glasgow Cathedral: plan of the nave and choir

strained and well proportioned, carved foliage being reserved for the capitals of the four supporting columns on the podium, and other sculptural detail for the ceiling bosses. These cover a number of subjects, the customary Christian symbolism, including a fine 'Lamb of God', vying with clerical and anonymous heads, vegetation and more complicated designs for our attention. Behind and around the shrine-tomb is an open ambulatory so that pilgrims could view the space from any angle, and this free arrangement is repeated in the choir.

The square chapter house opens from the crypt, its late-Gothic vaulting supported at the centre by a handsome pillar decorated with episcopal heraldry, its date being established thereby. The bosses here too are of particular interest and more elaborate, displaying the arms of Bishop Cameron and of James I of Scots and his Queen, Joan Beaufort, granddaughter of John of Gaunt. The ear-

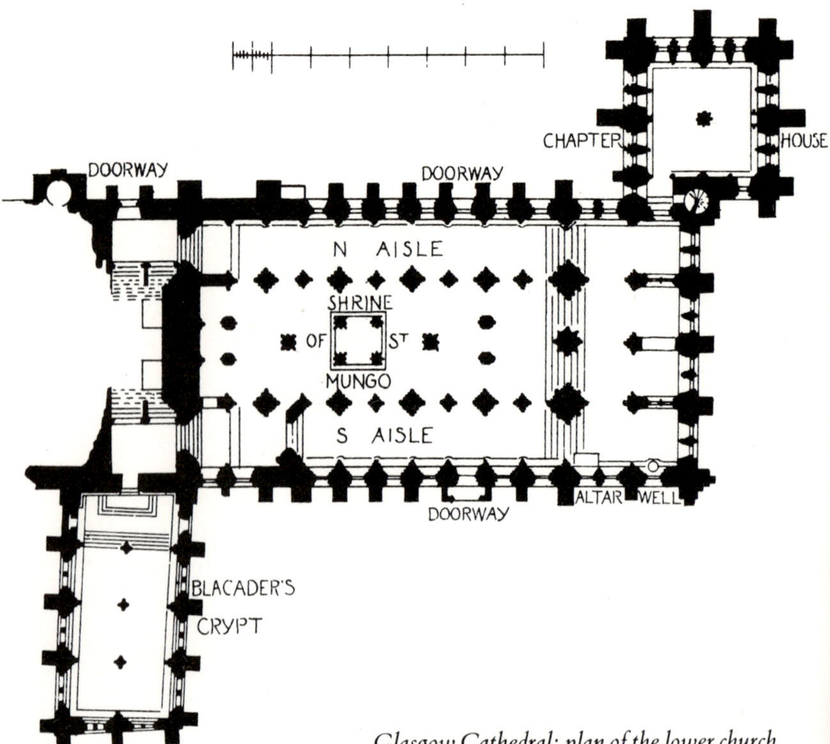

Glasgow Cathedral: plan of the lower church

liest date for this latter is 1424, as before then the King was still a prisoner in England. Above, on the level of the choir is the sacristy, which Bishop Cameron added in the mid-fifteenth century when he restored the thirteenth-century chapter house. This retains the Dean's seat, with ornately carved flamboyant Gothic canopy the arch of which is what the French would call *anse de panier*, or basket-handled, being nearly flat but not quite, and without the slight point at the centre that would relate it to English perpendicular. A similar arch on a much bigger scale spans the opening through the pulpitum between the choir and the nave, and was the work of Jean Moreau from Melrose, at least that was the opinion of Dr Richardson when Chief Inspector of Ancient Monuments in Scotland, under whose care Glasgow Cathedral was placed. The pulpitum has been linked with the name of Archbishop Blacader, whose coat of arms appears on the altars on either side of the steps leading up to the entrance, each also retaining its 'bleu de Tournai' marble top, but although these are undoubtedly contemporaneous with the nearby Blacader Aisle, the screen proper was erected by Bishop William Turnbull, founder of Glasgow University in 1451. The top balustrade is elaborately carved and divided into eight bays, the dividing features supported by decorative corbels which, ignoring the two ends, are said to represent a quaint amalgam of the 'Seven Ages of Man', the 'Life and Temptations of a Holy Man who was a Crusader', and the 'Lazy and Industrious Student'. Even Dr Richardson was puzzled by the apparent mixture of opposing material, though he does identify students being alternatively lazy and hard-working, marital bliss and 'The wife wearing the breeks', not to mention a knight and his symbolic lion of fortitude. He also mentions curiosities in some of the armorial treatment in the cathedral, mentioning especially the fact that the arms of Archbishop Blacader have for supporters the royal unicorns of James IV, while those of a later archbishop, actually the one who saw the Reformation in, and used the opportunity to get married, Alexander Gordon, retain the royal crown, and re-use an earlier royal shield.

The Blacader Aisle is often considered the greatest attraction to visitors to Glasgow Cathedral, though it does not rival the crypt either in architectural purity or refined detail, for here the effect is more from rich decoration than structural originality, the columns being clustered and carved lavishly and the ceiling bosses expressive to a degree, painted as well. The more correct name for this aisle, which is at an in-between level, between the crypt and the nave, is the Fergus Aisle, after either or both the hermit whom St Mungo buried here in the seventh century, or Fergus, the mason who carved the bosses and built the arches and vaulting, including that special boss I described in an earlier chapter. If the whole of this late-Gothic splendour, the last part of the cathedral to be completed, had ever appeared as proposed in an enlarged transept what a glorious display of masonic craftsmanship we would have seen here, yet the full extension would have stood well in front of the line of the existing buildings and hidden the choir entirely on the south elevation. It is interesting to note, incidentally, that the present transepts, as with most in Scotland, do not project beyond the line of the aisles in the nave and choir, making the church a basic parallelogram on plan, not cruciform. There is another peculiarity at Glasgow in the flat east end and generously planned ambulatory, replacing the apse and attendant circle of chapels one might expect to find in a pilgrimage centre like Canterbury, for instance, or most large Continental sanctuary churches. Just outside the Blacader aisle is a doorway leading into the crypt whose simplicity and ingenuity of construction is one of the more remarkable smaller features of the cathedral. In order not to obstruct the light by blocking up a whole bay between buttresses, the doorway, which is formed within a delightful porch with sloping roof, is placed asymmetrically to incorporate the base of the buttress, and a new, complementary buttress is introduced beyond. The whole device is a triumph of masonic skill and aesthetically entirely satisfying.

Both nave and choir of the cathedral were being built throughout most of the thirteenth century. The earlier structure consecrated in the presence of David I in the days of Bishop John is nowhere represented, nor is there much to show for its successor erected by Bishop Jocelin towards the end of the twelfth century. The flat-ended choir was the first part to be completed, under Bishop Bondington, though the nave was started first. Unfortunately the stone barrel roof with which it was ceiled became unsafe and began to push out the walls, some of which still show the effects of this, and had to be taken down. It now has, with the choir, a timber ceiling, the aisles alone being stone vaulted. The architecture too is not so good in the nave as the choir, a feature common to many churches, perhaps because the choir was for the clergy? In any event, the choir stood over the shrine of the founder-saint and its pillars and arcading repeated that of the lower church. The columns are richly clustered and carved, and both the triforium and clerestory have spaces behind and between. The triforium arches are divided by smaller double openings supported by clustered colonnettes, some sporting cusped arches, quatrefoil or trefoil in the spandrels. The clerestory reverts to lancet forms, in triplets, with narrow, blank arches at the ends. The east gable is renowned for its four tall lancet windows which look just right as one enters St Mungo's through either of the twin west doors, nearly 300 feet away. The arrangement in the nave is not dissimilar though executed with less care than the clerestory; it is lit by large single openings and the triforium arches are traceried, but there is little carving in the capitals, showing the effect of approaching conflict with England.

Glasgow Cathedral, whose western towers were removed by a tidying-up council with Government support, was saved by that council's predecessors at the time of the Reformation, they resisting orders from Edinburgh to reduce the building to the usual shambles required by the new, self-appointed authority there. It cannot be said that between that saving and the beginning of the nineteenth century, when the next attack came, St Mungo's was either properly used or properly maintained, particularly after the fall of episcopacy in 1690, when the building ceased to be a true cathedral and was divided up into several churches, like St Giles in the capital. It was too large for the purposes of one congregation, and Scott refers to the 'very singular place of worship' established in the crypt. His description in *Rob Roy* of 'extensive low-browed, dark, and twilight vaults . . . seated with pews' is happily a thing of the past, and the impression now is more of a forest of stone palm trees with fronds represented in the low bending arches of the pointed Gothic vaulting; well tended and much respected, without the pews and the site of the saint's shrine adequately marked. Other happy results of the forming of a Society of Friends of Glasgow Cathedral, and a renewed interest in Scottish architecture generally has been the removal of the German painted glass that used to disfigure and cloud the windows in the nave. These gave a good indication of the taste prevailing in the city in the nineteenth century, and provide more reason for rejoicing in the fact that once the western towers had been demolished at least they were not replaced at the time. Yet all is not light and sweetness, for that would be very difficult to achieve in Glasgow, not only on account of the dirt and grime of the city *per se*, but because of the overall gloom that descends upon one hereabouts, with those thousands of tombstones, marching like an army down that terrible hill with Knox on top, the ghastly Infirmary buildings, as omnipresent from the east as from the west, and that empty soulless expanse which does service as the Place de la Cathédrale, in this the former 'Second City of the Empire'.

Here was the episcopal centre of a Bishop's Burgh, as Glasgow was termed, the Bishop's Castle and the Clergy Houses, or Prebend's Manses, and here, as isolated and lonely looking as the cathedral itself is Provand's Lordship, last of the manses. The reason for its survival reads very like that for the survival of the domestic quarters of some abbeys, for it became the property of one William Baillie, titular canon of Glasgow and prebendary of Barlanark, an estate on the outskirts of the city, the little manor house of Provan Hall bearing testimony to that connection. This latter is the oldest purely domestic building of the fifteenth century still standing and roofed in Scotland and is now safe in the care of the National Trust. It is part of a new conservation area created in the wake of a vast motorway that cuts through the surrounding houses and has provoked long overdue re-landscaping. Provand's Lordship was William Baillie's town house, and also dates from the fifteenth century, when it was attached to the hospital of St Nicholas in Glasgow, founded by Bishop Muirhead, whose arms, three acorns on a bend, appear on one of the lower crow-steps of the roof. Baillie was a prominent member of the legal profession and became Lord President of the Court of Session, with the title Lord Provand, hence the nomenclature of his two houses. Mary, Queen of Scots is said to have spent a night in Provand's Lordship in January 1567, instead of the archbishop's castle, where Darnley lay sick of the smallpox, preferring the manse which had proved adequate for her grandfather, James IV, who was a prebendary of the cathedral in the past. It is even said she wrote one of the so-called 'Casket Letters' there, but we cannot go into that here; all one can say is that those who for their own purposes wished both her and Darnley away produced on the death of Darnley, a casket of letters seemingly implicating the Queen in her husband's murder. Nothing was proved, and the murder itself never properly explained. Provand's Lordship is not only the last of the manses attached to the cathedral but the oldest house in Glasgow, and has been set up as a most interesting museum, full of fine Scottish furniture, tapestries, documents, portraits and domestic utensils, and is maintained by a private society of well-wishers.

There is more than one opinion as to how medieval cathedrals, or indeed any ancient sanctuary-church should appear to pilgrims coming to worship in it and pay their respects at its saintly shrine. One theory is that it should be reached secretly and suddenly, like St Peter's in Rome used to be, when, after winding up narrow twisting streets one emerged into Bernini's great square and beheld the object of one's journey. Today one approaches the Roman Basilica via an enormously wide and windy boulevard which seems to be aping the Champs Elysées in Paris but lacks that thoroughfare's shops, trees, secondary roads and animated pavements. It is brash, touristy and unpleasant. Notre Dame, on the other hand, remains intact on its island in the middle of the Seine, though it has a small square in front useful for official arrivals and departures, even coronations, Napoleon was crowned there; and facing is the newly scraped-bare police headquarters. In fact Notre Dame itself has been cleaned so thoroughly it looks more like a Gothic ivory tower than a real church; but what of Glasgow? Did it stand alone on a green hill, separated from the city, or was it linked to the rest of the city by its own ancillary buildings, the turretted castle of its bishops, cobbled *place* of Prebend's manses, crow-stepped like the castle, consistory tower and chapter house, steep-roofed and picturesque in the Scots vernacular manner? One thinks of English examples, Salisbury in its almost hermetically sealed close, shut off from the outside world and ringed around its wide green by douce old houses, most still performing the function intended for them; of Canterbury, equally shut off but more intimately, less tidily; and York, the nearest metropolitan cathedral to Scotland. St Andrews, as we have seen, was entirely enclosed within its defensive priory walls, which remain, while the church itself has gone. Probably Glasgow was more like York, or even Durham, where the Bishop's Castle has survived, forming a distinctly clerical quarter within the town.

The danger to Scotland's largest and most complete example of medieval Gothic architecture did not come from the usual beauty haters, and it escaped, as by a miracle, the destruction of the Reformation. Instead it fell victim, fortunately on a minor scale, to the small-minded attentions of latter-day 'improvers', those who demolished the ancient episcopal castle and its neighbouring buildings, who removed the two western towers of the cathedral, burning the documents contained in one, presumably because they were of Popish origin. One can think of no other reason. The same folk caused the Old College of Glasgow, the University founded by Bishop Turnbull in the mid-fifteenth century, to be pulled down also, and replaced by that odd-looking structure on Gilmorehill that presently serves as a seat of learning and has itself even uglier twentieth-century adjuncts. All these things were done not in the spirit of vandalism but in the name of 'progress', which only goes to show how far we have to go before our historic architecture is treated neither as mere archaeology nor as an embarrassing survival from presumed less progressive ages. Glasgow's motto is 'Let Glasgow Flourish by the preaching of the Word', though for nearly a century only the first part of this has been adequately acknowledged, and the fact that the city was founded on a miracle performed by a Celtic saint more than 1300 years ago is often conveniently forgotten. It is probably the oldest Christian city of its size and importance in Britain and one of the most ancient in Europe; and it is at least some consolation to those who think it ought to be recognized as such, and who, like the present writer were born there, that its cathedral has survived so wonderfully and the site where that miracle occurred is still enshrined within its walls.

FOUR

'The Golden Age'

THOUGH labelled a 'sair sanct for the croun' David I was not merely a pious founder of abbeys and settler of dioceses, he was a warrior king and very much the 'father of his people'; and his religious foundations were created as much to educate his subjects and improve their life style as anything else. He was, as we have seen, very much *au fait* with the latest intellectual and cultural movements, as witness the almost imperceptible gap in time between some of his foundations and those in England and France. By bringing a variety of clerics and administrators north of the Border he hoped to provide a suitable base on which future progress in Scotland would develop in a balanced and orderly fashion. The monks, of course, not only built beautiful buildings and introduced sophisticated masonic techniques into the country but furthered agricultural activity, as well as studious pursuits, thus playing a salient role in forming the Scottish character and outlook and helping to give the country a sense of belonging to the wider Christian and feudal world.

Unhappily, David's second son, Henry, Earl of Huntingdon (his first had been strangled as a child by a jealous uncle), died before he did, and he was succeeded by his grandson Malcolm, nicknamed 'The Maiden'. This boy had inherited the family piety without its strength and coming to the throne at the age of twelve died childless at twenty-five. His principal contribution was to lose the three northern counties to England, which he voluntarily gave up while retaining the earldom of Huntingdon. It was in an attempt to restore the former situation that his more forceful brother William, called 'The Lion' because he rode into battle under the now familiar banner, invaded England in 1173, and again in 1174, when he had the misfortune to be captured at Alnwick Castle and ignominiously taken to France for an interview with Henry II. The result of this was that he was forced to swear fealty not only for his English property but for the whole kingdom of Scotland, a thing which no Scottish king had ever done before and which set a precedent that Edward I was subsequently quick to follow. William had been foolish to try and take advantage of Henry II's quarrels with Thomas à Becket and his own sons, and the fiery Plantagenet used the opportunity so provided to settle the matter of Scottish subservience once and for all, or so he thought. In practice neither King John nor Richard Coeur de Lion pressed the position, and in the end Richard, who was more interested in going on a Crusade than governing England, sold the three counties back to the King of Scots for a consideration.

Such a recitation of miscalculation and due retribution would not suggest a very lion-like monarch, nor a wise one, certainly not one given to careful government and the founding of selected clerical institutions in the manner of his grandfather. Yet it did result in the creation of one of Scotland's finest ecclesiastical structures and richest abbeys, at Arbroath, in Angus, which William the Lion founded in 1175, as soon as he got back from captivity; and in which he was buried in 1214. His real name, incidentally, at least the one by which he was known to his contemporaries, was Guillaume de Varenne, which title he held in the right of his mother, who was daughter of the Norman Earl of Surrey. It is doubtful if he could speak the educated English of his Saxon ancestors, let alone the Scottish version of that tongue which had spread from the mouth of the Humber to Caithness and which is still spoken with tolerable purity in the far north and extreme south, the intervening areas having become more mixed with Irish and Dutch contacts. His language was French, as it was of most of his associates, and he married Ermengarde, direct descendant of William the Conqueror. The lion banner he flew was not and is not the national flag of Scotland, though one might be excused for thinking so when one sees it on the bonnets of cars and buses, fishing boats, factories and in gift shops. Properly it was William's personal banner and is today still the personal property of the sovereign. The late Sir Thomas Innes of Learney, Lyon King, made it absolutely clear that any private person displaying it was liable to a fine of £10. The correct and only national flag of Scotland is the blue and white saltire of St Andrew.

One may perhaps be excused further excursions into Scottish medieval history, not only because it was William the Lion who first sported the rampant lion with a double tressure of fleur-de-lis as his royal banner, but because it was in his abbey at Arbroath that the celebrated Declaration of Independence, Scotland's Magna Carta was drawn up and signed and despatched to Pope John XXII in 1320. It came in response to that pontiff's excommunication of the entire Scots nation, an edict that carried with it the threat of eternal damnation, and which was the Pope's response to a request for support from Edward II of England in whose Continental domains he had been born. This, surely, was the formal birth of the modern Scottish nation, if indeed it had not already been brought into existence at Bannockburn. Here at Arbroath its 'arrival' was codified and expressed in classical Latin, indeed, the Three Estates, meeting in the abbey, put into diplomatic but meaningful language the whole essence of patriotism, not just Scottish patriotism but all patriotism. In 1951 the so-called 'Stone of Destiny', certainly not Jacob's Pillow and probably only a piece of sandstone palmed off onto a credulous Edward I in place of the genuine article, was stolen from Westminster by misguided Scottish 'patriots', and after being hidden was deposited before the site of the high altar in the ruins of Arbroath Abbey. The King, George VI, who took his coronation oath very seriously, and had, of course, been crowned sitting in St Edward's Chair with the Stone underneath, was particularly upset by the event, first, by the theft itself, and secondly by the manner in which the police bundled it into the back of one of their cars and transported it south again. It was after all a sacred object, made so by use if not by origin. The occurrence did, however, draw attention to the existence of Arbroath and of its Declaration, in which respect it did some good. Older guide-books and topographic works scarcely mention this magnificent exposé of the ideals of freedom and liberty which in its way is superior both to Magna Carta and the American Declaration of Independence, the wording of which it may have influenced.

Arbroath Abbey was dedicated to the Virgin Mary, and to St Thomas à Becket, ostensibly because the martyred archbishop had recently been canonized but also it is supposed because William the Lion was personally known to him in life and wished to show backhanded contempt for Henry II in a particularly obvious way. Be this as it may, the architecture is splendid, though not much of it is left, the abbey having become the usual

Arbroath Abbey: Abbot's House and fortified entrance

The vaulted pend under the gateway to the abbey

quarry for the townspeople, and parts actually sold as such by the burgh, who kept no records of the amounts paid in order not to incriminate themselves. It was a large cruciform building, flat roofed except in the aisles, which were stone-vaulted, ending in a presbytery projected at the east end to provide light on three sides around the high altar. There is presumed to have been a central tower as well, and two western ones of which the lower parts survive, opening directly into the roofless nave to show they were actually part of it, and not separate. This suggests a similarity with the west end of Kelso, whence the Tironensian monks came to Arbroath in the early thirteenth century.

The only roofed portion, other than the former Abbot's House and adjacent 'keep' or prison, is the sacristy, which dates from the fifteenth century and is placed to the north-east of the south transept, itself the biggest and tallest expanse of masonry surviving. In the sacristy is a strong-room, above floor level and entered via a ladder from both inside and out; and until removed to the museum in the Abbot's House there used to be a decapitated recumbent figure said to be that of the founder, William the Lion, or alternatively, a representation of Thomas à Becket. The first assumption is based partly on the fact that the feet rest on an animal which may be a lion, and partly because the workmanship seems too good to be local and has affinities with that of the tomb of Richard Coeur de Lion in the abbey of Fontevrault in France. The Becket connotation comes from the presence of Lilliputian personages, possibly knights, more probably 'angel' mourners or attendants, arranging the clothes; but as Dr Richardson has pointed out the apparel is not that of an archbishop so could belong to almost 'any bishop-saint in the Scottish calendar'. The south transept is the most conspicuous part of the abbey from the town, in fact from the sea, and especially for its great 'O' window above twin lancets. The massiveness of this remnant of transitional Gothic architecture is now revealed as it never could have been before, the roof mark of the second storey dormitory showing how the conventual buildings formerly interposed themselves between this prominent gable and the outer world.

There are a number of romantic legends attached to this 'O' window, which is not actually as large as the one over the west doorway but being placed high up in the structure can be seen for many miles around. The first legend is the most improbable and the one with which I was regaled as a child when my father and mother lived for a time in the town. This was to the effect that the abbot of Aberbrothock used to place a beacon in the round window in question to lure ships to their doom off the rocky Angus coast. In fact the opposite is nearer the truth, the abbot putting a light in his 'eye', which incidentally was not seen in the church below since it was purely decorative and came up in the attic storey, in order to save ships from being wrecked; a procedure matched by the bell he is supposed to have placed on a buoy attached to Inchcape or Bell Rock, way out in the Firth of Tay. Robert Stevenson, whose most famous lighthouse marks the traditional spot, said there was no foundation for thinking there had ever been any bell or buoy attached to this dangerous rock, which is completely covered at high tide. On the other hand, the poet Robert Southey made the legend the subject of a ballad which tells of the pirate, Ralph the Rover, removing the bell and himself becoming the first victim of his so doing. The abbot also owned the harbour at Arbroath and benefited from its dues; and the sight of his great red-sandstone abbey lit up not only by a beacon in the 'O' of the south transept, but throughout, as it sometimes was, must have been exciting and impressive in the extreme and a boon to mariners.

The cloisters and conventual buildings have practically all disappeared but for the secular Abbot's House, which was erected on top of the original vaulted kitchen, near Arbroath's version of the St Andrews 'Pends', the arched and fortified entrance. It was in a room in the gatehouse, above the portcullis arch, that the Declaration of Arbroath was signed and sent forth, after drafting and approval by the representatives of the Scottish nation in the abbey kirk. It is there, in the ruined choir, that an annual recreation of the scene is enacted in pageant form. At the southern end of the defensive walls is the old 'keep' or prison, with vaulted lower ceiling, leading out into the High Street. In Billings's day it was a butcher's shop, but today, with the rest of the abbey, it is in the care of the Department of the Environment. In fact Arbroath Abbey was one of the earliest sites to be tidied up and handed to the Board of Works as it then was to preserve and maintain. The west front of the church has at its centre what is probably Arbroath's most interesting and unusual feature. I refer to the tribune over the deeply recessed Romanesque west door. This is open to the inside

Arbroath Abbey: the arcaded tribune over the west entrance (R. W. Billings); the south transept and the Abbot of Aberbrothock's 'eye'

and the outside, and comprises six colonnaded openings facing the nave, two supporting columns in an intermediate position, and three outer openings, those latter cut off slightly having previously projected over the doorway and been finished under distinctive pointed gablets. Only the end walls of these now survive, the hoods having gone. No doubt trumpeters, instrumentalists and choirs would have assembled in this gallery when, for instance, the archbishop of St Andrews made his regular visitation, replete with gorgeous retinue, and on commemorative feasts and holy days. It would undoubtedly have been used during the consecration ceremony, in 1233, which the founder's son, Alexander II, attended.

The tribune would also have been used at some stage during the meetings of the lords spiritual and temporal who met with the king in the abbey to draw up the famous declaration, which was largely the work of Abbot Bernard de Linton, a staunch supporter of Robert Bruce and Lord Chancellor. It was he who carried the prized Breckbennoch, or holy banner of St Columba, which was kept at Arbroath, at the Battle of Bannockburn. He was the first mitred abbot, with a seat in the Estates. Other famous or notorious superiors of Arbroath included one, Abbot Malcolm, who so annoyed a visiting archbishop by questioning his display of wealth and power that he ended up in the archiepiscopal bottle-dungeon in St Andrews. Another was James Stewart, Duke of Ross, brother of James IV of Scots, archbishop of St Andrews and also Lord Chancellor. He was a considerable figure in his own right and immortalized in *Orlando Furioso* by Ariosto. He is not to be confused with another royal scion, Alexander Stewart, bastard son of James IV, who again was archbishop of St Andrews, and slain at Flodden with his father. He too was well spoken of in high places, having been educated by Erasmus, but like his predecessor he only drew the revenues of his ecclesiastical offices without performing the proper functions appertaining thereto, such was the state of the *Ecclesia Scoticorum* at the beginning of the sixteenth century. The story is not ended with these two pluralists, for three members of the Bethune, or Beaton family combined the abbacy of Arbroath with diocesan duties, two Jameses, both archbishops of Glasgow, nephew and uncle respectively of the third, Cardinal David Beaton, Primate of Scotland and chief supporter of Mary of Guise in her fight to stem the advance of the Reformation. His murder in his own castle at St Andrews set off a chain reaction that

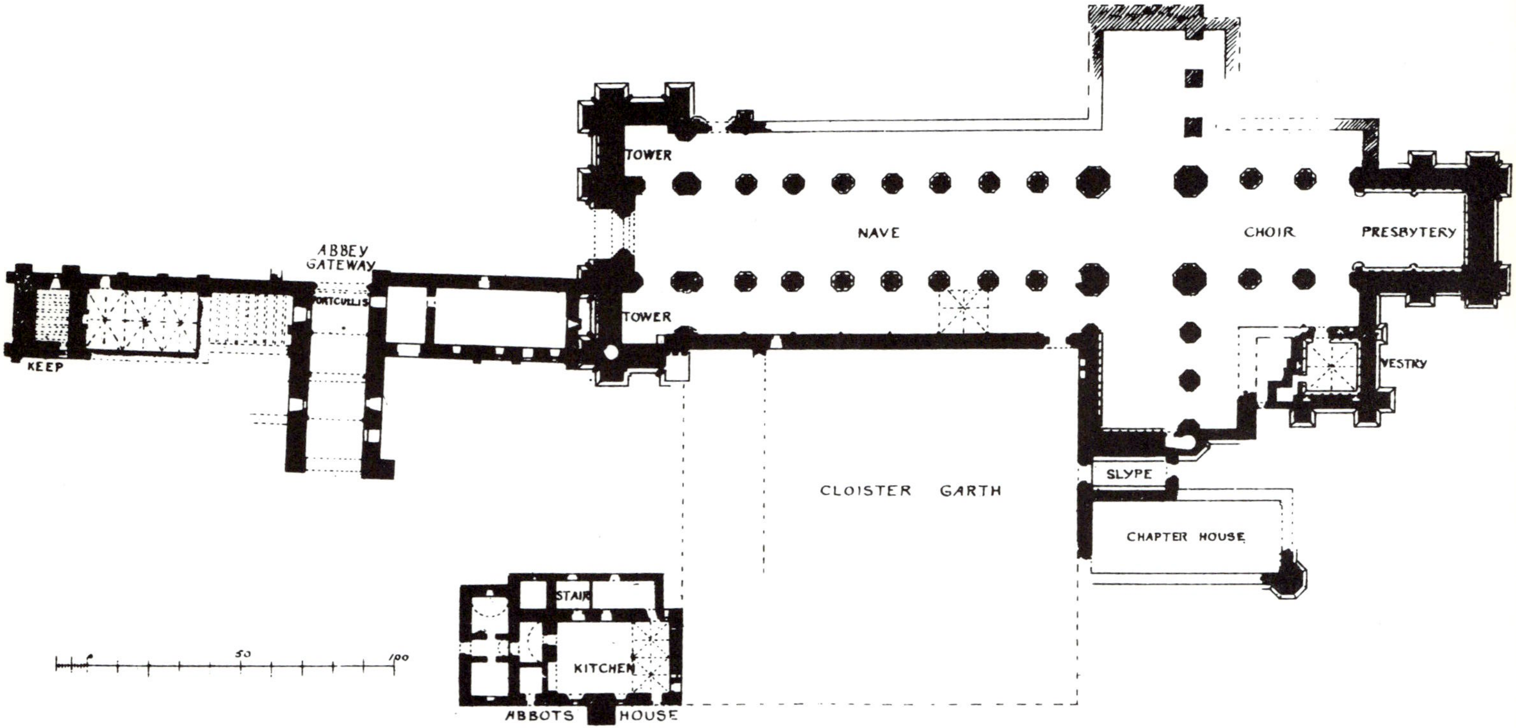

Arbroath Abbey: plan

ended after the Queen-Regent's death, in 1560, with the triumph of Knox and the 'Assured Lords', assured by Queen Elizabeth of England. One might end on a slightly more elevated note by mentioning that Gavin Douglas, one time provost, indeed the second provost of St Giles's Collegiate Kirk in Edinburgh, and afterwards bishop of Dunkeld, was abbot of Aberbrothock. He was the translator of the *Aeneid* and a gifted poet, but an unlucky politician who suffered the fate of all such, though he saved his life and died abroad. At the Reformation Claud Hamilton, already commendator of Paisley, became temporal abbot of Arbroath, to be succeeded by Esmé Stewart, Comte d'Aubigny, early favourite of James VI who made him Duke of Lennox. This French relative of the young king permitted the burgh to remove parts of the abbey in order to build a new Protestant church for themselves, but it took a long time to do and in the process much more masonry went than was strictly necessary for the purpose.

Arbroath was, as already indicated, founded for Tironensian monks from Kelso, with a complement of twenty-four, which was increased later. Stewart Cruden suggests that the arrangement of the western towers, with prominent Galilee or tribune between, and open to the nave as if a continuation of it rather than a separate feature, may repeat the idea of western transepts as at the mother church. It is difficult to see quite how this would have worked, especially as so little has remained of the abbey and there are no adequate pictorial records to make it plain. Unlike Kelso, the original appearance of which was discovered from a pre-Reformation sketch in the Vatican, and Elgin, whose central tower and main structure remained standing long enough for Captain Slezer to include it in his engravings at the end of the seventeenth century, Arbroath was already half gone before this sort of record was made. Thus all we have is the plan, one huge lump of masonry in the south transept, fragmentary links between it and the erstwhile three-bayed choir and nine-bayed nave, the late-Gothic sacristy, and part of the west front, with its remarkable tribune and richly decorated Romanesque doorway protected beneath tunnel-like vaulting. Indeed, the most upstanding parts of the abbey are its fortified adjuncts and Commendator's House, which survived the Reformation and were actually used after it, the house becoming a factory before being taken over by the Ministry of Works and made into a museum.

In 1226 the widow of William the Lion, Queen Ermengarde, founded in her husband's memory and as a suitable stopping place *en route* for Arbroath, the abbey of Balmerino, on the Fife shores of the Firth of Tay nearly opposite Dundee. She herself enjoyed the peace of this delightful spot and it became the resort of pilgrims using the ferry by which everyone had to travel to and from the north of Scotland. The Queen's foundation was confirmed by her son, Alexander II, who signed the requisite charter in 1231, some years after the first Cistercian monks had arrived from Melrose. The foundress died at Balmerino in 1233, and was buried before the high altar in the new church, her stone coffin being found in the nineteenth century doing service as a trough, and eventually reduced to a single piece used for floor-cleaning purposes in the kitchen of the farm built at one corner of what was once the cloister. The farm steadings deserve inspection for they include the monk's granary and doocot formed in the western gable, as well as an attractive red-pantiled mill, its hopper capped with a jolly fish finial. The monks, of course, were great fishermen and farmers themselves, and as at Lindores, further west, they introduced new methods of tilling the soil and planted orchards.

Like its mother abbey Balmerino was dedicated to the Virgin Mary, but also to St Edward the Confessor, thus emphasizing the royal and feudal associations established in Scotland by Queen Margaret and her descendants; and again like Melrose, Balmerino had its conventual buildings to the north, which was unusual but dictated then by the geography of the site. At Melrose the position of the River Tweed and the lade bringing water to the abbey was the governing factor, while here drainage problems were equally important, the land sloping gently down in a northwards direction towards the shore and the little harbour whence the ferry plied across the Firth of Tay. As always with Cistercian settlements the site was carefully chosen, both for its amenities and sheltered aspect, away from snell sea winds, but with air so pure and soft that the ailing Madeleine de Valois, daughter of François I of France and first consort of James V of Scots, was advised to come to Balmerino for her health, which, however, was so poor that she died only a month after arriving in Scotland, and was buried in the abbey kirk of the Holyrood in Edinburgh.

There is not much more of this abbey left than of nearby Lindores, it having been devastated by the English in 1547 when

Balmerino Abbey: vaulting in the chapter house

The ancient chestnut, planted by Cistercian monks, and abbatial remains

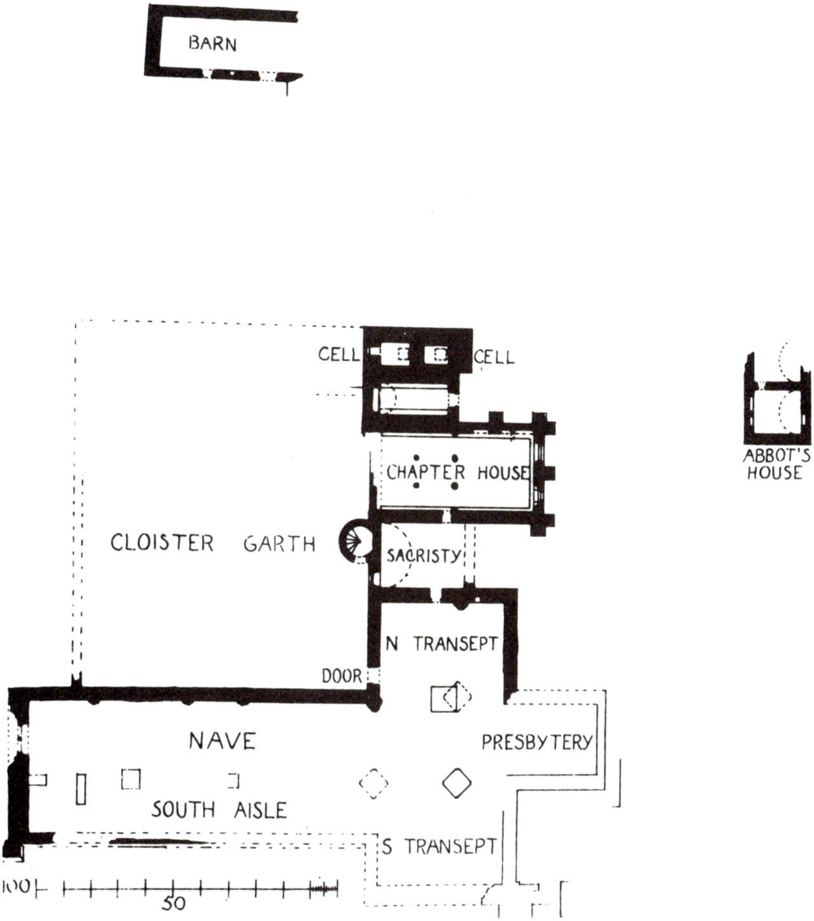

Balmerino Abbey: plan

they reached Dundee in their campaign of pillage and burning which had begun in the Borders, swept up through the Lothians and included Edinburgh and Leith. They came to the Tay by sea, when the monks themselves took up arms and called in help from the neighbourhood in an attempt to stop them landing from their ships. Though overwhelmed the defenders seem to have had some success in that the masonry survived sufficiently to be repaired, and the abbey continued to be occupied until the Reformation, when a determined gang of ruffians from St Andrews descended upon it on their way to destroy Lindores. What one sees today are the meagre foundations of a cruciform church on the Culross model, but with added south aisle, plus the slightly more substantial remnants of a chapter house, monks' parlour, or slype, and sacristy, which were incorporated in the secular abbot's residence when the local Naughton laird became commendator. Slype and sacristy are barrel vaulted, and the former has a stone seat on either side, while the chapter house is rib and groin vaulted and has good mullioned windows betraying fifteenth-sixteenth-century work. The capitals of the columns are elaborately and nicely carved, and in one corner is part of the day stair from the cloisters to the dormitory above. Beyond are two cells, with trap doors down to two more below, a *necessarium*, or lavatory, at one end and sewer at ground level. Mary, Queen of Scots probably stayed in this newer house when she came to Balmerino in 1565, not in the older abbot's quarters, a vaulted cellar of which is still visible to the east, in what was once an orchard.

The Queen's visit is traditionally said to have been commemorated by her planting a walnut tree, a rare enough species in Scotland in any case, and when the tree was blown down in a gale just before the last war the 'rings' gave it at least three hundred and fifty years of life, which rather proves the story. Another ancient tree, a Spanish chestnut, still stands in hoary majesty in the garden, propped up with poles and held together with chains, and is said to date from the time of Queen Ermengarde, and was either planted by her or the monks, most likely the latter as they planted similar trees at Inchmahome, preferring the edible variety of marron to the uneatable conker. The Monk's Well, sited beside a small burn running down to the sea, still functions, and until the introduction of a modern system provided water for the manse. The harbour pier is in a bit of a sorry state, however, and no ferry calls there now. Happily, the remains of the abbey and ancillary buildings have been preserved for posterity by the present owner of the land, the Earl of Dundee, who has placed those not adapted as part of the farm in the care of the National Trust for Scotland.

Elgin Cathedral, though smaller than either St Andrews or Glasgow, was in its heyday the most beautiful medieval structure in Scotland and amongst the finest in Britain. Its sad ruin was occasioned only partly by the ravages of the Reformers, for it had already been burned and sacked in the fourteenth century, notably by the 'Wolf of Badenoch', brother of Robert III, in revenge for his excommunication by the bishop for adultery. The Lords of the Congregation gave orders for the stripping of the lead off the roof and its transporting to Holland to raise funds and make bullets for their cause, while two generations later the Covenanters and Cromwell's troops 'had a go' at the building. The latter destroyed most of the remaining tracery in the windows and the former wrecked the interior, removing the magnificent wooden screen between choir and nave, together with a number of famous paintings. Ironically enough, the ship taking the stolen lead to the Netherlands sunk, so no good came to anyone from any of these exercises. Otherwise the cathedral stood empty but hale, gradually decaying but not irreparably, until the beginning of the eighteenth century, when the central tower collapsed crashing down onto the nave and transepts and generally reducing the building to the proportions we see today. It had not been used for more than a hundred years, the kirk of St Giles in Elgin being adequate for normal parochial purposes, and on the fall of official episcopacy the local Pisky congregation also found accommodation in a walled-off part of St Giles's, called the 'Little Kirk', before moving on to the old church of the Greyfriars, restored this century by the architect John Kinross for the third Marquis of Bute.

Elgin had not always been the seat of the Bishop of Moray, as it became in the thirteenth century, and the diocese already existed before the arrival in Scotland of Margaret, Queen and Saint. It was only after her son David I had established Benedictines from Dunfermline at Urquhart, a few miles to the east, and Cistercians from Melrose at Kinloss, to the west, that any decided change in ecclesiastical rule was apparent in this northern region, where the feudal system was resisted much longer than in many other parts of the country. It is interesting to note that the chief protagonists both of diocesan and baronial order in Moray came from the family after which both were named, the De Moravias, one of whom, Gilbert, was both statesman and cleric, Archdeacon of Moray before becoming Bishop of Caithness, and Lord Treasurer of the realm under Alexander II. Two other members of his family were bishops of Moray, which diocese was protected and dominated at one time by the Moravian castle of Duffus, between Elgin and the sea, where David I was lodged at the time of his founding of Kinloss Abbey in 1150.

Before 1224, when Pope Honorius III authorized its transference from Spynie to Elgin, the diocese of Moray had no fixed cathedral, the churches of Birnie, Spynie and Kinnedar being used at different times. The first was subject to attack by Highland marauders and the last to pirates from the sea, so that after a while Trinity Kirk at Spynie, between the two, was chosen as a permanent seat in 1207; and it was here that the bishops built their fortified palace the remains of which are such a kenspeckle sight on the way from Elgin to the mouth of the Lossie. It is curious that less than twenty years later a new position should have been chosen and a new cathedral was begun further inland, at Elgin. It is also curious that the constitution drawn up for the running of the Bishop of Moray's cathedral-kirk at Spynie should have been based on that pertaining to Lincoln, with which Elgin was to forge strong ecclesiastical and cultural ties. One reason for this may have been the episcopate of Richard de Lincoln, who was at Spynie from 1187 to 1203, but the commonest English model for adaptation north of the Border was Salisbury, whose usage was much admired, and indeed, the Sarum rite remained popular in Scottish churches until the latter-day introduction of 'pop' prayer-books and liturgies of lesser worth.

The Lincolnesque constitution went with the cathedral from Spynie to Elgin, plus an increase of canons from eight to twenty-four, with the dean, preceptor, treasurer, chancellor and archdeacon. With them also went the dedication to the Holy Trinity, in fact the new church incorporated part of an older one of the same dedication. The proclamation announcing the Pope's approval of the change was made by the bishop of Caithness, with the dean of Ross and the abbot of Kinloss in attendance, and Andrew de Moravia was the first bishop of Moray to be established at Elgin. Alexander II gave the necessary lands and grants and work was begun on the superb west front and choir immediately, Master Gregory being the mason employed. Disaster came in 1270, when fire swept through the new building and also damaged the clergy manses in the chanonry; but all was repaired and the cathedral complete by the time Bishop David de Moravia founded the Scots College in Paris in the reign of Robert Bruce. It was this beautiful early pointed church, made even more beautiful after the fire, that Alexander Stewart, Earl of Buchan, the so-called 'Wolf of Badenoch', sacked in 1390, when he singled out for his special attention as many religious structures as he could find between Forres and Elgin. Again the cathedral rose from its ashes, the most conspicuous alterations and additions being the reconstruction of the chapter house, a direct copy of the one at Lincoln, and the building of the central tower, which was begun by Bishop John Innes, whose colossal statue, one of four that once graced its corners, has survived in part. The 'Wolf' subsequently did penance for his acts, and after contributing to the cost of the repairs was absolved by the Bishop of St Andrews in the Kirk of the Blackfriars in Perth, in the presence of his brother the King. He probably lies buried, as we have seen, in the choir of Dunkeld Cathedral. In 1402 his nephew, brother of Donald, Lord of the Isles, tried to emulate his wicked deeds and burnt down the clergy manses, though he seems to have left the cathedral alone, it being still in the process of restoration. This frequent exposure to attack probably explains why the two western towers do not open into the church but constitute separate entities serving as defence points and refuges, like the old Pictish towers.

The west front of Elgin Cathedral has no parallel in Scotland and its twin towers though sturdily built and partly defensive have a refinement of line and proportion rarely achieved in the first half of the thirteenth century. That they were French inspired is obvious, but this inspiration may conceivably have two sources, one contemporary or near contemporary, the Cistercian work at Kinloss Abbey, the other Lincoln Cathedral itself, which derives in part from Franco-Norman examples in south-east England as well as the Continent. There is another odd coincidence in that the choir of the first great Gothic church, the abbey of St Denis, near Paris, begun by the Abbé Suger, inventor of the 'Gothic frame', is repeated at Elgin in a most extraordinary way, which I will describe in a moment. Lincoln Cathedral under St Hugh followed St Denis in the second half of the twelfth century, and apart from this and other influences has a plan devised by Yorkshire masons which recurs in miniature at Elgin, especially in the placing of the chapter house. One can assume, therefore, that some of the same masons or their apprentices probably had a hand in creating the cathedral of the bishop of Moray, as they definitely had in the building of Melrose and Melrose's daughter house at Kinloss. One ought really to be able to trace the journeys made by the various masons, Continentally based and British, as they travelled from job to job. John

The chapter house and towers of Elgin Cathedral from across the Lossie

Harvey does this to some extent in his *Gothic World*, and also mentions Master Gregory as the principal mason employed at Elgin, without, however, showing or mentioning from where he came. The international links are fascinating and surely explain, for instance, how the deeply recessed, richly ornamented west door at Arbroath recalls that of the cathedral of Lérida in Spain, and why Elgin's twin towers in the French manner are matched by a flat-ended east end derived from St Denis and a chapter house which more closely reflects Lincoln and York. It may perhaps be worth adding, as Douglas Simpson does when explaining French influence in thirteenth-century Scotland, that the Queen of Alexander II, in whose reign the best part of Elgin was built, was Marie de Coucy, one of the greater French ladies of the period, whose father's castle near Soissons inspired Gilbert de Moravia's design of Kildrummie, in Aberdeenshire, and which was only reduced to its present tumble-down state by the Kaiser's guns in the First World War.

Whitby Abbey, on the Yorkshire coast, was also hit, but not so badly, by the Kaiser's guns, firing from a cruiser in the German Ocean in 1914, which brings me to the astonishing peculiarity at the east end of Elgin, since Whitby's east end would appear to display a similar peculiarity, but to a lesser degree. It is this: that the masons, having copied original master drawings too slavishly, or at any rate more in the letter than the spirit, have actually incorporated as architectural features lines of a purely geometric or working nature, translating them into stone fillets between the windows, even to the extent of letting them cut through bases and capitals. The fenestration at Whitby is in the same early pointed style as Elgin, though having smaller triple lancets below taller ones, and with no rose window in the gable. Elgin boasts five tall lancets below five shorter ones, a design coming straight from that of the choir at St Denis which, however, is apsidal, while Elgin is flat, meaning that not only did the mason misinterpret the elevational drawings, but the groundplan as well, for the east end should have been rounded. Another odd bit of adaptation occurs in the considerable buttresses on the north-eastern and south-eastern corners of the towers, which are not supports so much as camouflage for the accidental projection of the double aisles beyond the original building line, which had to be masked somehow. There were, in fact, covered porches on the north and south

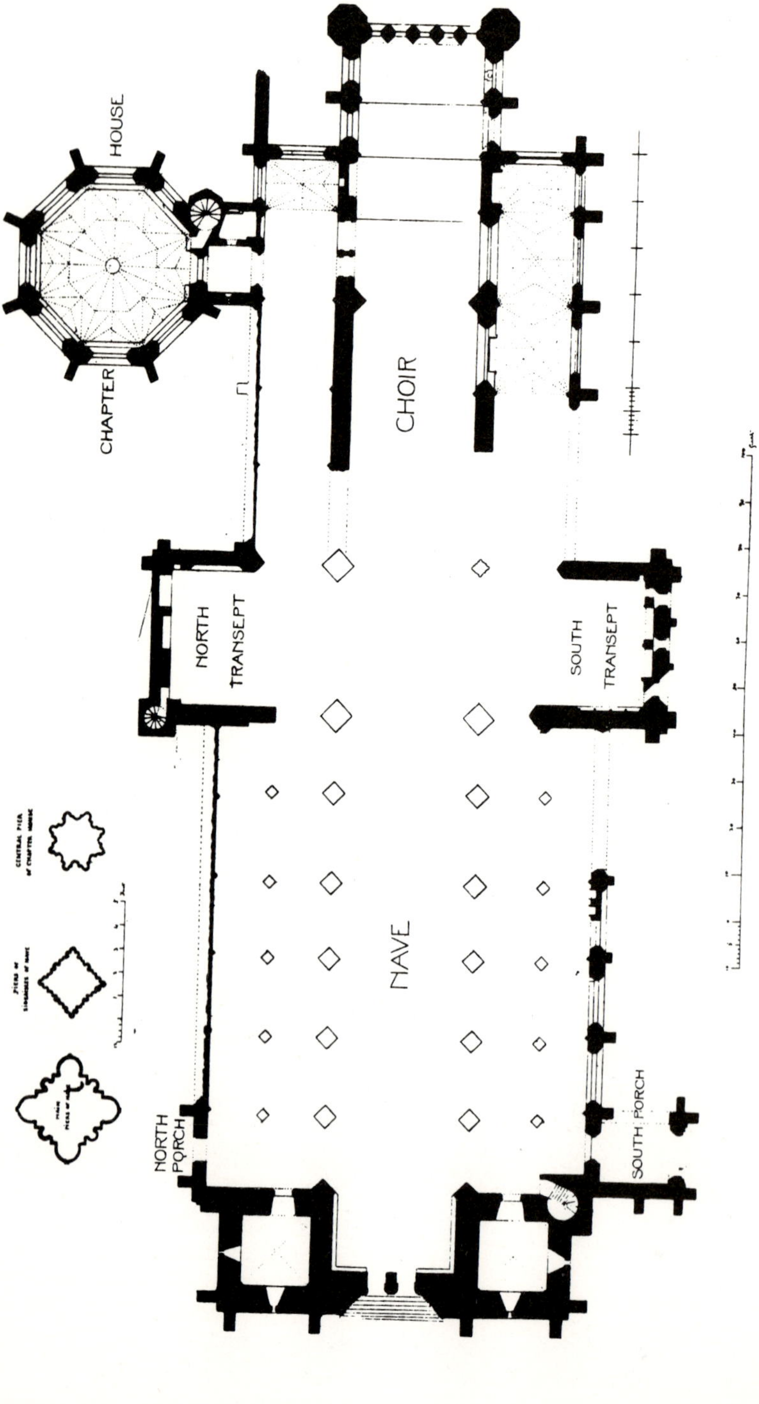

Elgin Cathedral: plan

sides of the nave, at the point of the artificial widening, and these will also have helped to hide the afterthought in the masonwork. The south porch is better preserved than the northern, or Marriage Porch, but neither are roofed any longer.

The centrepiece of the west front was the finest in Scotland, though in its present form it is much decayed and represents two stages in the building, pre-sacking and post. Originally the large central doorway, set behind nine receding arches and pilasters and contained within a sloping stone roof with three niched gablets, lacked the double openings and vesica that now divide it. Above too the big west window, only the broken ends of whose traceries survive, was enlarged and beautified under Columba de Dunbar, who succeeded John Innes as bishop in the early fifteenth century. He was responsible for the re-edification of the aisles and the north transept, where his tomb is. More splendid memorials, or the surviving portions thereof, can be seen in the Innes Aisle, or south transept, including that said to commemorate Alexander Stewart, Duke of Albany. He was the second son of James II of the Fiery Face, who escaped to France from imprisonment by his brother James III and married the daughter of Bernard de la Tour d'Auvergne, from whom descend the celebrated Franco-Scottish family which counted Marshal Turenne amongst its more distinguished members. This was in 1481; thirty-three years later the Duke of Albany and Comte d'Auvergne returned to Scotland to become regent during the infancy of James V.

The first cathedral at Elgin had no stone vaulting in either aisles or the main building, this was introduced in the reconstruction of the aisles, which in the nave were doubled, and in the single aisles of the choir, in the fifteenth century. The fine ribbed vaulting in the south aisle of the choir, called the Lady Chapel, survives, and here again there are the remains of arched tombs and monuments of the decorated period, notably that of Bishop John de Winchester, who ruled between 1437 and 1458, and of the Gordons of Huntly, whose burial place this was, the first Earl of Huntly being interred in the chapel in 1470. More remarkable late-Gothic work still, and unique in a purely Scottish context, exists in the octagonal chapter house, which stands detached from the rest of the building to the north of the choir, as its larger brethren do at York and Lincoln. It is actually a fifteenth- and early sixteenth-century reconstruction in an earlier style of the old chapter house which

Elgin Cathedral: the interior of the chapter house (R. W. Billings); detail of the west door (R. W. Billings)

was burned by the 'Wolf of Badenoch', and is famous for its handsome central column and lierne vaulting, in which the basic ribbing is linked by a spider's web of small ribs, not springing from the walls. This allows less substantial stones to be used for the infilling and lightens the load. It is the only example of its kind north of the Border and is complete internally.

The thirteenth-century chapter house was not vaulted in stone and accordingly when the masons came to reconstruct it for Bishop David Stewart and his brother Andrew at the end of the fifteenth century they devised a clever scheme whereby the new vaults could be supported by simply thickening and strengthening the existing walls at a point above floor level, permitting the same ground space, seats round and other features, including the arched entrance, to remain unaltered. This seems to have worked well and been adequate both to hold up the intricately patterned lierne ceiling and prevent the foundations from spreading, the whole being sustained by a single, octagonal column in the middle of the floor. The column is beautifully formed of alternate concave and convex curves, enriched with leaf moulding and heraldry, and has attached to its north-west side at an appropriate height a stone lectern, or reading ledge. The Scottish flair for amusing heraldry is seen here to advantage and as usual helps to date the various alterations and completions. In particular the emblems of several Stewart bishops of Moray are on show. There were four of them, all related and of the same family as the 'Black Knight of Lorn', Sir James Stewart, who married Joan Beaufort, widow of James I of Scots, in 1439.

Bishops David and Andrew Stewart were actually sons of the 'Black Knight' and Queen Joan, the first being the builder of the massive episcopal 'keep' at Spynie. The diocesan palace stood beside a now much reduced loch, but then connected to the sea, on which we are told swans swam, and from which they came to be fed as at Wells, in Somerset. Spynie was, at the end of the fifteenth century, amongst the most splendid non-royal residences in the kingdom, with terraced 'Italian' gardens and Continental furnishings, and comforts such as only princes, and not always they, enjoyed at that time. Indeed, even earlier, in the days of Bishop Dunbar, who visited Rome in state in 1433, it must already have been a place of unusual refinement and luxury, with a hunting lodge at nearby Gordonstoun, where the Duke of Edinburgh and the Prince of Wales were educated. Bishop Stewart's building, called 'David's Tower', was built in answer to a threat by the militant Earl of Huntly to 'pull him out of his pigeon holes' and exhibits all the latest military improvements, such as widely splayed gun-loops, six feet across at the front and two behind, thus allowing the maximum manoevrability. These martial qualities were, however, crude compared to those displayed by Bishop John Innes in the superb fortified gateway he erected in the first half of the same century, before the invention of firearms, and which in its sculptural details was undoubtedly the creation of craftsmen employed contemporaneously on the restoration of the cathedral in Elgin. Bishop Innes's arms appear over the central arch, which was once defended by a portcullis. From the same period and probably by the same craftsmen are the now blocked up windows of the former episcopal chapel at Spynie, which still show remnants of good decorated tracery.

Andrew Stewart succeeded his brother David as Bishop of Moray in 1485, after a notable career as Sub-dean of Glasgow, Provost of Lincluden and Keeper of the Great Seal. MacGibbon and

Spynie, palace of the bishops of Moray

Ross suggest that although the reconstruction of the chapter house was begun by David Stewart it was Andrew who completed it, this being symbolized in the figure of Scotland's patron saint carved on the north side of the central column, and the arms of the Stewarts of Lorn on both the east and west faces. The rampant lion appears on the south side, while the emblems of Christ's Passion are shown in between. Andrew Stewart was followed as bishop by the same Andrew Forman who combined offices so remarkably as prior of Dryburgh and Pittenweem, archbishop of St Andrews and of Bourges, in France, and whose very existence proclaimed the decadence which had set in by the beginning of the sixteenth century in Scotland, and which is even better expressed in the attitude of the last pre-Reformation bishop of Moray, Patrick Hepburn. An uncle of Mary, Queen of Scots's Bothwell, he had been prior of St Andrews, in which capacity he strengthened and rebuilt parts of the priory walls there, his arms being displayed on the Harbour Port. In Moray he alienated much of the diocesan property, granting church lands to his bastards and friends, and influential persons, such as the Earl of Moray, thus making himself well placed to weather any storm that might arise. In fact, he managed to retain the episcopal palace at Spynie as his private residence long after the Reformation, dying there in 1573, his coat of arms being added to those of the King and Bishop David Stewart's on the fifteenth-century 'keep'.

The cathedral at Elgin stands slightly apart from the town, to the east, rather like, say, Salisbury, only in a more countrified setting. Of the half mile or so of twelve-foot-high walls and three portcullised ports or gates that once guarded the precincts only a short run of masonry survives on either side of Pann's Port, the former Water Yett, down by the River Lossie. The old clergy manses have mostly gone, though recalled in the modern 'College of the Chanonrie', and in two quaint buildings on the north side of the precinct, one of which is called 'The Bishop's Palace' and the other 'The Deanery'. The first is an L-shaped structure with stair tower in the re-entrant angle and with fine gabled crow-steps similar to those of the episcopal palace of the bishops of Brechin at Farnell. This sixteenth-century building, however, was never a bishop's palace but the precentor's manse, while its near neighbour, more built upon and much restored, was probably the manse of Inverkeithy, one of the benefices attached to the diocese. 'The

Deanery' is also basically L-shaped and has vaulted rooms on the ground floor, and both are contemporaneous with the removal and rebuilding of the tall cathedral spire, which was taken down for safety reasons, apparently because it was thought to be too heavy for the piers at the crossing. It was replaced by a lower, saddle-backed top, with parapet not unlike that of St Machar's Cathedral, in Aberdeen, or Pluscarden Priory, on the south-western outskirts of Elgin.

On Bishop Hepburn's demise Spynie and its lands were formally secularized, but afterwards returned to the Reformed bishops by James VI, and they lived there until the end of the seventeenth century, Bishop Falconer dying in his palace in 1686. Three years later the last established bishop, William Hay, was forced to leave Spynie, which then became a ruin and has remained one ever since. Bishop Hay would be of the same family as William de la Haya, whose recumbent knightly figure lies in full armour at the entrance to the Lady Chapel in the cathedral. He died in 1422; his hands have been cut off and the lion of fortitude at his feet decapitated, but otherwise the effigy is reasonably whole by Scottish standards. His seventeenth-century namesake was made of quite different stuff, and was the very antithesis of the proud prelate of Presbyterian mythology; he tolerated both extreme Protestant and Papist brethren and advised his clergy not to oppose them but to 'excel them in life and doctrine'. At this time the Pisky congregation, the largest in Elgin, still occupied part of the parish kirk, but shortly afterwards moved to the disused Church of the Greyfriars.

Both the Blackfriars, or Dominicans, and the Franciscans, or Greyfriars, were brought to Scotland by Alexander II, son of William the Lion, the man most chiefly responsible for the building of the first cathedral at Elgin. The Blackfriars had a church in St Andrews, the charred skeleton of an apsidal transept of which survives in South Street as a permanent reminder to passers-by of the results of bitter religious contention, and a house at Perth, where the 'Wolf of Badenoch' did penance, and where in 1437 James I of Scots was murdered. The Dominicans were also established at Inverness, where for some curious reason the site is called after the Greyfriars, who had no house there, and where, in the graveyard, an effigy said to be of Alexander Stewart, son of the 'Wolf of Badenoch', has been placed upright instead of recumbent, and in

Elgin, whereas in the above-mentioned cases there is little left to show for it. The Franciscans were at Dumfries and Kirkcudbright, and in Edinburgh, but only here in Elgin have they left any substantial memorial in the church, which was restored towards the end of last century by John Kinross, architect to the third Marquis of Bute, a notable connoisseur and restorer of medieval buildings, including Cardiff Castle and Falkland Palace.

John Kinross was the ablest and most scholarly of Scottish restoring architects at the turn of the century, and after, and he managed to be as accurate as he was imaginative in both the Gothic and Renaissance styles. This was because he combined an unusual knowledge and understanding of the vernacular with a love of all things Italian, so necessary for the recreation of the Renaissance, even to taking in Italian newspapers, a thing he did to the end of his life. Thus his restoration of the long, aisleless kirk of the Greyfriars at Elgin, and his reconstruction of the friary buildings for the community of the Sisters of Mercy, who run a girls' school there, has an authenticity and authority about it rarely found in modern times. Indeed, the interior of the church probably represents the truest recreation of a medieval place of worship in Scotland, replete with barrel-vaulted timber roof, painted and gilded sacrament house, altars facing the congregation on either side of the screen entrance, high-level lepers' window, beautifully detailed choir stalls, altar, and above all the screen itself, which must surely have been inspired by descriptions of the one removed from the cathedral of Moray by the Covenanting minister and his friends in 1640. Half an hour in the restored kirk of the Greyfriars in Elgin will give the visitor a better idea of the interior of a Scottish church in the days before corruption and undue worldliness brought about the inevitable reaction than hours spent studying more elaborate reconstructions at Dunblane and Paisley.

Some years before the Cistercians were established at Kinloss, with results which became increasingly obvious in the later history of the old diocese of Moray, and especially in the high standard of building displayed in the first cathedrals at Spynie and Elgin, David I set up a Benedictine priory at Urquhart, a few miles to the east of Elgin, with monks sent from the royal abbey at Dunfermline. The priory did not flourish and eventually, in the fifteenth century, when the number of monks had fallen to two, it was merged with the Valliscaulian priory of Pluscarden, whose complement was six, and which henceforth was transferred to the Benedictine order. Pluscarden's links with the cathedral of Moray and the town of Elgin have always been close, and it was after restoring the kirk of the Greyfriars there that Lord Bute turned his attention to the decaying priory, which was open to the winds but was not destroyed, and showed promise to a restoring patron. The Valliscaulians, who first came here in 1230 at the behest of Alexander II in conjunction with two other foundations of his for the same order, one at Ardchattan, in Argyll, another at Beauly, near Inverness, originated, as one might suppose, in Burgundy. They constituted an even more austere breakaway from Cluny than the Carthusians in their Charterhouse between Chambéry and Grenoble, or the Cistercians at Cîteaux, devoting themselves to contemplation and grinding hard work in a secluded valley near Châtillon-sur-Seine, called the Val des Choux, or Cabbage Vale, their Vallis Caulium, in the diocese of Langres.

The hardy monks from France probably considered northern and western Caledonia just the right place for their austerities and a suitable challenge. In fact they did not thrive, except modestly at Beauly, where they were protected and encouraged by the Frasers of Lovat and other important local families, such as the Mackenzies of Kintail, one of whom, Alexander, became prior. He was the illegitimate son of Sir Kenneth Mackenzie, whose fifteenth-century

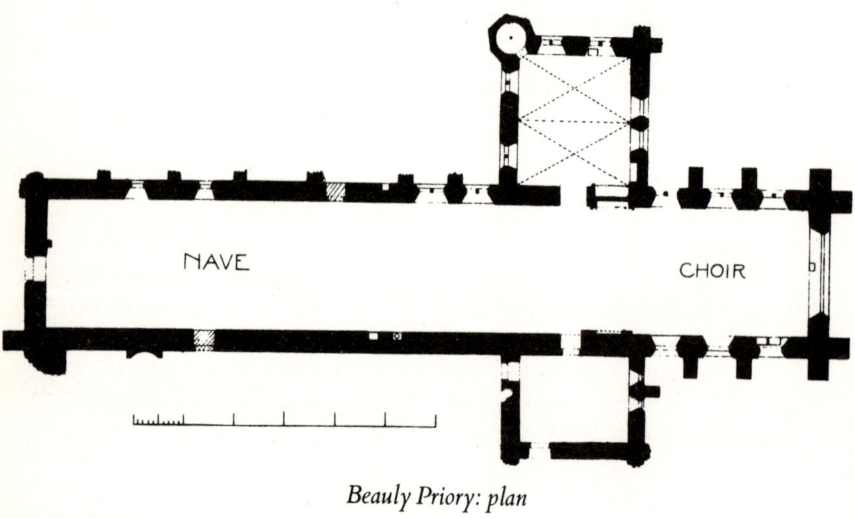

Beauly Priory: plan

arched altar tomb adorns one wall of the former north transept, now closed from the church. The roofless ruins of the red sandstone kirk stand at one end of the village of Beauly amongst a few trees and are in the care of the Department of the Environment. The building is aisleless and cruciform without tower or even bell-cot and much altered as well as decayed, the most recent restoration having taken place in the sixteenth century under Robert Reid, abbot of Kinloss and bishop of Orkney, whom we have met before. He was not a pluralist in the Andrew Forman sense, but an educated, responsible cleric of ability, and instead of letting Beauly fall down, as others might have done, and simply collected the revenues, he kept the church in decent repair and actually rebuilt the west end and much of the nave. His arms appear above the entrance and his work is easily recognizable by the round arches he inserted in place of early pointed ones, the fashion away from pointed architecture having by then become general in Scotland. Of the conventual buildings scarcely anything remains, not even the new Prior's House erected by Reid, though some of the corbels that supported the cloister roof still protrude on the west and south sides. At the Reformation Beauly's fate was much the same as that of Kinloss, when it became the property of Bishop Reid's nephew. Ardchattan is likewise bereft of sizable monastic adjuncts, and what does survive appears as a fragment of a transept in the garden of a modern house, plus the so-called Prior's Room inside. Here a small vaulted oratory has been uncovered which may represent the pulpit space of the refectory, which was otherwise roofed in oak; some beams have been discovered nearby, intact and undamaged, they are probably five hundred years old and possibly unique north of the Border.

All three Valliscaulian priories were founded in the same year and are the only ones known outside France. Perhaps it was the very smallness of their communities that militated against them (only seven monks were established at Beauly, the most promising), and the way in which they insisted on living and working. Whatever the reason, these severely unbending monks, who left the mark of the cabbage, or kail, carved in their buildings, either died out for want of recruits or were superseded by others; and even at Pluscarden, which was pleasantly sited and would have been their finest and most permanent settlement, they only completed the choir and transepts of the church, the Benedictines leaving things so. The setting is Cistercian in its perfection, in a sheltered vale with everything needed for a reasonable life provided one made proper use of the fruits of the earth as commanded in the Bible. There is nothing austere about the Vale of St Andrew, as it is called, the former Kail Valley; it is well wooded, well watered and the excellent soil and the present small colony of Benedictines who returned here after the Second World War have made the best of it, winning prizes at local agricultural shows and generally demonstrating how things were done in the 'Good old days'. They inhabit just a part of the buildings, and their re-roofing of the choir and transepts is likewise partial, but bit by bit they intend to get back to what was there in the fifteenth century, their brave experiment being the only return of its kind north of the Border. It is perhaps worth adding that this restitution is no mere amateur effort, any more than the restoration of Iona has been, work goes on with expert advice and according to architectural plans. Indeed, one of the oddities of such plans are the objects one is asked to design, for instance, boxes to contain bones and teeth and other relics. Odd to an outsider, since the monks seem so sensible otherwise, thrifty and practical. Yet this is part of the monastic tradition, and some monasteries were actually established for the purpose of venerating the carnal remains of saints and holy people.

The story of the return of the monks to Pluscarden is bound up with that of the third Marquis of Bute's ambition to restore the priory architecturally as well as functionally, and his difficulty in finding a community willing and able to come back and resettle the place. In his day the conventual buildings had already been partly refurbished as a hunting lodge and guest-annexe by the Duke of Fife; the cloister garth was walled in, market gardens flourished round about, the woods and fields were well tended and it seemed an ideal spot for resettlement. On the other hand, the period was not a propitious one from the point of view of enticing monks back, and the Marquis's son, Lord Ninian Crichton Stuart, was no more successful before he was killed in action in the First World War. In fact, it was not until the 1940s that any noticeable progress was made, when a group of Anglicans who went over to Rome in a body came to Pluscarden from Prinknash, near Gloucester, of which the priory is now an adjunct. These converts included Peter Anson, son of Admiral Charles Anson, who, perhaps with an occasional backward glance, like Cardinal Newman after

Pluscarden Priory from the east

his conversion, did not go all the way, but settled for the third Order of St Francis, and when he was not somewhere else, which was often, lived in Macduff, a fishing village on the Moray Firth. He became one of the best-known and best-loved figures in the North-east of Scotland and recorded in sketches and writing the then dying and now dead fisherfolk culture as it had survived when he first arrived. He died in 1975, and amongst his other works was the *Call of the Cloister*, which deals with the history and life of Anglican religious orders, towards which he clearly still had a sneaking attraction. I met him once, full of excitement and stories of Mother Superiors, and also the Abbot of Prinknash, an equally individualistic person but in an entirely different way. He made me think of what the Abbé Liszt might have been like, not only on account of his flamboyant appearance and long hair, in the days when long hair was not so popular, but his ability as a pianist; he smoked with a long cigarette holder, was full of anecdotes, not all of a religious nature, and carried in his pocket a small piece of stone, his portable altar, which he brought out in aeroplanes and elsewhere whenever he wished to say Mass.

It would be interesting to try and assess just how much these converted Anglicans contributed to their new church, and how much that church gave to them. Certainly we know that environment is more important than race, language or even past traditions, and I am sure no Italian monk, for example, would fail to find Pluscarden and its inmates somewhat distinct from what he was used to, perhaps closer to medieval Burgundy, when the Benedictines were evangelists rather than sustainers of a system and had to labour ceaselessly to maintain their position. In any event, I have visited no other revived religious site in Britain in which the primitive atmosphere of monastic life is so pervading, which makes one regret very much that John Kinross, who was a Presbyterian himself, was not employed to show his recreative skill so splendidly here as he did in the restored Greyfriars kirk in Elgin. What a marvellous job he would have made of it; but even if funds had been available, and the First World War had not intervened, it would have needed the monks to bring Pluscarden back to life, however complete and successful the architectural reconstruction.

At the present time the transepts of the priory kirk have been roofed in and the domestic quarters adapted by the monks, so that the calefactory, or warming-room, has become a combined kitchen and dining-hall, the chapter house remains as such, the slype is now a library, and joined to the south transept of the sacristy, which is used as a chapel. It may have been the Lady Chapel, since there is a squint through from it towards the main altar, though this could hardly have been for lepers as they were not usually allowed inside the building. From the south transept the old night stair to the dormitories has survived, and there are several examples of masonic cunning in the arrangement of a clerestory and triforium within a single set of openings. On the east side of the south transept this takes the form of elongated lancets whose supporting pillars reach down to triforium level, being cut through to make a passageway, while opposite, wider window openings are stopped and set back below their sills to keep a way clear. All this work is of the thirteenth century, when the church was being built at roughly the same time as the first cathedral in Elgin, possibly by some of the same masons; the four lancets at the

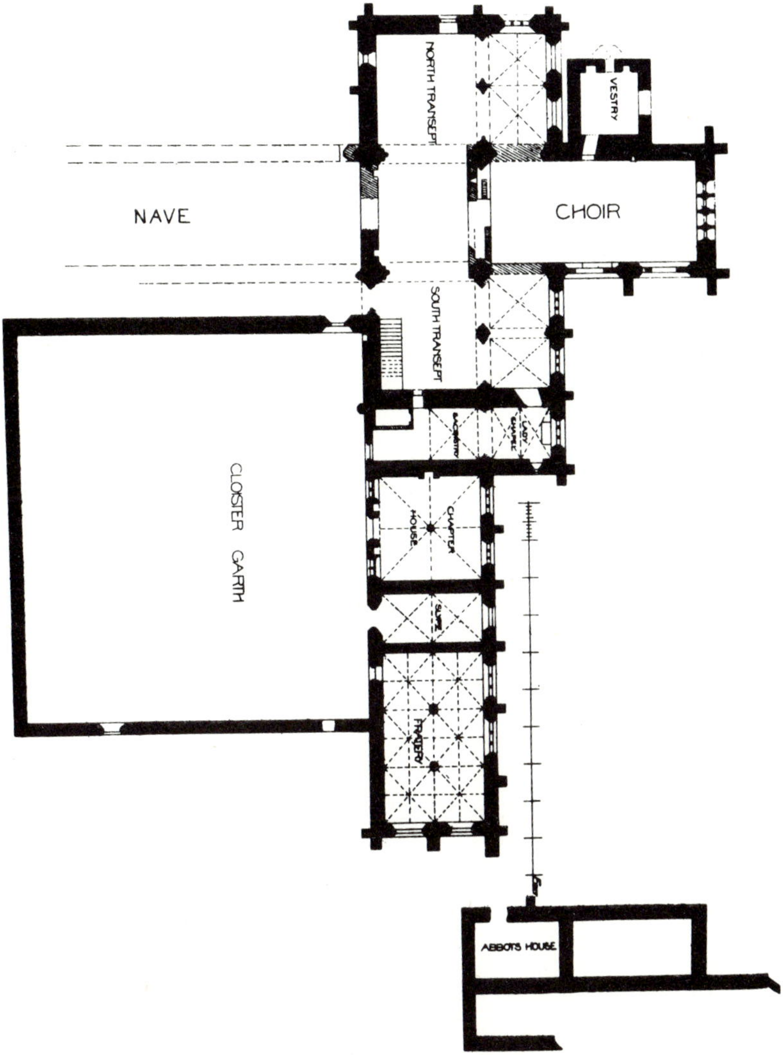

Pluscarden Priory: plan

east end having decided affinities with those at Pluscarden. It also suffered from the attacks of the 'Wolf of Badenoch', and the necessity for extensive repairs and the arrival of Benedictine auxiliaries in 1454 meant further changes.

Amongst the more obvious alterations was the rebuilding of the windows on a smaller scale, no doubt in case of further raids, the larger arches, which were filled in, being clearly visible on each elevation. At one period the church must have been 'all glass', like Gloucester, and very light indeed. It was also gaily painted inside, not the blinding whiteness of the early monasteries, but the blue and gold of a later age, traces of which can still be seen, though not the religious pictures and saintly figures recorded by past travellers. The tower was and is defensive, low, with saddle-back gables and corbelled parapet just masking the roof coping. It recalls Sweetheart, in Galloway, though the tower there is battlemented while this is plainly finished. It is probable that the beautiful central pillar in the vaulted chapter house was an elaborate replacement of an earlier arrangement and may have been influenced by Elgin, likewise the elegant tracery that remains in some of the decorated windows in the transepts and choir. Alexander Dunbar was the last prior and was placed in Pluscarden with the express purpose of making the transition from religious foundation to secular possession easy and profitable for his family and friends. He died in the very year the Reformation officially arrived, 1560, when the property went to Alexander Seton from Fyvie, future Lord Chancellor and Earl of Dunfermline, where he was already commendator. The monks were not molested and the buildings were neither sacked nor used as a quarry, they merely lay empty and became covered with ivy until rescued in the nineteenth century and more fully restored in this one.

To Abbot Dunbar has been ascribed the odd little vestry that protrudes on the north side of the choir almost touching but not quite the east wall of the north transept. More interestingly it was probably he who made the sacrament house, or aumbry, in the north wall near the high altar, as such features almost all date from the years immediately preceding the Reformation. They have a particular function and are not found anywhere else in these islands except in the east and north of Scotland. They are not tabernacles and were not used for the 'Adoration of the Host' or any other Counter-Reformation practice, but for housing the sacrament when reserved for the sick. There are a number of very fine specimens in the locality, the best being in the ruined kirk at Deskford, near Banff, which was made in 1551 for Alexander Ogilvie, the laird. It shows two angels in flowing robes holding aloft the chalice and elements, and round and below the aumbry, or cupboard, is ornate carving, the inscription and the armorial devices of the laird and his spouse. The sacrament house at Pluscarden is cruder but similar and again shows two angels holding up the sacred elements. Both John Kinross, in the Greyfriars kirk at Elgin, and Sir Robert Lorimer, in the Chapel of the Resurrection in St Mary's Cathedral in Edinburgh, have recreated complete sacrament houses, the first from an original design partly still *in situ*, whose door was replaced and whose carving was gilded and painted as it originally would have been. The second is the architect's own conception in which is blended the simplicity of the Pluscarden example and the sophisticated Renaissance details of the celebrated one at Deskford, which is in the care of the Department of the Environment and preserved behind glass.

It may seem a far cry from the 'Laigh o'Moray', as the district around Elgin is called, to that other 'Garden of Scotland', Galloway, but Scottish treasures are often found at the ends of roads, and so far as the South-west of the country is concerned three of our finest abbeys, plus Lincluden College, are there. The abbeys are Cistercian, founded from Melrose, the college, originally founded as a convent for Benedictine nuns by Ulchred, Lord of Galloway, was re-erected as a collegiate church with provost and canons in the late fourteenth century by the third Earl of Douglas, Archibald the Grim. Apparently the nuns did not pay enough 'dues unto Caesar' and were suppressed and evicted by the powerful local overlord. Of the Cistercian settlements we have already described Dundrennan, from which Sweetheart was colonized. It was the last such foundation and suffered from being built during the difficult years preceding the War of Independence, the form and style of its architecture being directly related to contemporary events. Glenluce Abbey, on the other hand, out on a limb geographically, the farthest west of the three and situated by Luce Bay, in Wigtownshire, had a peaceful existence until the seventeenth century. It was the creation of Roland, Lord of Galloway, who settled monks from Dundrennan there in 1192.

The Sacrament House in St Mary's Cathedral, Edinburgh, designed by Sir Robert Lorimer

The ironic thing about Glenluce is that the buildings, left undamaged at the Reformation, stood empty but hale until about 1640, when the local people, staunch supporters of the Covenant, suddenly decided to use the stones to build new houses for themselves, leaving the meagre remnants we see today. The site, in common with so many Cistercian foundations, is beautiful and inspiring, and this despite the order's professed hatred of beauty and anything that diverts man from the stern path of duty. The sands of Luce Bay are well known to perceptive holiday-makers, caravanners and campers, and famous for a curious natural phenomenon whereby the sand forms itself into rope-like patterns which legend tells us originated in the task imposed on some troublesome witches by the wizard, Michael Scott, who lived in the abbey in the thirteenth century. Scott was really a mathematician and wise man, or philosopher, in the medieval sense, rather than a modern wizard; he was a doctor of theology and studied both in Paris and Toledo universities. He was the friend and confidant of many famous men of his time, including the Emperor Frederick II, '*Stupor Mundi*', and is mentioned by Dante in the twentieth Canto of his *Inferno*. 'Michele Scotto' is buried in the abbey at Melrose where his effigy, or at any rate head, has been found, together with that of Jean Moreau, the Parisian master mason who, according to his memorial, had charge of all masonwork in St Andrews, Glasgow, Melrose and Paisley, Nithsdale and Galloway, the last two probably references to Lincluden and Glenluce respectively.

The first abbey, of which the high gable of the south transept, is about all of substance that survives, was an early pointed structure, like the mother church at Dundrennan, but the chapter house, the best-preserved part, dates from the fifteenth century, and could either be the work of Jean Moreau or one of his apprentices, probably the latter, as when examined in detail the rich decorations are more elaborate than refined. At a distance, just looking through the doorway to the central pillar and decorated window on the far side, one is reminded both of Melrose and Rosslyn; and if the French master mason himself was not directly responsible his influence is certainly apparent. The chapter house is slightly below ground level and is approached down a few steps; it is square and has excellent ribbed vaulting, plus a few original glazed floor tiles. Not so long ago it was a sheepfold and partly covered with turf, for which reason no doubt it has survived so well; it only needed cleaning out by the Ministry when they took over. It cannot have been the same vaulted chamber in which Michael Scott is said to have locked up a plague and starved it to death, as in its present form it did not exist then, but country people have a habit of seeking other-worldly reasons for strange events, as indeed they have for 'foreign' architecture, grotesque sculpture and other half-natural, half-artificial features such as one finds in this comparatively distant part of Scotland.

There are similarities in the late-Gothic work at Glenluce with that at Crossraguel, in Ayrshire, especially in the chapter house windows, and there is also an historical link of an unsavoury character relating to the nefarious conduct of that same fourth Earl of Cassillis, Gilbert Kennedy, who roasted the commendator alive to obtain his signature to the illegal transference of the lands to him. At Glenluce the abbot's signature was forged by an amenable monk, who was afterwards murdered in order to destroy the evidence, the earl then bringing the murderer to court to complete the circle of crime. Thus it would appear that Glenluce was important enough for him to go to so much trouble to obtain, though its revenues cannot have been very great after the Reformation; and as we have seen it stood empty and unused for nearly a hundred years before being pillaged for its free stone. The abbey did, actually, stand on a busy international cross-route used from prehistoric times until the sixteenth century, and this association is represented by 'finds' in the vicinity of Continental pottery, notably wine vessels of French origin. The presence of these and other high quality 'pots' may also have had some bearing on the first-rate design and manufacture of the baked clay drainpipes which are a special feature of the Glenluce site. The medieval system has survived and is operative, the pipes being formed with a narrow end which fitted neatly into a wider one; they are very nicely grooved and jointed, and laid in stone channels with proper inspection chambers as in modern drainage.

There was another way in which the extreme South-west of Scotland found itself linked to the outside world in a particular and unusual manner compared with the rest of Scotland. It lay on the missionary route to and from Ireland and Northern England. The first Scottish cathedral was, of course, founded at Whithorn in the fifth century, even before the Roman legions had departed, and later, when attacked by the Vikings, the monks came and went as conditions permitted, alternately fleeing and returning, coming back for sacred books and relics and transporting them both eastwards to Yorkshire and westwards to Ireland. Galloway was part of the ecclesiastical province of York, the only Scottish diocese to be so, almost to the Reformation; it was also the first place in Scotland to be affected by the teachings of John Wycliffe and the Lollards, and in the seventeenth century the most virulent hotbed of Covenanters. Whether these traits descended in any way from the mission of St Ninian or merely represented Celtic opposition to whatever establishment ruled in Edinburgh has never been satisfactorily explained, but hand-in-hand with religious mysticism went cruelty and bigotry of a most violent kind, and a mythology which, in the legend of the Wigtown Martyrs, who were said to have been tied to stakes in the bay at low tide and left to drown, is both emotive and imaginary. Careful examination of the parish records of the period shows no such episode, though it is true there was much persecution and suffering.

The nuns of the Benedictine convent which Uchtred, son of Fergus, Lord of Galloway, founded at Lincluden in 1164, on the banks of the Nith on the outskirts of Dumfries, were suppressed, as already mentioned, in the late fourteenth century, by Archibald the Grim, illegitimate son of the second Earl of Douglas and himself Lord of Galloway and third earl. Besides the usual reason given for this act, the lack of respect for himself by the Black Nuns, there was also the question of acquiring through their dispossession more lands and more revenue. The college he founded had a provost and twelve canons, which was later increased by the fourth Earl of Douglas to a complement of thirty-four, with eight canons, two dozen bedesmen and a chaplain, which was probably larger than the former convent had been and more amenable to the local lairds, being almost entirely under their control. What one sees today, at the end of a grubby cul-de-sac reached through a dreary council housing estate, are the ruins of the choir and part of the south transept of a beautiful fifteenth-century church, with the provost's and canon's quarters to the north. Behind the church, slightly to the south-east, rises what has been described variously as a Norman 'motte', and a Sacred Mount, or Holy Garden, with path winding up to the top, probably once lined with little sanctuaries in the manner of those found in Northern Italy and other parts of the Continent. If the latter description is correct this would be a very rare Scottish specimen, this ex-*Sacro Monte*, from which a good view of the ruined building can be enjoyed, and from which the most extraordinary discovery was made one frosty morning, as recorded by Douglas Simpson in *The Ancient Stones of Scotland*. 'One autumn morn a workman of the Office of Works, standing on the mote, looked down on this space all covered with frost and was astonished that the hoar had brought up a wonderful pattern on the soil. He hastily pegged out the pattern, and in due course that level space was excavated. It brought to light a medieval garden of remarkable design, exactly like the pattern in the frost.' In a footnote Simpson mentions that there was a herbarium, or herb garden, recorded here in the mid-sixteenth century. It would probably have been divided into parterres by box hedges and resembled a small formal Italian garden, but not, I think, the famous Knot Garden in the grounds of Stirling Castle, which is built up in terraces, and not level, nor, if it comes to that, the rounded tree-covered motte. The Sacred Mount at least must have been there in 1460, when Mary of Gueldres, widow of James II of the Fiery Face, acted as host to the fleeing Margaret of Anjou, Queen of Henry VI of England and daughter of the Good King René of the Two Sicilies. With her was her son, Edward, Prince of Wales, the future Edward V, who reigned only one year, being killed at the Battle of Tewkesbury in 1471.

As for the lovely brick-red sandstone of the college begun by Archibald the Grim and finished by his son, apart from the Provost's 'keep' and other domestic buildings, whose rude granite rubble walls contrast sharply with those of the smooth ashlar-built church, the principal object of interest is the altar tomb of Princess Margaret, sister of James I of Scots and widow of Archibald, fourth Earl of Douglas and Duc de Touraine in France. He fought for Charles VII and with his son was killed at the Battle of Verneuil in 1424. At that time the celebrated Garde Ecossaise was created as the Life Guard of French monarchs, and the duke, who had been created a Marshal of France, was buried with his son in the cathedral at Tours. His widow did not die until 1450 and was a great benefactor of the college at Lincluden, the choir being built partly during her husband's lifetime and partly in hers. It is entered through a stone pulpitum with an *anse de panier*, or depressed round arch in the manner of Glasgow Cathedral, and this, taken with the

The late-Gothic remains of the choir, Lincluden College

very fine sculpture remaining, either *in situ* or collected and set apart for preservation, from this screen and its erstwhile loft, would seem to be the work of Jean Moreau from Melrose. Indeed, all the sculpture is of a superior quality, including the window traceries, corbel-heads and springers of the now destroyed Gothic vaulting, but particularly the heraldry, of which this building has almost as much to show as Melrose itself, and of an equally high standard.

It is said the Duchess spent much of her time trying to obtain the widow's pension she felt was due from the King of France and not receiving any satisfaction, gave orders that the fleur-de-lis should be omitted from the armorial devices on her tomb. Be this as it may, the crowned lilies of France do appear higher up, together with the lion rampant of her brother, the Douglas heart of her husband and the fesse-chequey of the High Stewards, a pattern thought to express heraldically the addition and subtraction sums associated with their occupation. The tomb is set under an arched canopy, richly carved, and above is a triangular feature with an

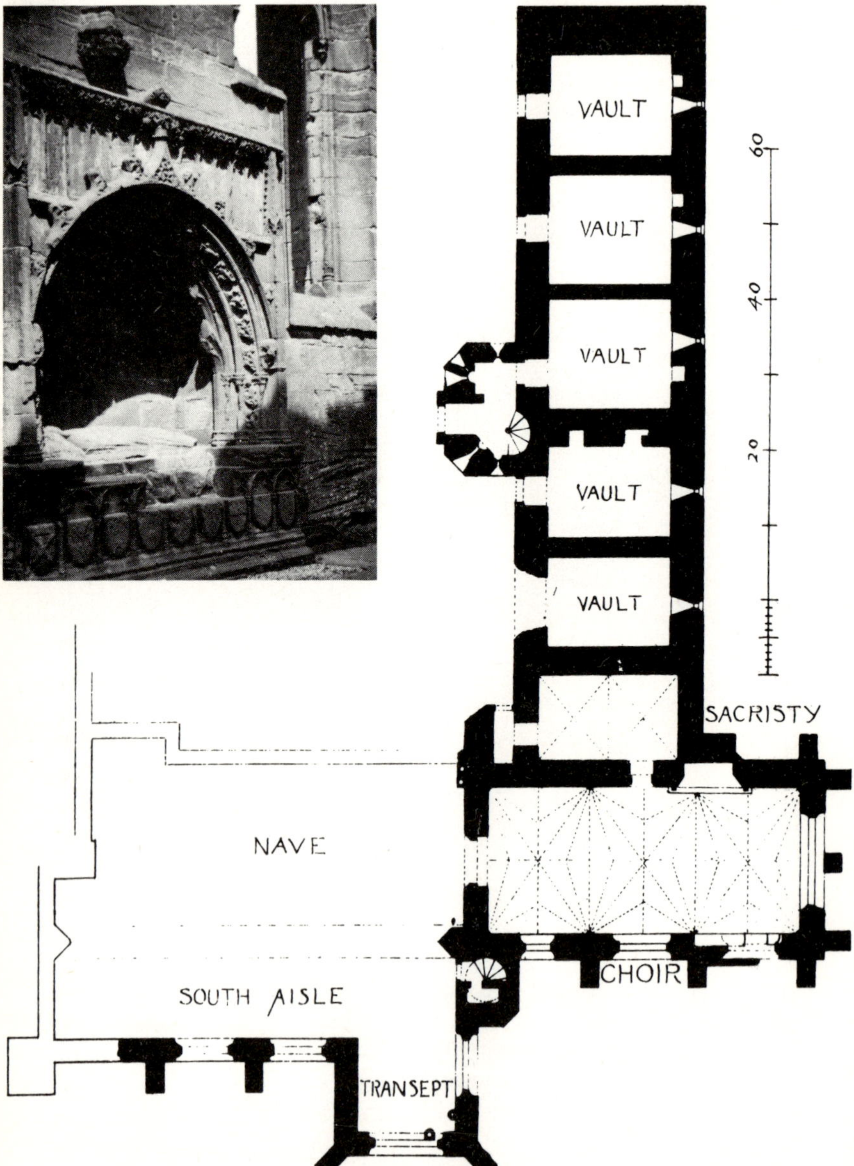

The tomb of Princess Margaret, Duchess of Touraine, at Lincluden College; plan of the college

oddly modern look about it showing three chalices all at different angles, chasing each other round a heart. MacGibbon and Ross suggest this may symbolize the Duke's offices, that of cupbearer to the king, but it need not necessarily be so. Much more remarkable is the decorative vaulting that once completely covered the choir, fully developed and elaborately conceived, its intricate pattern of ribs and panels hiding the timber floor of the roof space, while a sturdy barrel vault supported the heavy stone slab roof. Something of the same sort exists in St Mirin's Chapel at Paisley, only here the under-vaulting is separate and entire and fully in keeping with the late-Gothic architecture of the rest of the building.

At the east end, projecting from the wall below the vacant window are three heavy corbels, which could either have supported a stone *mensa* or a reredos, and might have included the sculptured saints in niches mentioned by MacGibbon and Ross and Douglas Simpson, but allocated to the loft of the pulpitum by the late Dr James Richardson. The latter identifies, amongst others, the curly-headed Saints John and Jude, one with a chalice, the other with a spear, and the bearded Matthew and Bartholomew, from a set which obviously included the twelve apostles; but whether they once stood on the face of the loft above the angel frieze of the pulpitum or behind the high altar is a matter of conjecture; there are supports in both positions for such an array of sculpture. The soft, red sandstone from which the choir is built lends itself admirably to sophisticated designs in leaf and emblematic patterns, of fine scrollwork around and below armorial shields, richly ornamented canopies and window tracery, and to a display of masonic panache not only in the execution of Princess Margaret's tomb but such functional items as the triple sedilia and piscina on the wall opposite. It is instructive to note also how weathering by wind and rain have affected different parts of the building, so that the carved stonework on the south side has survived much better than that on the north, where some features have been almost entirely worn away.

The effigy of the royal lady who was both Countess of Douglas and Duchess of Touraine was removed and damaged at the Reformation, but part of it has been replaced, and in fact the college, having the protection first of the Douglases and then of the Maxwells, suffered more from exposure than anything else. Stalls from the choir were taken to safety in the old parish kirk at Terregles, where the Maxwells had their principal seat, and a number of canons, plus the provost, remained in their quarters almost to the end of the sixteenth century. Amongst Lincluden's distinguished provosts were John de Winchester, who became Bishop of Moray, Andrew Stewart, son of Joan Beaufort and the 'Black Knight of Lorn' who, as already noted, filled the same post, and John Cameron, who as Bishop of Glasgow completed the chapter house and sacristy of St Mungo's. The poet Robert Burns found the site of the college conducive to the Muse, and in 'Ca' the yowes to the knowes' (in English 'Call the ewes to the hills'), conjured up scenes of fairies 'dancing sae cheery oe'r dewy bending flowers', and refers to 'Clouden's silent towers' though there never were any, except possibly the provost's 'tour of' fens, and the only portion still standing to wallhead height is the choir, with adjoining vaulted sacristy and part of the south transept. In a way, however, the most intriguing survival is the layout of the herbarium and motte, which may date from the time of the original Benedictine foundation and represent the nuns' veritable *Sacro Monte*.

Besides converting the convent at Lincluden into a college Archibald the Grim had a hand in the refounding, or at any rate resuscitation of the abbey of Dulci Corde, or Sweetheart, which had been created for the Cistercians earlier by Dervorguilla, Lady of Galloway, in memory of her husband, John de Baliol, and as a place for his and her burial. The refounding was perhaps more in the nature of a restoration of the buildings damaged in the War of Independence and a re-endowing of the property, after a contemporary 'Act of God', when Sweetheart was struck by lightning and many of the windows and much else had to be repaired. It is certainly not with the Black Douglas that the abbey is generally associated, but with the lady whose grandmother was the sister of William the Lion and whose son stood in the direct line for the Scottish throne, indeed ascended it for a short while. The Lady Dervorguilla scattered her patronage far and wide, in England and Scotland, and is remembered in Dumfries for the bridge over the Nith which she is said to have built, once nine-arched and now only six, and constructed of stone, when hers would have been of timber. She also founded a friary for Franciscans in the town, today represented by a modern Presbyterian kirk, standing on the site where Robert Bruce murdered his enemy and rival John Comyn, Lord of Badenoch, in 1306. There was also a Greyfriars kirk in Kirkcudbright of which a remnant, in the form of a transept and aisle of the church, is extant. The rest was demolished by Sir Thomas MacLellan of Bombie, provost of the burgh, in order to build his turreted town house nearby, the transept being preserved as a family burial place and containing to this day the arched tomb of himself and his dame. It was erected by their son in 1597 and is now incorporated within the local Episcopal church.

There is another Franciscan remnant in the Fife burgh of Inverkeithing. It is called the Palace of Queen Annabella, consort of Robert III of Scots, but in fact it is the domestic part of the former Greyfriars and medieval. The church has long since gone, which makes this three-storeyed survivor unique, though I wish the authorities when they restored it had not removed so many of its older neighbours and not municipalized its surroundings so obviously. The present condition of this relic, all scraped bare and looking almost as if it had been built yesterday, is a typical example of what happens when historic architecture is treated out of context. The

The former hospice of the Greyfriars at Inverkeithing, called 'Queen Annabella's Palace'

famous Greyfriars Kirk in Edinburgh was totally rebuilt in the reign of Charles I, reconstructed after an explosion in that of George I and again in the nineteenth century. It is, in any case, better known for the number and quality of its gravestones and memorials, including those of John Mylne, master mason to the Martyr King, William Adam, father of the famous brothers, and the Renaissance tomb of Sir George Mackenzie of Rosehaugh, who founded the Advocates' Library in Edinburgh and was nicknamed 'Bluidy Mackenzie' by the Covenanters on account of his rigorous implementing of the laws against them. The so-called 'Covenanters Prison', a narrow strip in Greyfriars graveyard, did not exist in the seventeenth century, nor were the prisoners ill-treated according to contemporary standards, the sick and wounded being taken to hospital and all those except a tiny hard core, who refused to accept the king's pardon, were released. The signing of the National Covenant is also associated with this former Franciscan site, not by the people of Edinburgh as traditionally stated but by a few noblemen and gentlemen, and not 'in blood from their veins'! The stone table on which this is said to have occurred was not there at the time and even details such as the age or manner in which individuals did sign has been greatly altered in the course of re-interpretation.

Sweetheart, or Dulci Corde, is sometimes known as New Abbey to differentiate it from Dundrennan, whence its monks were drawn, and this name is perpetuated in the village its roofless frame dominates; it was also used for his title by Sir Robert Spottiswoode, Lord New Abbey, lawyer son of the early seventeenth-century archbishop of St Andrews and Glasgow, when he acquired the lands on the collapse of the first Scottish episcopal government in 1638. It is remarkable for a number of things and astonishing for two in particular. Although the site was carefully chosen, like all those settled by the Cistercians, the buildings do not sit down quietly beside a burn as do those at Dundrennan and Glenluce, but stand on a high but flat plateau above, so that arriving from the north the abbey greets one suddenly and dramatically, rising over the houses and valley, its battlemented central tower looking extremely martial; and this effect is heightened by the presence of a vast perimeter wall made of huge granite boulders gathered from the approximately thirty-acre plateau by the monks when they cleared it. Criffel, nearly two thousand

Sweetheart Abbey: interior view with battlemented tower

feet high, rises rather grimly to the west, its summit often topped by a wisp of cloud or covered with mist, while the houses of New Abbey and the church of Dulci Corde nestle below, watchful towards the east and south, where the sea is not far away. The story goes that the stone for the abbey was brought across the Solway Firth in rowing boats from Cumberland, and certainly it is not the same as either the brick-red sandstone of which Lincluden and most of Dumfries are built, or the local granite, being of a softer, rosier hue, and making a nice contrast with the blue and white cottages round about and the ruder rubble of ancillary walls.

Of all the famous Scottish abbeys Sweetheart boasts the greatest amount of church standing, for almost all the claustral buildings have gone, and this is the reverse of usual. The reason is also unusual, since the main structure, against the south side of which a small parish kirk was erected in the eighteenth century, was spared from quarrying by a combination of local ministers and lairds who joined together and bought the property, saving it for posterity; leaving only the domestic quarters to the quarriers. The last abbot was the notorious Gilbert Broun, immortalized by Sir Walter Scott in *The Abbot*; so resolute was he in his refusal to be removed from office by the authorities in Edinburgh that despite threats of arrest and imprisonment he remained on the site well into the seventeenth century. He died in France in 1612 after a series of escapades in which he had the support of John Maxwell, fourth Lord Herries and Warden of the West Marches, as well as most of the ordinary folk, who on one occasion prevented his arrest by the King's Guard by arming themselves with guns and sticks and stones and obstructing 'the course of justice'. The abbot and his monks had, in any case, been appointed secular bailie and justiciaries by Lord Herries, who refused point blank to carry out the instructions of the Lords of the Congregation to destroy the buildings, giving as his reason that he was brought up there in his youth and was greatly attached to the abbey and its inmates.

The story that the stone or some of it came from across the sea is borne out by the position of the buildings *vis-à-vis* the pow, or burn, which runs eastwards from it to join the tidal Nith near its mouth, where the monks devised a small harbour and whence, not only stone, but lead and timber arrived from England and the Continent. The burn also drove the abbey mill wheel and flushed its drains. One result of Dervorguilla's foundation coming so late in time, it was the last begun before the War of Independence and suffered from the disturbances of the period, was that the first abbot found himself besieged by rival forces. He made his peace with Edward I only to bring the Bruce faction quickly on the scene and in hostile mood. In 1300 the abbey was occupied by the English king, who, however, was forced to depart when presented by his own Archbishop of Canterbury with a Bull of Pope Boniface VIII requiring him to remove himself and his troops from Scotland, which 'belonged to the Holy See'. He wriggled out of this by sending his son, the future Edward II but then Prince of Wales, with Welsh instead of English troops, the latter doing much harm to the abbey of Dulci Corde for which the abbot claimed compensation. Edward I died at Burgh-on-Sands on the Cumbrian side of the Solway, in 1307, within sight of Scotland but without having accomplished his mission of subduing it as he had done Wales.

The founding of Sweetheart Abbey constitutes one of the most romantic and edifying episodes in Scottish history, resulting from the model and loving relationship between Dervorguilla and her Norman husband, John de Baliol of Barnard Castle in County Durham. Inseparable in life, and in the event in death, the granddaughter of David, Earl of Huntingdon, caused the heart of her lord to be embalmed and placed in silver-bound ivory casket which she never allowed to leave her sight and which, when she died, was buried with her before the high altar of the Cistercian abbey kirk she had founded in his name. John de Baliol had large estates in France as well as Britain and was one of the foremost nobles of the age, but he fell foul of Mother Church and the Bishop of Durham imposed on him a penance, which he began to fulfil when he founded an almshouse in Oxford for four poor students, leaving instructions for the completion of what is today Balliol College. Why the two *l*s when the founder's name only had one I do not know, unless it is that in its French form the name is spelt Bailleul. In any event, in 1282, his widow, travelling everywhere with the casket containing his heart, confirmed and endowed the college that bears his name, taking the precious relic with her to the grave in 1289, that is, ten years after Edward Plantagenet's first appearance on the scene and not long before his second. Her tomb was destroyed at the Reformation, by whom must remain a mystery, for the abbey seems otherwise to have survived unwanted visitations by militant Reformers, and what remains is a partial reconstruction of what was left. It is also not now in its original position, but in the south transept; but it is her tomb, proof being provided by a portion of the thirteenth-century dedication which is clear enough to be deciphered.

The layout of Sweetheart Abbey followed very much the normal Cistercian plan, a cruciform church, with aisleless presbytery and eastern chapels in each transept. There was a pulpitum a third of the way down the nave separating the monks' choir from that of the *conversi*, or lay brothers, with an altar on either side of the entrance, facing west; and across a narrow passage was another screen, and the lay brothers' altar. The west front was entered

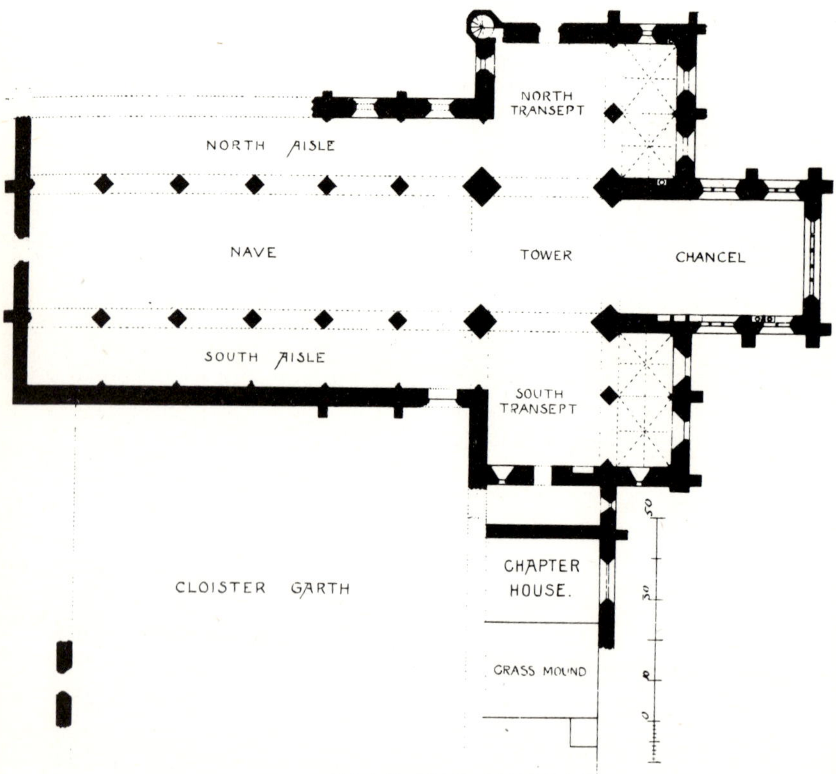

Sweetheart Abbey: plan

through a porch, with a lean-to roof, and the central tower, wholly defensive in purpose and appearance, was finished with a saddle-back roof and castellations like a fifteenth-century Border 'keep', or pele, the parapet being supported by corbels in the form of animals' masks and human heads. There were two night stairs to the dormitories, one near the west door on the south side of the aisled nave, for the lay brothers, another, for the monks, ascending the side of the west wall of the south transept. The covered cloister had quarters for the *conversi* on its western side, with a walk round, kitchen and refectory to the south, and novices' room, and upstairs dormitories beyond. Between this and the church were the chapter house, calefactory, or warming-room, monks' parlour and sacristy, the latter also serving as a library. The great granite barmkin, or outer wall, guarded the place, pierced by two gatehouses, one to the west and another to the south-east, on which side a deep ditch completed the defence. Of these domestic buildings only one small gate survives between the lay brothers' building and the cloister; there used to be a hospice for guests, a poorhouse and hospital, not to mention an abbot's house, none of which remain, only a fortified abbot's tower, about a mile to the north-east of the site, which was probably built by Gilbert Broun.

The placing of a big rose window above three lancets within an overall inset in the west front shows adaptations consequent upon the lightning and storm of 1381, but unlike Pluscarden, which also had to be repaired about this time, the architecture lacks finesse, indeed, romantic and charming though Sweetheart Abbey is it cannot compare architecturally with its sister at Dundrennan. Of the earlier, more refined features the triple trefoil windows above the arches of the nave are perhaps the best; they do service for both triforium and clerestory, but are without any through passage, and they are not represented identically on the exterior of the building. There were proper clerestory passages in the presbytery and those parts of the transepts that led either to the monks' quarters or in the north transept, to the tower and battlements, these being reached via a spiral staircase which still rises in a tall turret at the north-west corner. There are also a number of 'bodges' in places, not necessarily caused by thunder and lightning or resulting from fratricidal strife. On the gable of the south transept, for instance, where a rose, or 'wheel' window has been sadly mutilated by the insertion of a lower gable that comes up in the very centre of it and leaves only half a segment visible, while at the east end a badly proportioned but presumably early and experimental traceried window has a smaller one of five small lancets fitted in above, too close and altogether unhappily.

There used to be a lot of tombstones breaking through the green grass carpeting the floor, but these have now mostly been removed. They made a not unpleasant contrast with the warm almost crimson stonework round about; but the overall impression as one entered the nave by the comparatively small west door was, and is, of the size and strength of the crow-stepped bell-tower, against whose walls can be seen the watertable of the high-pitched open timber roof that formerly ceiled the building. The arches in the nave and the four large clustered pillars supporting the tower are of the pointed Gothic period, but only the aisles were vaulted, and the chapels on the east walls of the transepts now sport the only vaulting *in situ*. The work here is later, as the armorial bosses at the juctions of the ribs show; they display, with crossed crosiers, the Douglas heart and stars. The reconstructed altar tomb of the foundress has been placed in a chapel in the south transept, together with the top of that belonging to the first abbot, John, who saved his monastic patrimony by swearing fealty to Edward I, emulating thereby practically all the Scottish barons, bishops and abbots. The red-sandstone slab is decorated with Abbot John's crosier and cross of office, and it seems strange that of all the grave-slabs and tombs of abbots and monks, inside the church and in the cemetery outside, a portion of this alone should have survived.

FIVE

Post-Bannockburn

THE MOST FAMOUS Scottish abbey, and possibly the most beautiful in respect of its architecture, certainly in its detail, is Melrose, which would surely be well known even if Sir Walter Scott had not featured it in his *Lay of the Last Minstrel*; if the heart of Robert Bruce was not traditionally said to be buried before the high altar; and the Douglases, including Harry Hotspur's vanquisher at Otterburn, did not have their memorials there. Today it is, of course, one of the great 'musts' not only of Britain but of Europe, and being conveniently sited near Abbotsford is seen by thousands from all over the world. Not by moonlight, I hasten to add, as such visits have been halted by the regulation-bound government department that has looked after the ruins since they were handed over by the Duke of Buccleuch. Of the early Celtic monastery that existed as early as the seventh century, wherein St Cuthbert was reared and whence in later years the monks brought his body to be safe from the Danes, nothing remains. It was, in any case, in a different position, some two miles to the west of the present. Even of the Cistercian abbey founded from Rievaulx by David I, the veritable mother of Newbottle, Balmerino, Kinloss and Dundrennan, not to mention offshoots at Culross, Glenluce and Sweetheart, the merest 'footings' alone survive, near the unfinished west end of the fourteenth- and fifteenth-century kirk. The reason for this lies almost wholly in the post-Bannockburn history of Scotland in general and the Borders in particular.

Melrose lay right in the path of advancing and retreating armies and was sacked and burned on no less than three separate occasions, in 1322 by Edward II, in 1385 by Richard II, who, emulating Edward I at Dunfermline, spent a night there as a guest before burning the place down the next day and slaying his hosts. In 1545 the abbey was again the victim of English invaders, the Earl of Hertford and his minions leaving it virtually as we see it today,

Melrose Abbey: interior view looking towards the choir

except for the mutilation of the monks' choir, which was 'restored' in the seventeenth century as a Protestant church, and provided with a lower pitched, stone slab roof and barrel vault in lieu of a higher pitched and more handsomely vaulted antecedent. A certain amount of iconoclasm also occurred during the Covenanting period, but mercifully much of the best statuary, itself constituting the finest array of its kind in Scotland, and only exceeded in quantity but not quality in the collegiate kirk of St Matthew at Rosslyn, was beyond the reach of the axe-swingers and wielders of hammers. Thus one can still see on the third buttress on the south side of the nave, marking the point where the stone pulpitum divided the monks' choir from the rest of the building, the Virgin Mary, crumbling but not defaced or decapitated. On another buttress the patron saint of Scotland stands with his saltire in his appropriate niche; and within the church is some of the most remarkable late-Gothic sculpture in the country. Others have described each item in detail, the grotesques, the pig playing the bagpipes, angels making merry on stringed and reeded instruments and the homely curly kail carvings. Scots like to think that this latter represents something specifically local, and so it may, but the fact remains that vegetable sculpture is comparatively commonplace, one finds a whole cloister of cabbages and cauliflower at Batalha, in Portugal, and the Valliscaulians certainly left their mark in this fashion in many places.

Despite the collapse and spoliation of much of the original vaulting at Melrose a large number of carved bosses have survived, many resulting from the labours of Yorkshire masons sent north by a repentant Richard II, while others are French or Flemish inspired, the best of these being attributed to Jean Moreau, whose memorial is in the south transept, which he designed and built. Indeed, a comparison between the flowing lines and rich sculpture of that transept with the 'perpendicular' east window and 'flatter' architecture of the presbytery is an object lesson in the difference between contemporary Continental practice and Northern English. There is a very splendid Coronation of the Virgin in the triangular panel above the east window, set in the centre of some rather spiky-looking divisions containing bishops and angels, and topped by an even spikier coping, the so-called 'Crown of Thorns'. In roughly the same position on the gable of the south transept one finds the niches are deeper set, elongated, the flamboyant window tracery below not spiky but flowery; and the windows placed above a magnificent Gothic doorway which could only have come from the valley of the Oise, in the Ile de France. In the apex here are the royal arms of Scotland, but with the lion turned in reverence towards the high altar, in the opposite direction to its normal posture. Acolytes and apostles fill the niches on either side. Elsewhere at Melrose are a number of forward-inclined, or 'bowing' ogee-shaped niches, the trick being in the shape of the canopy, which leans out from the main line of the wall as if in a slight nod.

Melrose was the only large church in Scotland to be completely stone-vaulted. Today little of this has survived, of course, but good examples of developed Gothic vaulting may yet be seen in some of the side-chapels in the nave, of which there were once eight, each divided from the next by a solid stone wall. Externally this arrangement expressed itself in a series of flying buttresses, unique in Scotland; but the nave was never finished after the second sacking

Part of the cloister at Melrose

Detail of the south transept

at the end of the fourteenth century and several of the chapels have since become the burial aisles of local families. The ugly barrel vault over what was the monks' choir needs no description, nor the disfiguring walls built against the original Gothic pillars and arches to support it. The pulpitum itself, however, is intact, and rather plain after Glasgow and Lincluden, but with stair still leading up to the missing loft. Better, and more authentic vaulting can be seen in the south transept and in the presbytery, which, as was quite common in Scottish churches of the period, was short and lit on three sides. Here there is also a sophisticated English form of the barrel vault in which the ribs, like those at Lincluden and in St Mirin's Chapel at Paisley, are decorative and non-functional, light and fanciful, presaging in their clever criss-cross patterns Tudor fan-vaulting. It could almost as well have been done in timber. The rib vaulting in the south transept, by contrast, repeats the more usual ribbed and groined forms, with both basic and secondary ribs all being structural in purpose.

The vault supports at Melrose are especially nicely designed and executed, rising as slender stone fillets from the bases of the main pillars and breaking unobtrusively through the capitals to spring into arches above. There is also a clever scheme for the clerestory-cum-triforium by which the two are combined rather ingeniously. Here the internal and external fenestration is not identical, the outer windows finishing well above the walk-way, with larger inner windows reaching down to the bottom, and replete with protective balustrade, a thing forgotten in most cases. The principal builder of the existing abbey kirk was Abbot Andrew Hunter, who was amongst the foremost statesmen-clerics of the fifteenth century. Ambassador to France for James II of the Fiery Face, whose confessor he was, and Treasurer of the Realm. His arms appear in at least three places in the abbey, being represented by hunting horns in between crossed crosiers. The rule of Abbot William Turnbull, afterwards Bishop of Glasgow and founder of the university, is recalled in one of several ornately canopied piscinas, of which there are no less than a dozen including a double one in the south wall of the presbytery. Naturally, the royal arms are carved in a number of places, but notably on the last, westernmost buttress of the nave, the red sandstone clearly still showing the date 1505 and the monogram I.Q. for James Quarto. This marks the limit of building; and the date is further confirmed by the discovery nearby of a French coin of the reign of Charles VIII, who died in 1498. Originally it had been intended to extend the west end beyond the present line, the old wall being retained until its successor was finished, but the work stopped suddenly after Flodden and was never taken up again.

There are peculiarities in the lay-out of Melrose which the casual observer might miss but which, taken together with the dates and subjects of the armorial devices, give some indication of the history of the building and the alterations made necessary by frequent sackings and repair. The most obvious of these is the alignment of the buildings, which although cruciform on plan is asymmetrical, there being two aisles on the south side of the nave and only one narrow one on the north. The reason for this was the position of the cloister against the north wall, itself an unusual arrangement but occasioned by the position of the River Tweed and the means of bringing water for drinking and drainage, and to drive the abbey mill. The door from the church into the now roof-

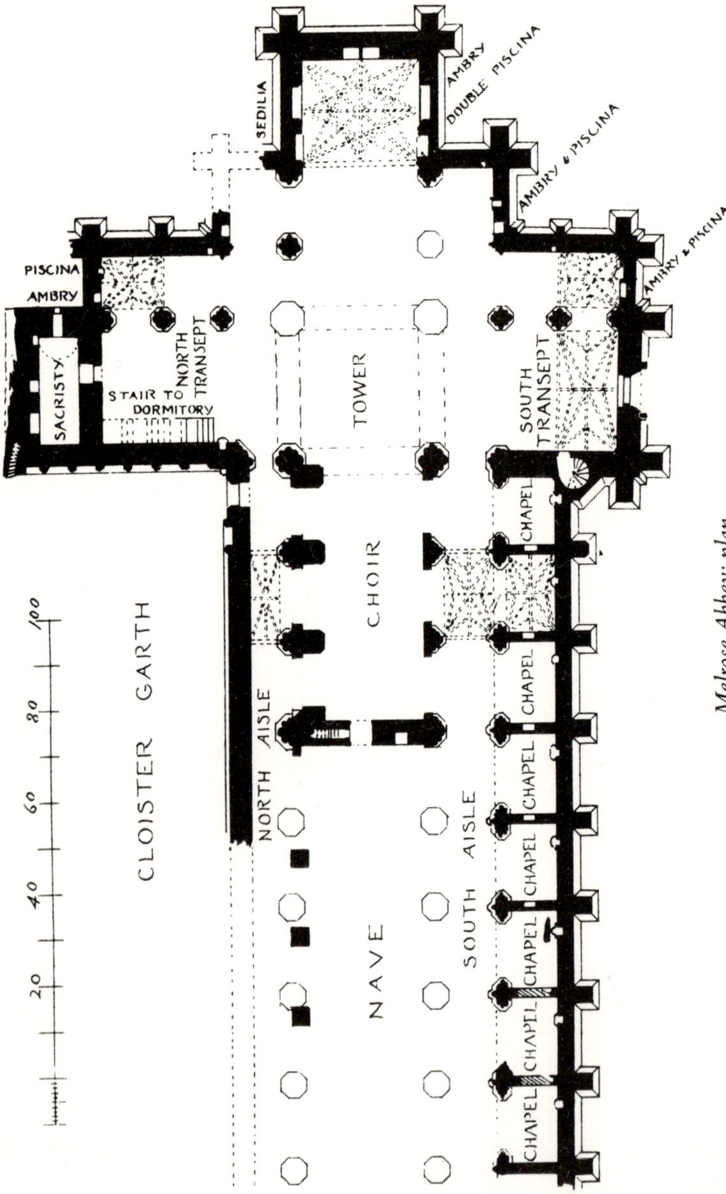

Melrose Abbey: plan

less and fragmentary claustral quarters is round arched and seemingly of Norman inspiration, but closer inspection will show it to be of the same late date as much of the rest of Melrose, and just another typical example, therefore, of the Scottish return to roundnesses during the final stages of Gothic and its merging with the Renaissance. The beautiful run of flamboyant arcading that reveals itself outside that door is particularly fine; and despite the ravages of war and time, and the lack of substantial walls around, some contemporary floor tiles remain *in situ* in the erstwhile chapter house.

In an earlier chapter I have already said something about the plan of Melrose, how the lay brothers' quarters joined the west end of the church, protruding from it and across what is now the public road. This was the most extensive of Scottish Cistercian establishments counting more than a hundred monks and *conversi* in the days of Abbot Hunter, and coming down to eleven at the time of the Reformation, these being granted pensions when the property went to the crown. It was a sad fate for so rich and powerful a colony, one which had perhaps gone too far in the manner of cultural display and possessiveness and no longer reflected very closely the teaching of the monks of Cîteaux in the twelfth century. Yet the abbey, both in its pre-Bannockburn state and post could probably no more escape becoming powerful and grand, and full of patronage, than it could avoid being sacked by the envious and the revengeful. Alexander II was buried within its walls, his first queen too. The monks, who held land on both sides of the Border, did homage to Edward I and 'enjoyed' his protection, and it was near the high altar that the heart of Robert Bruce was destined to be buried, though no one knows whether it ever got there, and whether it was interred by the high altar or in the chapter house, close to the shrine of St Waltheof, second of the old Cistercian abbots. Bruce was excommunicated for his part in the murder of John Comyn in the kirk of the Greyfriars at Dumfries and hoped to expiate his crime by making a pilgrimage to the Holy Land. He died without accomplishing this ambition but gave instructions to Sir James Douglas, his paladin and the so-called 'Good Sir James', to take it to Jerusalem in his stead, and bring it back and have it buried at Melrose. As fate would have it Sir James was killed in Spain, but managed to pass on the king's heart to William St Clair, Earl of Rosslyn, who is thought to have come back with the precious object and had it buried in the abbey. Sir James is also said to have been buried at Melrose with his ancestors, whose tombs were despoiled in the sixteenth century by invading southern troops. It is not known where either Michael Scott or Jean Moreau were interred, but Queen Joan had her tomb in the earlier church in the north transept near the door to the sacristy.

The long straight canal of clear flowing water marking the position of the mill lade divides the purely abbatial site at Melrose from the house and garden of the secular commendators, one of whom was no less a personage than the Cardinal de Guise, brother of the Queen-Regent, and uncle of Mary, Queen of Scots. The latter, as arbitrary as anyone when it came to the diversion of clerical revenues, subsequently appointed her lover, James Hepburn, Earl of Bothwell, as 'abbot' of Melrose; but it is unlikely that either of these notorious characters ever inhabited the house we see today. This is complete and scarcely ecclesiastical in any respect, being a seventeenth-century domestic building, but attractive, and set up as a museum by the Department of the Environment, wherein a number of very interesting things may be seen, lead piping for instance, from the medieval drainage system. Then, besides the expected sculptural exhibits, 'pots' and pans, there is a notable display of comparative objects from Yorkshire and Scotland, showing the close links between Melrose and the mother house at Rievaulx which were maintained throughout the pre-Reformation history of the two abbeys.

If Sweetheart Abbey was the last to be founded and Melrose the last to be completed, the last cathedral to be built in Scotland before the Reformation was at Fortrose, on the Black Isle, near Inverness. The diocese was ancient, may even have been in existence in the ninth century, when St Boniface, having baptized King Nechtan of the Picts, and retired to Rosemarkie, died there at the age of eighty. Boniface is also associated with the cult of St Peter, which he brought north from Brechin and established on the shores of the Moray Firth in pre-Norman days. The more modern diocese of Ross, of which Fortrose eventually became the cathedral, was founded by David I in 1126, but nearly two hundred years were to elapse before bishop and chapter were transferred from Rosemarkie to the new site, indeed, the church at Rosemarkie was still being called the 'kyrk cathedral' in the fourteenth century, when safety as well as administrative considerations triumphed and a charter setting up a dean, treasurer, archdeacon and six canons finally established Fortrose as the episcopal headquarters.

Of the new or possibly greatly extended buildings built at Fortrose in the late thirteenth and early fourteenth centuries all that remains of a once large and handsome cathedral is the south transept and a curiously isolated two-storeyed red-sandstone shed. This latter has done service as town house and tolbooth, but before that must have been part of the church for it retains in its lower floor some good late Gothic vaulting. It is thought to have been the chapter house and sacristy, the first above the latter, and to be older possibly than the surviving transept, though more altered. Its free-standing position also gives some indication of the original extent of the cathedral, to which it was connected by a doorway from the choir. The form of the remaining aisle gives the impression of being a single entity, complete in itself, and to have been all there ever was. The polygonal bell tower and turret contains the original bell of 1460, which still rings at curfew, and the time is told by the burgh clock. Each end of the transept retains a high-pitched gable, and there is very little to suggest any previous attachment to a parallel and larger building, so completely was it removed by Cromwell to build his fort at Inverness that practically nothing remains even to show where it stood. The handsome remnant we do see is beautifully vaulted in stone in the late-Gothic manner, with an unusual feature, rarely found in Scotland but more common in England, whereby the transverse ribs cut straight across the vault above the arches, meeting the others at right angles. All the architecture is decorated and very splendid, an explanation for this being found in the name and standing of the creator of the transept.

Euphemia, Countess of Ross, was extremely well connected, being related to Robert II, the first Stewart king, and marrying as her second husband Robert's brother, Alexander, Earl of Buchan, the so-called 'Wolf of Badenoch'. When he died, in 1394, she became a religious and it was no doubt then that she endowed and commissioned the existing south aisle at Fortrose. It could not have been built much before the end of the fourteenth century and was not completed until the fifteenth, the foundress's tomb taking the form of an open-arched structure which would have been visible both from the defunct cathedral and the aisle. Bosses carved with

Fortrose Cathedral: south aisle; plan

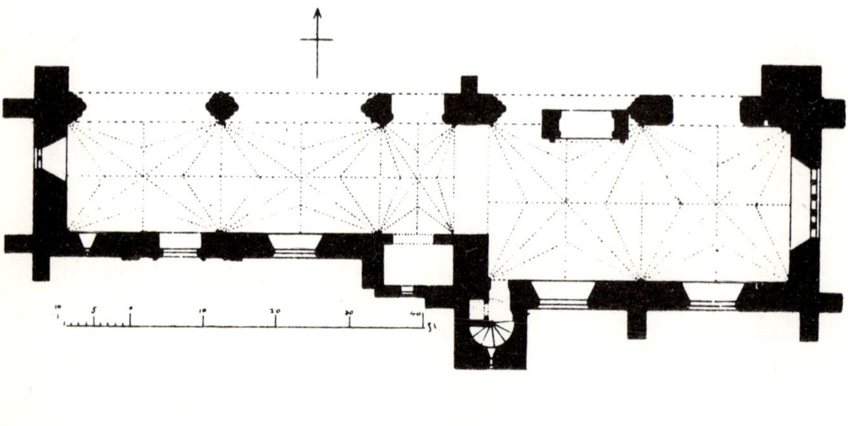

the arms of her first husband, Sir Walter Leslie, and of Bishop Tulloch, who reigned here between 1420 and 1439, appear on the ceiling and the theory is that her son, the Earl of Ross, finished the building and placed his mother's tomb in it. On the same wall, to the west, is the arched altar tomb of Bishop Fraser, who lived in the early sixteenth century, and this is much more ornate, being in the flamboyant style, but again open on two sides. An odd-shaped octagonal font, amongst the very few such objects remaining from before the Reformation, has survived, and despite the stripping of the lead from the roof at the same time as Elgin, Fortrose Cathedral was repaired in the early seventeenth century and was still in use in the reign of Charles I, which makes Cromwell's depredations all the more greedy and inexcusable. The little town at whose centre the old south transept and former chapter house rise is the capital of the Black Isle, which, despite its name is not black at all, boasts a mild climate and produces some of the best oatmeal in Scotland. The village green, for that is what it really is, is surrounded by charming old red sandstone houses many of them with ecclesiastical associations, including that formerly belonging to the Dean, while further away is Chanonry Point, with its handsome neo-classical lighthouse beaming across the Moray Firth to Fort George.

We have now dealt with all the medieval abbeys in Scotland of substance and all the cathedrals except St Machar's in Aberdeen and St Giles's in Edinburgh, which enjoys honorary cathedral status even though it has no bishop. The first stands on the site of an older edifice and represents a restoration of the nave of that earlier building, while St Giles's did not become a cathedral until after the Reformation, though it had ancient monastic connections, having been attached to the priories of both Lindisfarne and Scone. Raised to a diocesan seat by Charles I in 1633 it was afterwards divided into several separate kirks, a meeting place, a gaol, a court, coffee-house and shops, all sorts of things, before being cleared out and thoroughly restored on two occasions, both in the nineteenth century and both so drastic as to reduce the exterior, except for its inimitable crown-sire, to a brand new building. The famous spire was last repaired and restored when St Giles's became the cathedral of the Carolean diocese of Edenburgen. However, before going on to describe these interesting but very late structures it may be as well to dispose of one or two others which are neither cathedrals nor abbeys yet associated with monastic life in pre-Reformation times. I refer to the buildings erected by the preaching friars, of whom the Franciscans and Dominicans are the best known, and which had precedents in the priories of the Augustinian canons regular. The canons lived together in a community but went out into the world to work, not unlike a group of priests or vicars living in one place instead of separate vicarages, or clergy manses. The preaching friars carried this idea a stage further, and besides the Black and Greyfriars there were Whitefriars, or Carmelites, and Redfriars or Trinitarians, not to mention two priestly orders of knighthood, the Templars and Hospitallers.

The Carmelites had a dozen houses in Scotland of which one, the friary church of St Mary of Mount Carmel at South Queensferry, near Edinburgh, is a unique survival, the only original foundation still in use as a place of worship in Britain. The order was very old, in fact one might say it went back into the mists of time, even to the pre-Christian era, for it was based on the eremitical life of the Hebrew prophets as exemplified by Elijah and Elisha. So there must have already existed some sort of hermitage on the slopes of Mount Carmel when Christ appeared, to become in due course a Christian cell. Initially the hermits seem to have continued living in isolation until the time of the Crusades, when the Patriarch of Jerusalem took them under his wing and provided them with a 'rule' and a liturgy, the latter following the Rite of the Holy Sepulchre. In these days when the Church is busy changing its kalendar, its rites and its liturgies, as often as fashion dictates, it is instructive to note that the Carmelites not only used a liturgy and rite as ancient as the church on the site of their master's birth, but numbered the Sundays after Trinity as in the old Anglican kalendar, not the Roman one, in which the Sundays are numbered from Pentecost. The failure of the Crusades meant that the Carmelites were dispersed and had to leave Palestine for the first time in their history, and thus they joined the preaching friars, being invited to South Queensferry in the fourteenth century by the laird of Dundas, whose castle still stands a few miles to the south of the friary kirk.

The Carmelite kirk has survived because at the Reformation it was handed back to the Dundas family who continued to use part of it as a burial aisle, their memorials adorning the walls of the choir. In the nineteenth century the remaining buildings, consist-

Carmelite Friary Kirk at South Queensferry

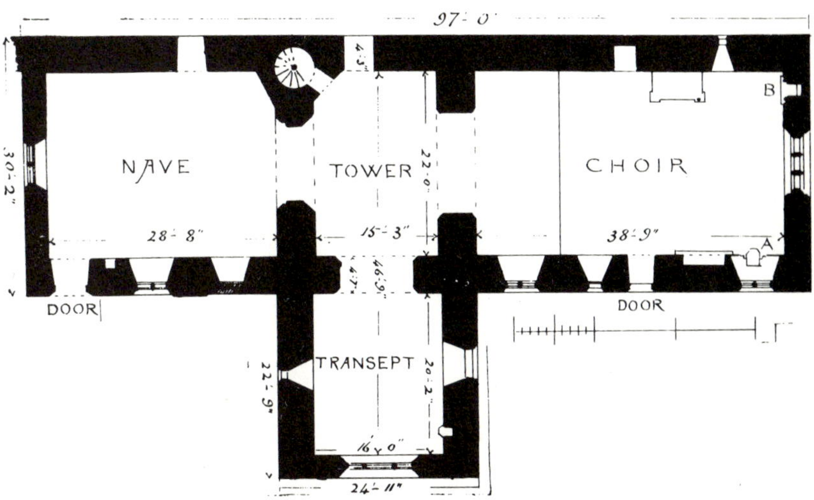

Plan of the kirk

ing of choir, tower and south transept were restored under the aegis of Bishop Dowden of Edinburgh as the local Episcopal church. John Kinross began the work which was completed by the late Ian Lindsay, whose 'wee bookie' on the church is invaluable. There was a scheme for recreating the whole friary complex as it originally was, but funds were not available. What remains is a stumpy building, very martial but somehow in keeping with the ethos of an austere order having its roots on the shores of the Mediterranean and born into its latter-day function through war with the Saracens. The heavy stone slab roof is typical of the fifteenth century, as too is the not quite square tower, which is the same width as the choir and barrel-vaulted, tunnel-wise across its long side, the choir vaulting running in the opposite direction. The two parts would probably have once been divided by a stone screen. There is a triple sedilia on the south wall by the altar, also a wall aumbry, or sacrament house, while outside, on the gable of the east wall, there is a niche, now empty, in which the figure of Our Lady of Mount Carmel would have been. There is a special sundial, with twenty-four radiating lines but missing its gnomon, on the side of the easternmost window to the south of the choir, which had the purpose of telling the people the time for services, being called a 'Mass Clock'. The height of the tower, which has a simple, low-pitched roof, hipped at the corners, would have been greater in the past, saddle-backed like Elgin and Pluscarden, and it still contains a vaulted upper floor divided into two rooms with fireplaces, plus a doocot which today houses a bell. The priory, or friary as it should properly be called, is right beside the Firth of Forth and had its own landing stage where the modern boat harbour is.

The Redfriars, or Trinitarians, were founded in Rome in the twelfth century in order to combat heresy in the face of pressure from the Infidel and particularly to emphasize the indivisibility of the three persons of the Godhead. In 1218 they were invited by the Earl of Dunbar to settle on his land and there is a curious building extant testifying to their having done so. It is a doocot but was clearly something else in origin, probably the central area and bell-cot of the church, which was adapted to its present utilitarian use when the Redfriars removed themselves to the Borders in the reign of James IV. They are said to have been invited by a later Earl to settle at Luffness, between the existing Jacobean house of that name and the village of Aberlady, but most authorities are now agreed that this was a Carmelite convent, the confusion probably deriving from a common respect for the Trinity and association with the Crusades. In any event, there are fragmentary remains of the Luffness convent, including a doorway and an arched tomb on the north side of what was once the altar space. It is said to be that of the founder, while immediately before the site of the high altar is the grave slab of Kentigern Hepburn, who held the barony and lands towards the end of the fifteenth century with a number of other superiorities, including that of Elstaneford. This is interesting because that is how the East Lothian village of Athelstaneford is still pronounced; clear indication of what one has always suspected, namely a change in spelling made in recent times in order to bolster up the story of a mythical battle that occurred hundreds of miles away, a hundred years earlier and between different people.

The Knights Templars were founded in 1118 for the purpose of protecting the Holy Places and those making pilgrimages to them, but were suppressed by the Pope at the behest of Philip the Fair of France, in 1314, on the grounds they had become too powerful. In general they built their churches circular, in imitation of the Church of the Holy Sepulchre in Jerusalem, and we have in this country a notable example in the Temple Church in London. Oddly enough their church at Temple, in Midlothian, is not circular but rectangular, though why this should be so is a mystery. The building sits nicely down beside a bend in the River South Esk, inland from Dalkeith, and served as the parish kirk until 1832 when the present ugly replacement was erected not many yards away. It was then stripped of its roof and contents and left to the winds as we see it today. It dates partly from the twelfth century, when David I first brought the Templars to Scotland, and retains its simple pointed traceries and lancet windows, with inside, on the north wall nearest the site of the altar, an arched sepulchre which probably once contained a representation of Our Lord's entombment, sometimes called an Easter Sepulchre. On the suppression of the Knights Templar their property in Scotland went to the Hospitallers of St John of Jerusalem, an even older order, having been formed as early as the year 1092 and already boasting a preceptory in England by the turn of that century. They came to Scotland at the invitation of David I and had their principal headquarters at

Torphichen: preceptory of the Hospitallers of St John

Torphichen, in West Lothian.

The preceptory at Torphichen has survived in part, joined to a modern parish church and maintained by the Department of the Environment. What remains is in fact the central area, with transepts and crossing of a formerly cruciform building with crow-stepped, saddle-backed tower of purely domestic aspect. One says domestic, as opposed to ecclesiastical, but one really means military for the church displays even more than the Carmelite friary at South Queensferry those characteristics that remind us of the Mediterranean and of the fact that the builders had houses all the way from here, through England and across France, to the walled city of Aigues-Mortes, which St Louis created in order to have a free port for his Crusade to the Holy Land in 1240. Torphichen also has rooms in the tower, replete with bulky chimneys, the effect of which, if one discounts one or two traceried windows at a lower level, suggests a baronial edifice of the late Middle Ages. There is some good ribbed and groined vaulting under the crossing and an amusing mason's drawing showing how the arches were worked out. The Hospitallers were suppressed at the Reformation, when the preceptory became the temporal Lordship of Torphichen, but since then there has come into being a Protestant branch of the Order of St John of Jerusalem, members of which sometimes meet in the old preceptory.

The twin towers at the west end of St Machar's Cathedral in Aberdeen are also martial-looking like those of Templar and Hospitallers churches, and they are defensive, with heavily corbelled parapets, stepped-up battlements and granite steeples, the whole supported by massive buttresses. These towers date from the fourteenth century and, with the nave as far as the crossing, represent all that remains of a much bigger building of tall central tower, choir and transepts, which was demolished in the seventeenth century to make yet another of Cromwell's forts. Not that the local Covenanting ministers did not enjoy themselves aiding and abetting in the work of destruction, hacking away at the 'images' and woodwork, taking advantage of the temporary eclipse of the dominant pisky faction in the city. Aberdeen was and is a pisky stronghold, and the bishop's throne from St Machar's is one of the things rescued from the philistines and taken to safety in King's College Chapel in the university. The woodwork in the chapel constitutes the most important assembly of pre-

Reformation fittings to survive in Scotland, and can be precisely traced to the work of sixteenth-century Aberdeen craftsmen working in the Flemish style. The name of John Ferdour, for example, has been associated with some of the furnishings, together with that of James Winter, who actually came from Angus and made the magnificent oak ceiling in St Machar's Cathedral. This is flat, and displays at the intersections of the panelling the arms of the great of Christendom, including the insignia of the Medici Pope Leo X, the Holy Roman Emperor, the King of Scots, James IV, other kings and princes as well as the bishops and barons of Scotland, not forgetting the golden cross on a blue ground set with martlets which was the assumed coat of Margaret, Queen and saint, lineal heir of King Edward the Confessor.

The present cathedral is not only not the original building but is not on the original site, which was some distance to the west of the town, near where the late Dr Douglas Simpson had his tower. Indeed, that tower stands almost where the old episcopal motte was, built to protect the building works of the first Norman cathedral and replaced by a stone bishop's palace in later years, first in the middle of Loch Goul, remnants of which fortress can still be seen, and then adjacent to the existing cathedral. The whole of Aberdeen was burned by Edward III in 1333, so that whatever survives today dates from after that disaster, except possibly the celebrated Brig o' Balgownie, which is said, and Simpson supports this view, to have been built in the reign of Robert Bruce and to be the work of Bishop Henry de Chen, or Cheyne. The bridge has a single magnificent Gothic arch of more than sixty feet spanning the River Don, and is both ecclesiastical in appearance and foundation. Elsewhere, in *Scotland's Historic Buildings*, I have mentioned how Byron defied the curse on only sons crossing the Brig o' Balgownie; but as he himself cynically remarked, he was going to hell anyway, not being of the elect, while Robert Burns, who was of the elect, would go to heaven whatever he did!

It is thought that some of the timber centring used in constructing the Brig o' Balgownie's splendid pointed arch may have been re-used in vaulting the Royal Castle at Drum, on Deeside, but if so just a small part of it, for of course the span is very much less. It is nice to think, however, that this could be so and that Richard Cementarius, whose name has been associated with both structures, might have had a hand in other contemporary ventures,

Old Aberdeen: the Gothic arch of Bishop Cheyne's bridge, the Brig o' Balgownie

possibly in the cathedral, a tiny fragment of which survives at the east end of the present nave, built of red sandstone, not granite, and much more delicately designed and executed than its successor. The granite church of St Machar is probably the only cathedral built entirely of that material in Europe, certainly in Britain, and no doubt part of its simple massiveness derives from that fact. The stone is employed sensibly and plainly, not over elaborately as one sees in, say, the Marischal College in Aberdeen, with its lacy pinnacles and mock Gothic features reminiscent more of Milan Cathedral than a Scottish building. Before it was engulfed in this complex there stood on the site of the Marischal College the kirk of the Greyfriars, which was founded by Bishop Gavin Dunbar shortly before the Reformation and was subsequently adapted as the College chapel. Unfortunately, it was afterwards reconstructed and has since been incorporated in the modern buildings. Aberdonians are proud of the Marischal College, but they only have to look at St Machar's, the houses in the Chanonry and old university quarters to see how much better granite appears when treated simply, and also, incidentally, how much better the warmer, older granite was than the cold, grey modern variety, which does not sparkle or glisten in the same manner.

St Machar's was rebuilt by Bishop Lychtoun, also spelt Leighton, in the first half of the fifteenth century, and completed by Bishop Gavin Dunbar in the early sixteenth, when the oak ceiling was erected with its forty-eight armorial shields. It was a cruciform structure with central tower, and immediately joined to the Bishop's Palace, a square building with four large corner towers. The choir was demolished at the Reformation, though few Aberdonians supported the extreme Knoxian faction and the bishops remained *in situ* until the arrival of Oliver Cromwell and his Roundheads, when the building was pulled down to provide stone for garrison purposes. In 1688 the central tower, which had a saddle-back roof, not a spire, collapsed, partly as a result of the removal of the choir and its supports at the crossing, and with it went the transepts of the older church, leaving the nave and western towers. The interior had been gutted fifty years earlier, though as already indicated some of the furniture was saved, including the episcopal chair, and taken to King's College Chapel, where it still is. The Aberdeen doctors, university professors and lecturers, refused to subscribe to the Covenant and suffered for their obstinacy, but at least it was through their influence that so much was preserved both of material and intellectual substance. The tomb of the penultimate Caroline bishop, Patrick Scougal, an elaborate and somewhat crude baroque erection of 1685, with effigy, stands undamaged just inside the main door at the west end of the south aisle of the cathedral.

The nave of St Machar's, without its timber ceiling and just looked at on its own, is a somewhat dully conceived rectangle with side aisles, not well lit and with tiny insufficient round-arched clerestory windows. The main arches are completely out of period, being pointed but supported by plain round columns which, did one not know differently, might belong to the thirteenth century instead of the fifteenth; and there is a curious piece of adaptation in the spandrels above, where the thicker wall is cut back to the line of the pillars, so as to keep the latter as slender as possible. As there is only a timber roof, and slates, this would appear to be strong enough, but barely so. Much more interesting and indeed characteristic, and also showing off the glistening sur-

The battlemented towers of St Machar's Cathedral, Aberdeen

Plan of the cathedral

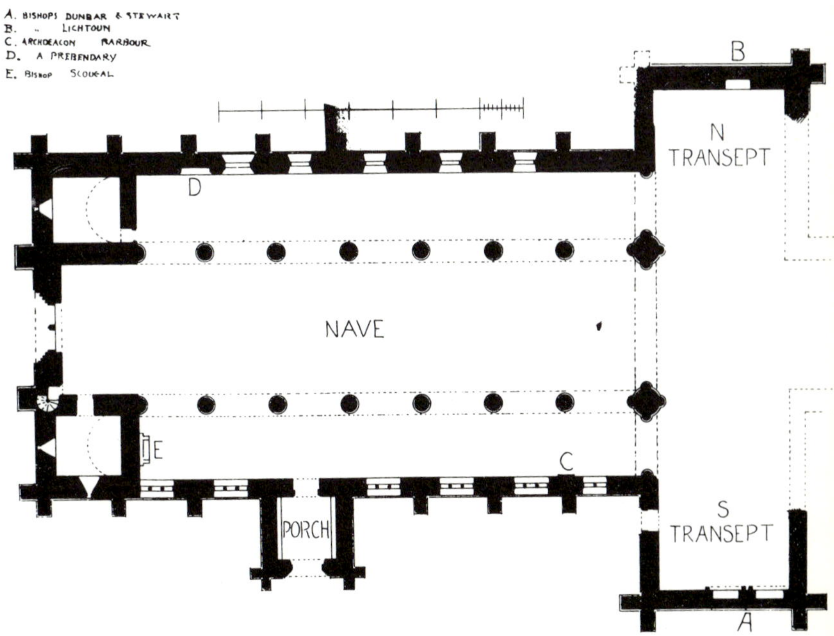

face of warm, pinky-grey granite to perfection, is the porch, which is crow-stepped and built out from the south aisle, with its own separate gabled roof matching the twin towers at the west end. Military-looking as far as their battlements, these rise from a square base to become octagonal, with castellated circlets above and numerous little stone dormers, or lucarnes. The result almost verges on the inspiring, is extremely Scots and impressive, and makes up for many of the less well-thought out features elsewhere.

About the time Gavin Dunbar was finishing the cathedral one Thomas Franche, of French origin, but probably born at Linlithgow, where his father served as master mason to James III, was employed by the bishop on the building of another episcopal bridge, the many-arched Brig o' Dee. A little earlier he had designed the lovely crown-spire of King's College Chapel at the university. This was founded by Bishop Elphinstone, acting under the authority of the Borgia Pope Alexander VI, the same who, in 1494, presented James IV of Scots with the sceptre, which with the crown of Bruce and the Sword of State given by Pope Julius II in 1507, completes the 'Honours Three', or regalia of Scotland. The engraved designs on the rod of the sceptre are in the Italian Renaissance mode, and it is interesting to see similar features appearing in the carved woodwork installed in the College Chapel, finished in 1505. The building is, of course, neither episcopal nor monastic but collegiate, so need not concern us here in detail, except for its remarkable crown-spire, of which Scotland boasted three others at one time, at Linlithgow, from which this one in Aberdeen may have been derived, at Haddington, which must have been inspired by the fourth, in Edinburgh, crowning the collegiate kirk of St Giles. The Linlithgow crown was removed as unsafe in the nineteenth century but has since been replaced by a dubiously successful replica in wood and metal, the Haddington example no longer survives and all four have been associated with the crown-spire of St Nicholas's Cathedral at Newcastle-upon-Tyne, which is certainly medieval and was studied by John Mylne at Charles I's suggestion in 1633 before he restored St Giles's. The original spire of King's College Aberdeen was also restored about this period, after storm damage, when the existing most attractive Renaissance crown cupola was added to the larger crown below. Indeed this top feature, itself surmounted by a smaller, imperial crown with multi-angled cross, is amongst the

Thomas Franche's crown-spire of King's College Chapel, Aberdeen, (compare with St Giles's)

The crown-spire of St Giles, Edinburgh, and the statue of Charles II

most refined exercises in Renaissance style in Scotland, albeit on a modest scale and much superior to the flamboyant pinnacle that finishes St Giles's crown in Edinburgh, with its crescent-like finial, more reminiscent of the 'jingling Johnny' in a Turkish band than any Christian symbol.

The construction of these crown-spires is simple enough, if ingenious, consisting of four flying buttresses turned towards each other to meet at the centre. The Aberdeen crown has arches only from the four corners and is supposed to represent not the crown of Scotland, or even of Great Britain, but that of Charlemagne, symbolizing the universality of the university, and of Christendom. The spire in Edinburgh, on the other hand, is an imperial crown in the generally accepted sense, having intermediate arches between the four main ones, and much more elaborate than either Aberdeen or Newcastle. Without it St Giles's would simply not be St Giles's, and especially since the building suffered so badly at the hands of restorers in the nineteenth century as to be almost unrecognizable for what it once was. The way in which the entire outer surface of the Carolean cathedral was re-incased in smooth, standardized masonry, with niches lacking saints, pinnacles without structural meaning and the protecting side chapels, roofed with individual gablets as at Elgin, sliced off if they stuck out too far or interfered with the revised scheme for the building. The removal of the deeply recessed Norman doorway of the north or Marriage Porch, was perhaps the greatest crime of all, since it was the one remaining link between the late-Gothic kirk and its tiny Romanesque ancestor, a stone shed not unlike St Regulus's at St Andrews or twelfth-century Coldingham. St Giles's has always had a special status, and began life as an ecclesiastical appendage of Lindisfarne. Even after Edinburgh ceased to be the capital of the Northumbrian kingdom of Bernicia it remained under the jurisdiction of Durham, indeed, as late as the mid-fifteenth century, the Perpetual Vicar was Nicolas de Otterburn, a native of Northumberland.

While the exterior of St Giles's fell victim to the Victorian penchant for tidying up medieval waywardness the interior, which ever since the eighteenth century had been divided up into various kirks and compartments, fortunately was not only spared too utter a restoration but actually benefited from being cleared out of all the unseemly clutter that had accrued. Thus it was made into the present much more acceptable church and became at the same time a suitable place in which to erect memorials to the great and the not so great figures in Scottish history, making it a sort of Caledonian pantheon. Odd though that Jenny Geddes, who in the form usually described never existed, should have her tablet, not far away from that of the Dean of Edinburgh whom she apocryphally accused of 'saying mass at my lug'. In 1975, during the Edinburgh Festival, a Roman Catholic bishop was asked to assist at the opening service, which is normally an ecumenical event, when extremists entered the church bearing a banner with the same words upon it and caused such a commotion that the poor man retreated and left so that order could be restored. History does repeat itself as I have remarked before, even false history, for Dean Hannay was not a Roman Catholic and Jenny Geddes was first recorded in an entirely different context as having burnt her luckenbooth, or stall, against a wall of St Giles's, with joy on hearing of the restoration of Charles II!

The High Kirk is like Melrose, a place of detail rather than for general observation, its plan has been altered so much in the course of time that its basic form has been lost, with many altars, a double aisle on the south of the nave and a narrower single one on the north. It resembles Melrose in other particulars, in its sackings by Edward II and Richard II, and by Edward III. No wonder its shape was a bit odd when the restorers got back to the original masonry, in the interior at any rate, the exterior they recased and smoothed over. Happily the remarkable and complete vaulting of the church was rediscovered beneath much plaster and paint, together with some magnificent heraldry, most of it dating from the same time as similar armorial decor at Lincluden and Melrose, and possibly by some of the same hands. The vaulting is by no means all of a piece, the finest, copied by Lorimer for the reconstructed chancel at Paisley, is in the choir and is ribbed and groined in the best fifteenth-century manner, springing from slender fillets rising from corbels between the arches. It replaces some slightly lower vaulting, the original height of which can be seen by the plain cross-vault under the tower. The nave ceiling is later again, and not so good, replacing an even lower vault which did not allow any clerestory or other fenestration above aisle level. In the Chepman Aisle, which branches off from another more famous one, founded and named after Sir William Prestoun of Gorton, who obtained an

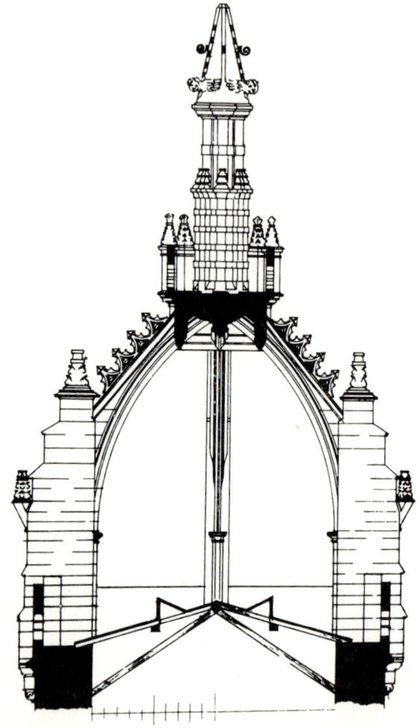

St Giles's: section through crown; plan before the nineteenth-century alterations

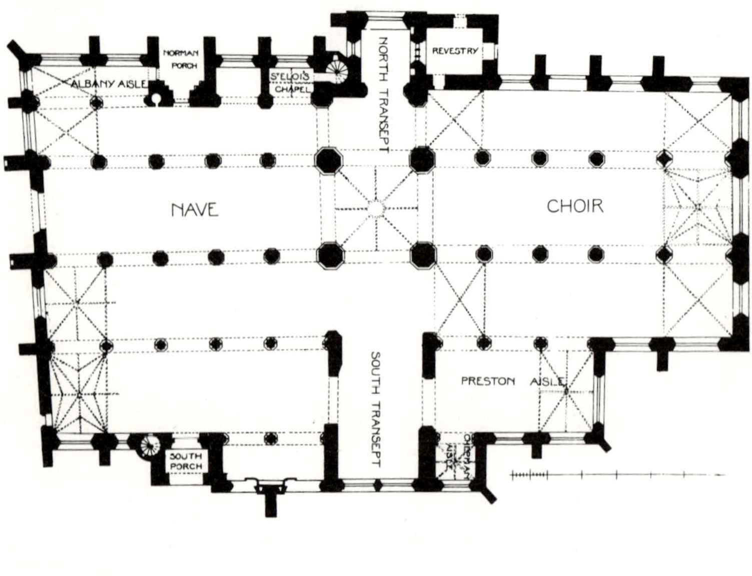

arm bone of St Giles on the Continent and donated it to the church in 1454, the vaulting is a simple barrel with false ribs as at St Mirin's Chapel at Paisley and the choir of Lincluden. This aisle, really a chapel, as they all were, was the creation of Walter Chepman, who with his associate Andrew Myllar brought the first printing press to Scotland from France in the reign of James IV. He was buried here in 1532 and the chapel is dedicated to St John the Evangelist, whose emblem, an eagle holding a pen, appears on one of the vault corbels, with the Latin words that begin his Gospel, 'In Principio'.

The vaulting in the Preston Aisle is different again, giving very much the feeling of Angevin practice, with its domical form, leaving no flat spaces between the arches but instead coming straight down in a curve onto them. The arm bone which the donor obtained with such difficulty, and only after assistance from the King of France, was housed in the chapel, but lost at the Reformation, plus the effigy of the church's patron, which was taken out and ducked in the Nor 'Loch and afterwards destroyed. St Giles was a Greek who preached in the south of France, near Nîmes, where he saved the life of a hind from the hunters and lived with it in his hermitage. The links with Edinburgh are somewhat remote, though many nobles journeyed to the Holy Land via the valley of the Rhône and it is known that Matilda, Queen of Henry I of England and sister of David I of Scots, founded St Giles's Hospital for lepers in London in 1117; and St Giles's hind is symbolized in the supporters of the arms of the city and in many other legendary forms in Edinburgh. The arm bone came from Bruges, and it is perhaps no mere coincidence that early in the sixteenth century a chapel dedicated to the Holy Blood was made between the south porch and adjacent transept, remembering that the festival of *Le Sacré Sang* was and is one of the greatest in the Low Countries, the relic having been brought to Belgium after the Second Crusade. In Bruges too the other bit of the saint's arm bone is still venerated in the church of St Giles.

All trace of any chapel to the Holy Blood in St Giles's in Edinburgh has long since gone, together with the ancient chapel of St Eloi, patron saint of smiths and hammermen, whose chapel this was. It existed on the north side of the nave on the easternmost side nearest the north transept, but was swept away in the restoring mania of the nineteenth century. It had been founded by ex-servicemen on their return from the Crusades, when Alexander the High Steward led the Scots contingent under the banner of St Louis. Their original banner, dedicated to the Holy Ghost, used to hang in the chapel, until James III gave them a new and very special one which James VI nicknamed the 'Blue Blanket', on account of its blue and white saltire background and the hammermen's habit of hoisting it whenever they wished either to show their displeasure at royal actions or to ask for further privileges. By this time the chapel of St Eloi had been desecrated and the hammermen repaired to the Magdalen Chapel, founded in the Cowgate in Edinburgh in 1541 as part of a hospital under their patronage. The building is particularly interesting since it has retained some of its furnishings, the tomb of the founder and his wife, plus the only sizeable remnants of pre-Reformation glass in Scotland, secular and displaying the royal arms of Scotland with those of Mary of Guise, together with those of the founders. The 'Blue Blanket' has also survived and can be seen in the Museum of Antiquities in Edinburgh, near the stool which a mythical Jenny Geddes is said to have hurled at Dean Hannay in the organized riot that took place in the cathedral in 1637.

The Albany Aisle, just inside the west door of St Giles's, on the north side, is still extant, with its fine late-Gothic vaulting, in two sections, supported by a handsome central pillar on which are the arms of Archibald, fourth Earl of Douglas, Duke of Touraine, and Robert, Duke of Albany, brother of Robert III of Scots and with Douglas the probable murderer of David, Duke of Rothesay, at Falkland Palace in 1402. The chapel, or aisle is supposed to have been founded in expiation for this crime, if so it also confirms and pin-points responsibility for it. The King, Robert III, attached St Giles's to the Abbey of Scone, more to the advantage of the latter than the former, since the intention was to transfer revenues and property from the wealthy Edinburgh foundation to the much less well-off monastery near Perth which was expected to welcome and entertain not only royalty and government officials but visiting ambassadors and clerics from abroad. At that time Edinburgh was some way from becoming the capital and seat of the court, which was wherever the King happened to be, but mostly at Scone.

Historic heraldry is a particular feature of the interior of St Giles's, particularly at the east end, which was enlarged by two bays in the mid-fifteenth century, the new columns on either side of the former altar space bearing the most interesting show of armorial devices. The northern column, called the 'King's Pillar', tells its own story, for on it are the monarch's arms, the lion rampant, plus those of the King of France, whose ally he was, the differenced arms of James, Prince of Scotland, the future James III, and the arms of Gulderland, or Gueldres, impaled with the Scottish lion, representing the coat of Mary of Gueldres, consort of James II of the Fiery Face and herself foundress of the collegiate kirk of the Holy Trinity in Edinburgh. The southern pillar is equally instructive in telling the story of this famous church in that it displays the three otters' heads of Nicolas de Otterburn, Perpetual Vicar of St Giles's and the man principally concerned in bringing Mary of Gueldres to Scotland in the first place, he having visited the Continent in 1448 especially for the purpose of choosing a suitable bride for the young 'Fiery Face'. The arms of Sir William Prestoun of Gorton, who discovered and presented the relic of St Giles to the kirk, are recognizable by his three unicorns' heads, while on another face are the arms of the burgh, a castle. A fourth shield, on the west side of the same pillar, is that of Bishop Kennedy of St Andrews, whose Jerusalem crosslets bounded by a double tressure of fleur-de-lis express his royal lineage, he being the son of Sir James Kennedy of Dumure whom Princess Mary, daughter of Robert III, married as her second husband in 1405. He was one of the better members of the Kennedy clan, perhaps the best, Chancellor of Scotland and founder of St Salvator's College, but not the university at St Andrews.

Elsewhere in the church will be found the arms of Thomas Cranstoun, who was chief magistrate when the enlargement took place, and of Napier of Merchiston, the Provost and ancestor of the Jacobean inventor of logarithms. These do not exhaust the heraldic details with which St Giles's is plenteously sprinkled, nor have I described the beautifully carved bosses and capitals, which deserve to be considered in the same category as many at Melrose and Lincluden, with both of which establishments the main part of the church is architecturally and historically associated; but this is not meant to be a guide to St Giles's, which contains, besides much old Scots heraldry and fine emblematic sculpture, a host of monuments ranging from those to the 'Great Marquis', Montrose, through Robert Louis Stevenson to the inevitable John Knox, who thumped its pulpit cushion and was buried in the graveyard to the south. The site has since been paved over and serves as the forecourt of Parliament House, the hub of the Scottish legal system, which was last used for the purpose its name proclaims in 1707, but is not destined as the seat of any proposed new assembly. Knox's statue stands against the wall of the church, facing the mounted lead figure of Charles II, a seemingly unlikely companion whose day, 29th May, used to be celebrated with gusto by the boys of Heriot's Hospital well into the nineteenth century, when they had a holiday and decorated the 'Merry Monarch' with greenery.

It was in Parliament Close, beneath the statue of King Charles, and almost on the spot where John Knox was supposed to have been buried, that the bishops of the Scottish church suddenly found themselves gathered in a huddle, as Stevenson describes in his *Picturesque Notes*, rejected by a Parliament that denounced James VII and II and welcomed William of Orange. Since that day in 1690 St Giles's has ceased to be the seat of a bishop, though still calling itself a cathedral. The only parallel one can think of is Westminster Abbey, which has neither abbot nor monks; but it was founded as an abbey, whereas St Giles's was never a cathedral until after the Reformation and then only for a few years. On the other hand, it has always enjoyed a rather special position, and at one time was actually declared independent of all local ecclesiastical jurisdiction and under no one other than the Bishop of Rome himself. This was shortly after its raising to collegiate status, with a 'chapter' like a cathedral only ruled by a provost instead of a bishop, with sixteen prebendaries, precentor, choristers, sacristan and bedesmen, which, together with the extra chaplains needed to say mass at nearly forty altars made up an establishment of more than seventy clerks; almost as large a complement as Melrose and larger than that of the average Scottish cathedral. The second provost was the contentious but gifted Gavin Douglas, the poet and translator of Virgil's *Aeneid*, afterwards Bishop of Dunkeld.

A fine oriel window that once projected from the south porch was removed during the renovations of last century, refashioned and put back in an entirely different position, when the porch itself was removed, and with it a handsome round-arched doorway, richly carved and Romanesque-looking though actually late-Gothic in date as with so many Scottish examples of the kind. The doorway became part of the new royal entrance and now leads not only to the Royal Pew but to the Thistle Chapel, which Sir Robert Lorimer designed, and for which he was knighted by King George V in 1911. In *Scotland's Historic Buildings* I explained in some detail what happened, how money was left for the restoration of the abbey kirk at Holyrood, but the scheme of reconverting it for use by the Knights of the Thistle was abandoned, and after some argument and in agreement with the donor's family, went towards Lorimer's new chapel. One does not wish to be too unkind about this, but Sacheverell Sitwell and Francis Bamford are surely quite accurate in describing it in *Edinburgh,* published in 1948 and still the best work of its kind, as 'that excessive exercise in pseudo-Gothic now used as the Chapel of the Thistle in St Giles's Church'. The style chosen for this exercise is flamboyant-Gothic of the most elaborate and eclectic kind, with every conceivable space, panelled walls and stalls, ceiling and windows, carved and traceried, groined and ribbed, so that the inside of the tiny chapel resembles more the interior of an exotic jewel box than a work of architecture. Lorimer's mice and rats and other rodents are well to the fore, as are his birds and angels and floral and fruity features, not to mention so many ceiling bosses and so intricate a pattern of ribs, main and subsidiary, that one scarcely knows which way to turn to examine so much concentrated detail. It is redeemed by the craftsmanship, which is first rate, and shows that the skills acquired by pre-Reformation Scottish masons did not die out completely then, but only needed resurrecting as here, and later, after the First World War, in the Scottish National War Memorial and in the restoration of the choir of Paisley Abbey.

The most original part of St Giles's is, of course, its superb crown-steeple, an early sixteenth-century design restored by John Mylne for Charles I when the church became the cathedral of the new diocese of Edinburgh which the king carved out of the large archdiocese of St Andrews. I have already described its overall form and relationship to other towers of similar design, notably in Aberdeen and Newcastle, both of which are extant, only this one is 'imperial', with eight arches in place of four, signifying neither the crown of Charlemagne nor of James IV, in whose reign it was completed, but of Christ the King, whose crown of thorns is symbolized in the prickly finish of the parapet and macelike pinnacles. The spire, with its quaint finial, has become both the emblem and chief architectural ornament of the capital of Scotland. From it the

New Year used to be brought in from tubular bells, now fortunately done away with; and more familiar to the present generation of Edenburghers, as it must have been to those of the fifteenth century, is the old great bell of St Giles, which was cast in Belgium and bore the arms of Mary of Gueldres, who died in 1463. The inscription, erased in a recasting, read in translation from the Latin: 'Honourable men, burgesses of the town of Edinburgh, in Scotland, caused this bell to be made in the year of our Lord one thousand, four hundred and sixty, Johannes and Wilhelm Hoerhen made me and determined that I should be called Giles' bell. I mourn the dead; I summon the living; I disperse thunder.' St Giles's bell still rings the hours, though it should be heard on Sunday or at night, when the traffic is less and its archaic echo resounds to best effect. The so-called 'Mary Bell' was lost at the Reformation, but another, sometimes known as the 'Angelus Bell of St Giles' and probably the one that called folk to Vespers, remains in the steeple. It was made in 1504 and is inscribed with the words 'Mater Dei, Memento mei'.

When St Giles's ceased to contain a bishop's chair, or cathedra in the reign of William and Mary, the congregation moved with its clergy to a site now occupied by the church of Old St Paul's, on the north side of the High Street, at the foot of the ridge running down from the castle to Holyrood. It is almost joined to the former collegiate kirk of the Trinity which Mary of Gueldres had founded in the fifteenth century but which was subsequently removed, stone by stone, as it stood in the path of 'progress', in the form of the North British Railway. Its splendid ribbed and groined vaulting and polygonal apse, as fine as anything in St Giles's, and contemporary with the best in that church, now serves as a reading room attached to the Edinburgh Central Public Library, which is as good an ending as could probably have been devised under the circumstances. The side panels of a triptych by Hugo van der Goes, showing the first Provost, the Queen and her son, from Trinity College, survived the Reformation and are on loan from H.M. The Queen in the Scottish National Gallery.

The Bishop of Edinburgh, who on a visit to London had been somewhat cagey about support from his church for the new regime, became itinerant and his flock disestablished all over Scotland. They represented the largest religious body in the country at the time, and would probably have stayed so but for continued espousal of the Stuart cause and involvement in the two Jacobite rebellions in 1715 and 1745, after which they were proscribed, along with the wearing of the kilt and other expressions of Scottishness, until returned to favour in the reign of George IV. The idea of building a cathedral in place of St Giles's did not at first occur to anyone, or at any rate not before the middle of the nineteenth century, when numbers and funds were greater and a considerable revival of episcopalian fortunes took place. It was then that a series of cathedrals was planned and most of them built; some were modest and almost bijou, like Butterfield's St Ninian's in Perth, the first Scottish cathedral begun since Fortrose, or St Andrew's in Aberdeen, which was designed in Gothic-revival style by the local architect, Archibald Simpson, and later re-edified by Sir Ninian Comper in this century. The cathedral in Inverness was the work of the provost of the town, Alexander Ross, who also entered the competition for a big new diocesan seat in the capital. He did not win this largely on account of the fact that his chief rival was none other than the famous Sir George Gilbert Scott, the most fashionable and sought-after architect of the age, who, unlike Ross, who faithfully fulfilled the conditions laid down in the competition, simply designed what has become his masterpiece, irrespective of cost or amenity; and this was accepted almost certainly because from the very start those promoting the competition wished him to do the job.

St Mary's, Edinburgh, the resulting church, is the largest building used as a cathedral in Scotland; boasts both western towers and central spire and is not in the Gothic-revival style but represents an extremely able re-creation of authentic Gothic architecture, medieval methods of construction being employed throughout. Indeed, Sir George Gilbert Scott showed a remarkable knowledge not only of those methods but applied them particularly imaginatively in raising such a vast church in the nineteenth century, one which will in four hundred years' time scarcely seem any different to the beholder than many much more ancient structures, such as St Mungo's Cathedral in Glasgow. The design of the central tower was the architect's main worry and main success, for rather than take any risks of failure, as had happened in so many medieval examples, he studied what occurred at Ely and made sure it would not happen here. At Ely, Alan de Walsingham had strengthened the central tower after collapse by connecting the four main piers

The twin spires of St Mary's Cathedral, Edinburgh

to four outer arches, thus making the uppermost shape an octagon instead of a square; he also ceiled it in oak instead of the more usual stone vaulting and kept the overall height comparatively low, as we see it today. In St Mary's, Edinburgh, Scott adopted the idea of the extra supporting arches, but went a stage further, providing a central spire that rises nearly three hundred feet above the street. To the arches he added giant buttresses, one at each corner of the building, at the point where the transepts break through to the line of the side aisles, so transferring the load from the inner square of four columns onto the outer foundations. It was a stroke of genius and exceeds in masonic skill anything done in medieval times by the Gothic masters. It helps to explain too why the architect had the largest and most thriving practice in Britain, he was clearly very clever.

Sir George Gilbert Scott has his memorial in this great Scottish cathedral church just as much as Sir Christopher Wren has his in St Paul's in London, the only other big cathedral built in Britain after the Reformation and before St Mary's. In describing how he set about his task the architect declared: 'I desired that it should be not in the least discordant with the finest of the Scottish examples of early Gothic architecture. I have myself been most impressed by the earlier phase of the early pointed period, which especially unites the architecture of Scotland and Northern England, and is capable of the greatest possible degree of dignity, united with a remarkable amount of simplicity and any amount of beauty.' It is interesting after reading this statement and examining the building that arose as a result of it to compare Scott's interpretation of early Gothic art with that of William Butterfield, architect of the Tractarian Movement and the Camden Society, whose minor masterpiece is also in Scotland, in the Cathedral of the Isles, at Millport on the Isle of Great Cumbrae. The contrast with St Mary's is considerable, not only in architectural terms but in size, one being the largest building of its kind north of the Border, the other the smallest cathedral in the British Isles. I will return to that theme later. Meantime I must say something about Scott's more practical incorporation of historic Scottish ecclesiastical features in his Edinburgh design, notably in the triforium and clerestory of the choir, where there are distinct echoes of Dunblane in the former and Coldingham in the latter; and throughout the building the observant visitor will detect things that remind him of other

The west door of St Mary's Cathedral (compare with that at Elgin)

Scottish churches, abbeys and cathedrals. Perhaps the most successful of these blends occurs at the magnificent west entry, where the gablets above recall those of both Elgin and Jedburgh, and the pointed blank arches on either side relate to Dunblane, Inchmahome and Paisley. The central doorway itself, divided in two as at Elgin, has the vesica above filled with a Christ in Majesty and a lintel clearly derived from that of the west door at Holyrood, replete with chanting angels linked by scrollwork.

The cathedral was not completely finished in the architect's lifetime, nor in that of its principal creators, the Misses Walker of Easter Coates, whose father had been White Rod at the coronation of George IV and assisted in that monarch's triumphal but comical progress through the streets of Edinburgh in 1822. The manor house of Easter Coates, sometimes called a hunting lodge, since it used to be in the midst of the ancient forest of Drumsheugh, a few trees from which have been preserved nearby, is a typical turreted Jacobean laird's house, with amusing additions brought from the old residence of the French ambassador to the courts of Mary, Queen of Scots and James VI by Sir Patrick Walker when that building was demolished. It is now partly the Verger's House and partly the headquarters of the only official Choir School in Scotland, itself the successor to the 'Sang Schules' set up by James III to supply the music for the Chapel Royal at Stirling, in the fifteenth century, and the later one created by James VI at Holyrood. Formerly attached wholly to St Mary's Cathedral, the school is now associated with Yehudi Menuhin's more widely based ventures and takes girls as well as boys, who are taught music in all its branches, to play and sing, besides the usual educational curricula.

The Misses Walker resided in this delightful old manor house, bequeathing it and the fortune they made by feuing, or letting off the bulk of their estate during the latter stages of the creation of the 'New Town' of Edinburgh, to the church. At least the profits went to create a splendid work of architecture, a memorial both to

Easter Coates Manor, now the seat of St Mary's Music School, Edinburgh. Note the cathedral chapter house

its architect and founders, the two western towers, completed in 1917, being named Barbara and Mary after them. This was during the episcopate of Bishop Walpole, father of Hugh the novelist, and some forty years after the main building was opened for worship in the year of the architect's death, 1879. At that time the chapter house, another remarkable design by him, had not been erected, largely because of the cost of the rest, but in due course it too was built in accordance with the original plan, which is square at the base becoming octagonal above, no doubt inspired by the shape of the central tower, the vaulted interior again recalling older Scots models and supported in the middle with a single slender column. It contains the Dowden Library, or that part of it not moved for greater security to the National Library of Scotland; and since the cathedral is the lineal successor of St Giles's and the diocese founded in 1633 by Charles I there are valuable souvenirs of this period, including a contemporary copy of the Scottish Book of Common Prayer issued in 1637, which was made the excuse for the celebrated riot and stool-throwing episode. In fact, this so-called 'Laud's Liturgy' was mainly the work of two Scottish bishops, Wedderburn and Maxwell, who gained for their efforts the King's, and finally Laud's grudging approbation. There is also a chapel dedicated to the martyrd founder of the diocese in the cathedral, but it was not part of the original scheme.

Sir George Gilbert Scott designed smaller cathedrals for the diocese of Brechin at Dundee, and another at Glasgow, but neither has quite the proportions and daring of St Mary's in Edinburgh, far less its dimensions, and they resemble more the architect's work elsewhere, in New Zealand, for instance, where the cathedral at Christchurch in the South Island might almost be St Mary's in Glasgow, but for the setting. Christchurch's lawns and river recall Oxford or Cambridge more than any Scottish background, as the inhabitants intended. Neither did Scott introduce other adaptations of the local northern style, and both Dundee and Glasgow are almost run of the mill standard Gothic designs. St Mary's, Edinburgh, incidentally, has some very fine stone vaulting, none in the nave, which is of timber, but in the side aisles and crossing and in the choir, which is finished with a false apse, by which I mean the east end is flat but the vaulting is very cleverly arranged to suggest an apse, the arches and ribs coming down between the tall lancets to create a curved effect. There can be little doubt that such skilful exercises could only have been undertaken by a master of re-creative Gothic such as Scott, and that although one has a sneaking bias in favour of Alexander Ross, being a native, his entry lacked imagination and was certainly not truly medieval in concept. Amongst other things he introduced the idea of triple crown-spires in imitation of St Giles's, a fairly obvious thing to do and one which one is glad was not adopted. What he did provide for was lavatories and vestries which were stipulated for in the competition and which the greater man had more or less ignored in order to get his general plan accepted. One has to chose what one wants in such cases, and what one can afford, and the Episcopalians of the second half of the nineteenth century chose the grand design, which is marvellous from one point of view but has become in this century almost as much of an embarrassment to those who have to maintain it as the large cathedrals and abbeys of Scotland became in 1560 to the Reformers. The failure to make provision for vestries and other functional offices has resulted in all sorts of makeshifts, none of them really satisfactory.

Provost Ross did get the job of designing St Andrew's Cathedral

Inverness Cathedral, apse and chapter house

in his home town of Inverness, modern seat of the Bishop of Moray, Ross and Caithness, and although his first scheme was more ambitious than that which was eventually accepted, and included a very fine apsidal chancel, what did eventuate, looks well beside the River Ness and gives a momentarily French impression, perhaps a little like Notre Dame. Admittedly bijou, and lacking the spires that were meant to top its western towers, as well as the tall *flèche* that until after the Second World War graced the crossing, it is on a good site and is as complete as any other cathedral in its appurtenances, notably in its handsome octagonal chapter house which is roughly in the same semi-detached position as that of Elgin. Whatever else one may say about Ross's design at Inverness it is that of a cathedral, while the existing episcopal seat in Aberdeen could easily be mistaken for just one more of the Gothic-revival kirks with which the 'Granite City' is plentifully supplied. It stands at the southern end of busy King Street, without imposing front, tower or other feature to set it apart from other churches in the neighbourhood. A much more impressive structure is the Roman Catholic cathedral, which has a tall spire and a peal of bells, though the interior is so bare that it might almost conform to the austere requirements of 'the sanctified bends of the bow' which Sir Walter Scott refers to in his *Bonnie Dundee,* an extremely strict calvinist sect from the West Bow of Edinburgh who occupied the whitewashed Tolbooth Kirk within St Giles's in the eighteenth century when that building was still divided up.

The Roman Catholic community in Scotland dates in its present form from the setting up of the first Counter-Reformation bishop in 1695, a few years after the dis-establishment of the Episcopal church and its official supplanting by the Presbyterian one. Their numbers were negligible until the second half of the nineteenth century and the influx of Irish emigrants into the west of Scotland, indeed, apart from a few remote pockets that survived the two Jacobite rebellions, they scarcely existed at all. Even in the Western Isles, which now comprise several almost wholly Roman Catholic areas, they had no roots, the people having been Protestant for more than a century when proselityzing priests arrived from Rome, only to find what amounted in some districts to pagans, without churches or ministers of any kind. It may be on account of this unusual history and rapid development at a later stage that the policy of the Roman Catholic hierarchy in Scotland has been quite different from that in England or Ireland. In the latter huge and ornate Roman Catholic cathedrals have been built in opposition to the older Church of Ireland ones, while in England, though not permitted to use the same nomenclature as the Anglican Church, the Roman Catholics erected Westminster Cathedral in clear rivalry to Westminster Abbey; and intended their new Liverpool Cathedral to rival the large Anglican one, though Sir Edwin Lutyens' grandiose design was actually found too ambitious at the end of the day and a smaller more interesting cathedral was built on his foundations. It is perhaps worth adding that Lutyens, who designed a Roman Catholic cathedral in imitation of St Peter's in Rome for Liverpool, was an Anglican, while Sir Gilbert Scott, grandson of the architect of St Mary's Cathedral in Edinburgh and architect of the outsize Anglican cathedral at Liverpool, was a Roman Catholic. He actually designed the only Scottish cathedral of his persuasion that was built as such, at Oban, whose typically sturdy but modest silhouette graces the shore to the north of the town. Generally the Roman Catholics have not been cathedral minded in Scotland, the theory being that they will one day get back, if that is the right expression, the old ones, including St Giles's; but I doubt that. More interestingly, they have revived or founded new abbeys, at Nunraw, near Edinburgh, at Pluscarden as already described, and at Fort Augustus in Inverness-shire. This latter began life as one of Wade's forts created to pacify the Highlands between the 1715 rebellion and that of 1745. It fell to the Jacobites, however, and although afterwards repaired and re-occupied by government troops was subsequently sold to Lord Lovat in 1876; and in the following decade it became a Benedictine abbey. Building went on from then until the first half of this century and Pugin is credited with a posthumous hand in the work.

St Andrew's Episcopal Cathedral in Aberdeen was intended to be rebuilt on a much grander scale to commemorate the 150th anniversary of the consecration of Samuel Seabury, the first North American bishop, in 1782, in secret in a room near where the Marischal College is now, by three non-juring Scottish bishops. The reason for this was that after the American War of Independence the former colonial clergy could no longer take the oath to George III, and since the Archbishop of Canterbury was unable to impart any authority to them without that they sought the help of the Scottish Episcopal Church, whose own disestablishment had been occasioned by its loyalty to the House of Stuart, and whose bishops and clergy still refused to pray for the House of Hanover. Thus, the Anglican communion we know today was born in an obscure upper room in Aberdeen, when the apostolic succession was transmitted from the old to the new world, with Samuel Seabury of Connecticut becoming the first overseas bishop independent of Canterbury. It was to honour this event that in the '30s of this century American Episcopalians sought to build a large new cathedral in the city whence their church originated, and Sir Ninian Comper was asked to draw up plans for it. Comper's father had been a parson in Aberdeen and he himself had designed the convent of St Margaret in the city as a memorial to him, incorporating many traditional Scottish features in the architecture, and especially in the internal arrangements, which make the chapel almost as good an example of such a recreation as the kirk of the Greyfriars at Elgin. A particular feature is the oriel window above the stalls for the Mother Superior, which is copied from the one removed from the south porch of St Giles's in Edinburgh in the nineteenth century, while in the stained glass at the east end Sir Ninian Comper's father appears, kneeling at a desk which is draped with the arms of St Margaret impaling those of Scotland.

Sir Ninian Comper was, of course, the foremost ecclesiologist of his day, and was responsible for the Warrior's Chapel in Westminster Abbey as well as many other splendid ventures in which he put into practice his own strongly held beliefs, and chiefly the one that a church does not acquire sanctity by merely having existed for a long time, but must acquire it through the spirituality of the designer. Accepting this certainly explains the lack of atmosphere in so many modern churches. In Aberdeen Comper had a splendid opportunity to prove his case in a vast new building, which would certainly have been his *chef d'oeuvre* but which in the event was not built owing to the Wall Street crash. Instead, St Andrew's in King Street was enlarged and improved and given an internal face-lift, the most notable decorative additions being the arms of the American states, designed by the architect, and the burnished gold ciborium over the high altar, with its four columns supporting a vaulted dome. From this hangs a veil, or handkerchief, shrouding the Reserved Host, the idea of a hanging pyx being recreated in preference to the more modern wall aumbry, or sacrament house.

(left) *Sir Ninian Comper's design for a new cathedral in Aberdeen.* (right) *Interior view showing the ciborium, now in St Andrew's Cathedral, Aberdeen*

Precedents for both ciborium and pyx go back at least as far as the fourth century, though very few original pyxes survive from medieval times. There is one at the abbey of Valloires, in Picardy, where the bodies of slain knights were brought after Crécy, which takes the form of a small wrought-iron abbot's crosier suspended over the altar, while in the cathedral at Amiens there is another in the shape of a dove, a more common device. Sir Ninian Comper's splendid ciborium is one of the few things intended for the larger cathedral that was actually made, the design being for a cruciform church of the decorated period, with a fine tower and spire at the crossing, something the architect particularly desired as in his youth he had witnessed the destruction by fire of the old lead-covered spire of St Nicholas parish kirk in Aberdeen, and thought of this as some sort of restitution.

Best known for his work at St Cyprian's, Baker Street, dating from 1903, Sir Ninian Comper, who died at the age of ninety-six in 1960, was the last ecclesiastical architect of note to retain complete freedom from professional bodies, including the Royal Institute of British Architects, which he resolutely refused to join. In effect he was made an Honorary Fellow, and also accepted a knighthood, under pressure, but he always maintained that a builder of churches did so to the glory of God, not to anyone else. What he would have said of people who applaud performers of music in churches goodness only knows, and personally I think it would be a bold person who could defend this practice unconditionally. One recalls his story about Disraeli, who, rather than spoil the atmosphere in Hughenden church for his guests, explained in the porch what they were to see, then simply opened the door and let them enjoy the interior in silence. Comper was employed in a number of Scottish churches, his minor masterpiece being that of St Margaret, his favourite Scottish saint, at Braemar, which is reminiscent of medieval French churches lost in the deepest champaign; but he built no cathedrals, though he assisted in the re-edification of St Andrew's, Aberdeen, and St Ninian's, Perth, which was begun by William Butterfield and where Comper designed the choir screen and all the vestments and plate, banners and processional cross. One should have a look at these, though they are modern, for they are true re-creations of the medieval such as one could not find in many places, their creator having an authority rarely surpassed.

St Ninian's, Perth, is not especially happily sited, being on a double corner plot, which the main road to Inverness cuts round in two right-angles, giving the cathedral prominence without displaying its architecture to advantage. It certainly is bijou in the way the late Provost of the Isles, George Douglas, implied when he compared it with the same architect's quite superb layout and design at Millport, on Great Cumbrae. St Ninian's actually came first, and was the product, the first in Scotland and one of the earliest in Britain, of the Oxford Movement. Its sponsors were the Hon. Frederick George Boyle, afterwards sixth Earl of Glasgow, and the Scottish Judge, Lord Forbes of Medwyn, who went up to university together, one to Oriel and the other to Christ Church, George Boyle being the Secretary of his College Architectural Society. Here they fell under the influence of the Tractarians, of Keble, Wilberforce and Hook, and their associates Newman, Manning and the future Liberal Prime Minister W. E. Gladstone, a fellow Scot. Two of the number went over to Rome, but not the rest, and especially not Mr Gladstone, amonst whose other interests was the furtherance of the Episcopalian cause in Scotland, he encouraging the lairds to revive Pisky congregations and set up new churches. His father, Sir John Gladstone, took a part in the founding of Trinity College, Glenalmond, in Perthshire, which was intended as both theological seminary and secular school, the latter function alone surviving to this day. Glenalmond is amongst the better-known Scottish public schools, though still attached to the church and having bishops on its board. It was the Glenalmond venture that really inspired the Hon. George Boyle to create something of a wholly ecclesiastical nature on his estate on the Island of Great Cumbrae, in Buteshire. His idea was for a revived Iona as it might have been in the days of St Columba and the Celtic monks, a romantic notion which might have worked many centuries earlier but which in the middle of the Industrial Revolution, with the west of Scotland filling up with foreign migrants, was doomed to failure in this particular form. Later in the century Lord Glasgow's scheme developed into something different, the Church of the Holy Ghost, which had been intended to serve his latter-day Celtic monks, became the Cathedral of the Isles, and the collegiate buildings the Provost's House, dormitory for visitors on retreat, the refectory and other offices also coming in useful.

There had not been a Cathedral of the Isles since Iona was wrecked at the Reformation, and this beautiful church by the principal architect of the Oxford Movement, William Butterfield, was an admirable successor. The curious thing is that here is a frankly Gothic-revival group of buildings, conceived in a revivalist atmosphere, which is simpler and more in keeping with the true spirit of the early Middle Ages, of the first Cistercian foundations of Melrose and Dundrennan and King David's cathedral at Dunblane, than anything else created in Scotland in the nineteenth century, and a great deal more in the spirit of the old Iona than the revived Iona of today. The form Butterfield chose was that of a cross, not simply for the church but for his whole layout, with the nave joined at the transepts by the Provost's house and library, to the south, and the dorter, or dormitory wing jutting out to the north. Behind he placed the choir and cloisters. Every detail is as plain and perfectly proportioned as could possibly be imagined, nothing is extraneous, thus making the architecture fully Gothic in struc-

Millport, Isle of Cumbrae: the Cathedral of the Isles and Provost's House

ture as well as appearance. The influence of early pointed architecture in Scotland, especially the then ruined but soon to be restored nave of Dunblane, is clearly visible, notably in the fenestration of the cloister, which is enclosed within plain, trefoil windows, and in the clear-cut framing of the south porch to the church, with five tiny lancets contained within a single low-segmental arch. A similar arrangement can be seen in the former sacristy at Dunblane, which is probably the oldest part of that cathedral and dates from its foundations by David I.

Although small the cathedral is not bijou, the scale and proportion being such that if anything it looks quite large; and the church which only seats just over a hundred persons, is complete, with tower, miniscule chapter house, vestries and other necessary adjuncts. The setting is superb and clearly affected the layout, while the use of local stone and Ballachulish slates helps enormously to place college and kirk in a Scottish background. It sits most comfortably on a grassy podium overlooking the Firth of Clyde, looking towards the mountains of Arran. The situation is sheltered and charming in every possible way, and below, enclosed by its own stone wall and ivy-draped Gothic archway is the graveyard, a big Celtic cross marking the burial place of the founder, the sixth Earl of Glasgow. Something of this Arcadian setting seems to have guided the architect in his work, differentiating it strongly from that of his more famous designs, especially All Saints, Margaret Street, in London, and Keble College, Oxford, where brick and stone are used contrastingly and a wealth of Victorian polychrome tiles and coloured marbles decorate the interiors. Reposeful reticence is the keynote on Cumbrae, multicoloured tiles and contrasting bands of masonry are used sparingly and on the whole successfully, while the ceiling joists are gay in orange and green, displaying in formalized patterns the wild flowers of the island. In the church, incidentally, are some very ancient Celtic stones, remnants of the era Lord Glasgow so romantically sought to recreate.

A little off the beaten track, the buildings at Millport have for some years now been rather wasted, they do not stand near any large centre of habitation and Great Cumbrae itself only comes to life in the holiday season. In fact it was this which brought George Boyle here in the first instance, when he made his summer retreat out of a former Preventative Cutter Station and so loved the situ-

The Cathedral of the Isles: the former seminary, before the fire in 1976

William Butterfield's cloisters

The oriel window in the Provost's study, Cathedral of the Isles

ation and its climate that the site seemed ideal for his tractarian schemes. Today the house is the centre of a funfare and most of the activity around is concerned with entertaining tourists from the mainland. Even the twentieth-century 'monks', students toying with the notion of becoming priests, but not quite, have not benefited Cumbrae much. There has been a lack of respect for trees and shrubs and 'hippies' have decimated the bird population, while the beautiful buildings, the most beautiful of their kind in Scotland, perhaps in Britain, stand waiting to play a genuinely progressive role in the religious life of the community. At the moment they are at the disposal of a Pentecostal mission of North American provenance which, however worthy, is clearly unlikely to rekindle the spirit of St Columba in the district, or fill the Church of the Holy Ghost, limited though its accommodation may be, with regular worshippers.

The last provost of Cumbrae, and dean of Argyll and the Isles in the old dispensation, was George Douglas, who died in 1974 and was buried in the college graveyard with others who had served the place long and faithfully. I visited him shortly before his demise, when he was still maintaining regular services in the church, on weekdays as well as Sundays, still polishing the cutlery, airing the beds and keeping the library tidy and in order. He entertained guests to excellent coffee in his study, with its latticework oriel window designed not by William Butterfield in the best pointed-Gothic but by his master mason in a more picturesque style. Douglas was a contemporary and friend of my father, both staunch supporters of the historic Scottish Episcopalian tradition, which, though different from that of the Church of England, contained within it the seeds of the existing Anglican communion. They were proud to belong to the most ancient church in Britain, with its roots going back to the days of St Ninian and the Roman legions, yet always open to new ideas if these appeared to further the cause of evangelical truth and apostolic order. In many ways a building such as the Cathedral of the Isles at Millport represents their approach more closely than Sir Ninian Comper's, whose definition of a church as a tent to contain an altar, though basically true, plays down the function of history and art, and man's need to express himself materially as well as spiritually.

List of Religious Buildings described in the Text which are Regularly or Periodically Open to the Public

Buildings under the care of the Department of the Environment (Secretary of State for Scotland)

Aberdeenshire (Grampian Region)
*St Machar's Cathedral, Old Aberdeen

Angus (Tayside Region)
Arbroath Abbey (Tironensian)
Brechin, Round Tower
Restennet Priory (Augustinian)

Argyll (Strathclyde Region)
Ardchattan Priory (Valliscaulian)

Ayrshire (Strathclyde Region)
Crossraguel Abbey (Cluniac)

Berwickshire (Border Region)
Dryburgh Abbey (Premonstratensian)

Dumfriesshire (Dumfries & Galloway Region)
Lincluden College

Fife
*Culross Abbey (Cistercian)
*Dunfermline Abbey-Nave (Benedictine)
Inchcolm Abbey (Augustinian)
St Andrews Cathedral-Priory, and Castle (Augustinian)

Inverness-shire (Highland Region)
Beauly Priory (Valliscaulian)

Stewartry of Kirkcudbright (Dumfries & Galloway Region)
Dundrennan Abbey (Cistercian)
Sweetheart Abbey (Cistercian)

Lanarkshire (Strathclyde Region)
*Glasgow Cathedral

Midlothian (Lothian Region)
Holyrood Abbey-Crown Property (Augustinian)

Moray (Grampian Region)
Elgin Cathedral

Orkney
Kirkwall, Bishop's Palace

Perthshire (Tayside Region)
*Dunblane Cathedral
*Dunkeld Cathedral
Inchmahome Priory (Augustinian)

Ross & Cromarty (Highland Region)
Fortrose Cathedral

Roxburghshire (Border Region)
Jedburgh Abbey (Augustinian)
Kelso Abbey (Tironensian)
Melrose Abbey (Cistercian)

Stirlingshire (Central Region)
Cambuskenneth Abbey (Augustinian)

West Lothian (Lothian Region)
Torphichen Preceptory (Knights of St John)

Wigtownshire (Dumfries & Galloway Region)
Glenluce Abbey (Cistercian)
Whithorn Priory (Premonstratensian)

* Partly closed on Sundays during services.

Regular Religious Buildings open out of service time

Aberdeenshire (Grampian Region)
Aberdeen, St Andrews Cathedral (Episcopal)

Argyll (Strathclyde Region)
Iona Abbey (Iona Community)

Berwickshire (Border Region)
Coldingham Priory (Church of Scotland)

Buteshire (Strathclyde Region)
Isle of Cumbrae – Millport, Cathedral of the Isles (Episcopal)

Inverness-shire (Highland Region)
Inverness Cathedral (Episcopal)

Stewartry of Kirkcudbright (Dumfries & Galloway Region)
Kirkcudbright, Kirk of the Greyfriars (Episcopal)

Midlothian (Lothian Region)
Edinburgh, Kirk of the Greyfriars (Church of Scotland)
High Kirk of St Giles (Church of Scotland)
St Mary's Cathedral (Episcopal)

Moray (Grampian Region)
Elgin, Greyfriars (Roman Catholic)
Pluscarden Priory (Roman Catholic, Benedictine)

Orkney
Kirkwall, St Magnus' Cathedral (Church of Scotland)

Perthshire (Tayside Region)
Perth, St Ninian's Cathedral (Episcopal)

Renfrewshire (Strathclyde Region)
Paisley Abbey (Church of Scotland).

West Lothian (Lothian Region)
South Queensferry, Carmelite Friary Kirk (Episcopal)

Note: Balmerino Abbey, in Fife, is in the care of the National Trust for Scotland but can only be seen externally.

Provan's Hall, near Glasgow, also belongs to the Trust and is open at the usual hours.

Provand's Lordship, opposite Glasgow Cathedral, is run as a museum by the Provands Lordship Society, and open daily, except Sundays, in summer.

The Great House at Pittenweem can usually be seen on written application to; Representative Church Council, 21 Grosvenor Crescent, Edinburgh 12. St Fillan's Cave is open in summer, key from Mrs Dougal's shop in the High Street.

Spynie Palace, Moray, is under restoration by the Department of the Environment and not yet open to the public, but it can be seen from the outside.

Index

Index

Page numbers in bold indicate illustrations